Theatre Studies

WITHDRAWN FROM
THE LIBRARY

UNIVERSITY OF
WINCHESTER

D0416297

Palgrave Foundations

A series of introductory texts across a wide range of subject areas to meet the needs of today's lecturers and students

Foundations texts provide complete yet concise coverage of core topics and skills based on detailed research of course requirements suitable for both independent study and class use – *the firm foundations for future study.*

Published

A History of English Literature (second edition)
Biology
British Politics
Chemistry (third edition)
Communication Studies
Contemporary Europe (second edition)
Economics
Economics for Business
Foundations of Marketing
Modern British History
Nineteenth-Century Britain
Philosophy
Physics (second edition)
Politics (third edition)
Theatre Studies

Further titles are in preparation

Also by Kenneth Pickering:

Studying Modern Drama (Palgrave Macmillan)
Key Concepts in Drama and Performance (Palgrave Macmillan)
From Page to Performance (Trinity College)
Drama Improvised (J. Garnet Miller)
Drama in the Cathedral (J. Garnet Miller)
Thinking about Plays (with G. Auckland-Lewis) (Dramatic Lines)

Theatre Studies

KENNETH PICKERING AND MARK WOOLGAR

UNIVERSITY OF WINCHESTER
LIBRARY

palgrave
macmillan

© Kenneth Pickering and Mark Woolgar, 2009

All rights reserved. No reproduction, copy or transmission of this publication may be made without written permission.

No portion of this publication may be reproduced, copied or transmitted save with written permission or in accordance with the provisions of the Copyright, Designs and Patents Act 1988, or under the terms of any licence permitting limited copying issued by the Copyright Licensing Agency, Saffron House, 6–10 Kirby Street, London EC1N 8TS.

Any person who does any unauthorized act in relation to this publication may be liable to criminal prosecution and civil claims for damages.

The authors have asserted their rights to be identified as the authors of this work in accordance with the Copyright, Designs and Patents Act 1988.

First published 2009 by PALGRAVE MACMILLAN

Palgrave Macmillan in the UK is an imprint of Macmillan Publishers Limited, registered in England, company number 785998, of Houndmills, Basingstoke, Hampshire RG21 6XS.

Palgrave Macmillan in the US is a division of St Martin's Press LLC, 175 Fifth Avenue, New York, NY 10010.

Palgrave Macmillan is the global academic imprint of the above companies and has companies and representatives throughout the world.

Palgrave® and Macmillan® are registered trademarks in the United States, the United Kingdom, Europe and other countries.

ISBN-13: 978–0–230–21141–4

This book is printed on paper suitable for recycling and made from fully managed and sustained forest sources. Logging, pulping and manufacturing processes are expected to conform to the environmental regulations of the country of origin.

A catalogue record for this book is available from the British Library.

A catalog record for this book is available from the Library of Congress.

10   9   8   7   6   5   4   3   2   1
18   17   16   15   14   13   12   11   10   09

Printed and bound in Great Britain by CPI Antony Rowe, Chippenham and Eastbourne

UNIVERSITY OF WINCHESTER

03579670   792
            PIC

Contents

List of Illustrations and Tables

Acknowledgements

The authors acknowledge with thanks the permission granted to use copyright material as follows: Indiana University Press for the extract from *That's Life*; Oxford University Press, New Delhi, India, for the extract from *The Journey Within*; David Casteal and Bryan Harnetiaux for the extract from *York*; Philip Dart for his article on 'Adapting for the Stage'; the late Dr. Paul Ranger for his article on Theatre History; Nicola Savarvese, Adela Karszinia-Karpowiczan and the Grotowki Institute for the photographs of Grotowski at work; Steve Rodenbough for the photograph of *York*; Peter Simpkin for the photograph of *The Death of Margaret Thatcher*; ExFeat Productions for the photograph of *Return Journey*; David Willis for the photograph of the Canterbury Cathedral piece; and Lisa Crew at Thames Valley University for the photograph of the 'single performer'.

We would also like to express our sincere thanks and appreciation to the following friends and colleagues for their constant support and encouragement: Charlotte Emmett at IATE; Jayne Thompson, Paul Allain and Patrice Pavis at the University of Kent; Philip Dart at Chalkfoot Theatre; Keith Miles; Michael Herzog at Gonzaga University; Tim White at Warwick University, June Abbott at the Courtyard and our editors Karen Griffiths and Frances Arnold at Palgrave Macmillan.

K.W.P. and M.W. 2009

Introduction

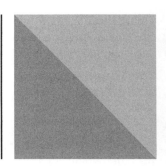

■ The aims and scope of this book

This book is designed as a companion to undergraduate studies. It is *not* a substitute for private study, reading, thinking or practical work but it is a guide to all these activities. The book is intended for students following entire courses or programmes of Theatre Studies or for those who have elected some modules or units of Theatre within English Literature, Joint Honours degrees or degrees in Acting. Theatre Studies may be located within a department of Communications Arts, possibly including such disciplines as Journalism, Broadcasting or Film Studies, each of which has its own distinctive terminology and forms of discourse. We shall certainly be drawing upon insights from the field of Communication Studies in this book, in order to explore issues which cross the boundaries of a single subject. Similarly, it is equally possible that in your institution Theatre Studies is located within Performing Arts, where its natural companions are thought to be Dance, Music, Theatre Technology or Design for Performance. We shall also be drawing upon elements of the comparatively recent discipline of Performance Studies to assist in our investigations into aspects of Theatre. We acknowledge that there has been some tension between the disciplines of Theatre and of Performance Studies but we believe that the two areas are, in fact, complementary and not in opposition. Performance Studies has drawn significant insights from Social Psychology and Anthropology just as Theatre Studies has been enriched by an understanding of elements of History, Aesthetics, Psychology and Archaeology. Because Theatre often operates through images, texts and media other than the 'live stage', we shall also find ourselves intersecting with Film Studies and Media Studies: again, this can only help us to make the connections that are so vital for the thorough understanding of any aspect of human artistic activity.

It is quite probable that the course you are following is of a modular nature and that a particular selection of modules will achieve an emphasis reflecting your interests and ambitions. However, the entire field of Theatre and Performance does not necessarily fit comfortably into modules and you will discover that it is virtually impossible to study this subject without one area overlapping on another, revealing a sense of inter-relatedness. As an example of this you will find that, although this book does not include specific sections on directing or theatre design, both these specialist areas are frequently mentioned. We shall be encouraging you to 'make connections' throughout your study. For our examples of both scripted and devised drama we have drawn from a very wide range of material including the 'canon' of substantial plays in the Western tradition.

1

Our deliberate strategy of also using texts from non-Western sources and new plays by playwrights whose work may be unfamiliar to you is an attempt to celebrate the richness and ongoing creativity of the international phenomenon of Theatre.

How to use this book

We suggest that you survey the contents quickly to see which of the areas of Theatre you have elected to study are discussed here. You will find that each chapter may well cover the requirements of a single module and that the book, like any good course, has a sense of progression.

Each chapter lists its learning outcomes and these should be used to assist in determining the relevance of a chapter to your needs and as a final self-assessment check once you have completed using that chapter.

Many of the chapters contain suggested activities which may be undertaken as individuals or as part of a group: this is an indication of the fact that Theatre Studies is an active, not passive, subject and certain forms of learning require practical participation.

Key terms are highlighted in **bold** text and these are then listed and defined in the Glossary at the back of the book. A short conclusion also lists the main points covered and will naturally lead to topics for discussion and reflection which you should use, in consultation with your tutor, as one of the means of exploring ideas further.

Each chapter concludes with suggestions for further reading and will not only point to the books from which we may have drawn material but also to important areas of research and critical thinking.

The book's bibliography contains details of all the plays and books mentioned in the text.

Further help and ideas for students and tutors

Although this book is complete in itself, a distinctive feature is the provision of a dedicated website: www.palgrave.com/foundations/pickering acting as a supplement and resource for further information, examples and activities, together with guidance and suggestions for their use. If we are offering supplementary material for a particular chapter, this will be indicated clearly at the conclusion of the further reading section.

Initial Explorations

Studying any subject involves understanding the nature and definition of that subject. In this chapter we shall be introducing some definitions of Theatre and illustrating its essential elements by considering the work of key thinkers in the field and by exploring examples of types of performance and of dramatic texts drawn from contrasting traditions.

Learning outcomes

By the conclusion of this chapter, you should be able to:

► work towards a definition of 'Theatre';

► identify the key elements of Theatre;

► become familiar with a number of texts for a single performer;

► acquire key terms for discussion, reflection and discourse about Theatre;

► understand the concept of the 'reflective practitioner'.

■ What is unique about Theatre?

For many years now, the term 'Theatre' (derived from the Greek word *theatron* – a seeing place) has been used to describe a building, a location, a profession, an event or activity and even a way of life. However, it is only comparatively recently that Theatre has also been thought of as a subject for study and research; it is therefore perfectly reasonable that we should ask precisely what it is we are studying.

The term 'Theatre' may now occur in unexpected places. For example, in a recent radio broadcast, the art critic Lisa Jardine described a visit to a large London art gallery as 'a promenade theatre event'. We shall encounter both the concepts of **promenade** and **event** at a later stage but we would suggest that, in its most elemental form, an act of Theatre takes place when a performer finds a space and an audience gathers to observe some form of action. We shall be examining the implications of this throughout this Chapter.

3

Cities, towns and villages throughout the world have many **found spaces** in which various kinds of presentation or **street theatre** take place. In Britain, one of the most popular locations for such performances is in London's Covent Garden, on the open piazza outside the 'Actors' Church' (so named because of all the memorials to performers it contains) and also in an area near a wine bar. In the former space the performers initially have to attract an audience by playful banter and loud announcements and in the latter they have to engage a potential audience who are already seated at tables but equally quite likely to walk away at any point. In such situations, performers may have to accept that audiences will come and go as they please and performances of this kind are sometimes termed **durational**, with no particular starting or ending point.

In certain cases, performances are created to have a particular association with the history or nature of a particular space and this is often known as **site-specific** or **site-sensitive**.

Where there is nothing but a single performer, a space and a gathered audience the onus is on the performer to interact with the spectators in order to retain their attention for long enough to see what has been prepared. This often requires extensive improvisation, direct address and an ability to respond to the audience's comments or level of attention. In theatrical terms this might be described as **actor-generated text** or what the Italian-born director, Eugenio Barba (1994), considered to be part of what he termed the **dramaturgy of the actor**. The power of such performances lies in the minimalist element: the simple ideas of display, narrative and directness in a chosen empty space without any of the sophisticated technology of theatre buildings or a comfortably seated audience committed to remaining. The relationship between performers and an audience must involve the possibility of multiple perceptions on the part of both. This is illustrated in the short piece *Street Scene* (1936) in which the German director, dramatist and theorist, Bertolt Brecht, shows how the various witnesses of an accident will relate their experience from a number of varying perspectives, each of which will contribute to creating an entire picture of the event.

To illustrate the points we have made so far, we might consider the following illustrations of street performers in Barcelona who use a similar situation to that pertaining in London's Covent Garden and ask if these comprise acts of Theatre and what elements of Theatre they contain (see Figures 1.1 and 1.2).

Elements of Theatre

The concept of a single performer creating an act of theatre has produced many variations in approach ranging from 'stand-up comedy', single 'variety acts', minstrels or troubadours, jugglers, story-tellers, mime or escape artistes to short 'monologues' and very extensive 'one-person' plays. However, all these forms containing the elements of 'Theatre' rely equally on the ability of a single person to engage an audience in a chosen space. Most frequently this is achieved by a conscious recognition that the audience is present and may be addressed as if in conversation. This, of course, contrasts with styles of performance in which the actor appears to pretend that the audience is not actually present but is eavesdropping on the action.

Figure 1.1 A crowd gathers around this simple black box in the expectation that something will happen. At certain times the doors on the front of the box suddenly open and a white-faced figure screams at the spectators, making them jump. The doors close and the figure disappears. Some of the onlookers remain to see this process repeated or to see if anything else happens. Is this Theatre?

Source: © Kenneth Pickering

Figure 1.2 A static figure in an elaborate costume appears to be a statue: then she responds in gestures to spectators and approaches some of them. Some of the spectators are clearly uncomfortable, others watch from a 'safe' distance. Some remain for a long time, others move on. What elements of Theatre are present here?

Source: © Kenneth Pickering

In order to progress their understanding and exploration of Theatre, a number of recent practitioners have insisted on a return to what they consider to be the main elements and universal characteristics of Theatre, sometimes examining a wide variety of forms and cultures to inform their debate. Probably the most influential of these thinkers have been the British director, Peter Brook and the Polish director, Jerzy Grotowski. If we consider the writings of either Brook or Grotowski, who worked closely for many years, we can see them asking or implying similar questions and we would recommend that you follow their example:

What is the theatre?

What is unique about it?

What can it do that film and television cannot?

Is there a distinction between the concepts of 'an event' and a 'performance'?

In order to attempt to answer these questions we can consider typical passages from the works of Brook and Grotowski. Peter Brook says:

> Part of the splendour of theatre, at least, of the possible theatre, is that anyone can come. It is always an unknown mixture of people coming together round a core. You don't know who's going to be there, and at the moment of the event all are welcome. So actually, at the moment of performance, the actor is in an ambiguous relationship with the audience. He needs the audience, he wishes the audience to be there, yet he doesn't trust it and he feels it is basically hostile.
>
> (Brook, 1988, p. 126)

Whereas Grotowski both poses some questions and offers some answers:

> What is the theatre? What is unique about it? What can it do that film and television cannot? Two concrete conceptions crystallized: the poor theatre and theatre as an act of transgression.
>
> By gradually eliminating whatever proved superfluous, we found that theatre can exist without make-up, without autonomic costume and scenography, without a separate performance area (stage), without lighting and sound-effects, etc. It cannot exist without the actor–spectator relationship of perceptual, direct, 'live' communion. This is an ancient theoretical truth, of course, but when rigorously tested in practice, it undermines most of our usual ideas about theatre.
>
> (Grotowski, 1969, pp. 18–19)

As you read and re-read these key passages, you should note the use of the following terms that underpin much of our discussion about Theatre:

◆ event

performance

relationship with the audience

'live'

communion.

Suggested activity

After reading these passages, consult the Practitioner Profiles for Brook, Grotowski and Barba and construct your own definition of Theatre. You may find it helpful to consider and decide what is meant by some of the following terms from Brook and Grotowski:

◆ the possible theatre
◆ the poor theatre

◆ an act of transgression
◆ 'he feels it is basically hostile'
◆ autonomic costume
◆ scenography
◆ stage
◆ 'our usual idea about theatre'.

Figure 1.3 Eugenio Barba (centre) in conversation with Dario Fo (left) and Jerzy Grotowski (right) in 1981
Source: © Nicola Saravese

Practitioner profile

Peter Brook (b. 1925)

The contribution of the British director Peter Brook to critical thinking about the nature, purpose and practice of Theatre is almost incalculable. Even though he directed his first play in 1946, his productions are still remembered, discussed and analysed. He was invariably controversial and provocative; rebelling against the systems and attitudes of the conventional commercial theatre that he dubbed 'the Deadly Theatre' in search of a purer and more elemental form. In his *Manifesto for the Sixties*, he wrote:

The trouble is not that we want entertainment, but that we don't. If audiences truly insisted on nothing but entertainment, the world's theatres would: (a) be completely emptied, once and for all; (b) start delivering much more serious work.

(1988, p. 53)

Brook reduced his concept of the theatre to its essentials: the actor and a space and elucidated his ideas of this 'Holy Theatre' in lectures published as *The Empty Space* in 1968. This book has remained a key text for students of Theatre ever since.

He is probably most remembered for his innovative productions of Peter Weiss's *Marat/Sade* (1964), the devised piece *US* which challenged the need for the Vietnam War and in which he invited Jerzy Grotowski to work with the actors (1966), and Shakespeare's *A Midsummer Night's Dream* employing circus skills and staged in a white box (1970). Brook once said of Shakespeare:

> We need to look to Shakespeare. Everything remarkable in Brecht, Beckett, Artaud is in Shakespeare. For an idea to stick, it is not enough to state it: it must be burnt into our memories. *Hamlet* is such an idea.

Brook's many productions of Shakespeare have been extensively documented and regarded as some of the most influential of modern times.

Brook's other experimental work included the London 'Theatre of Cruelty' season in which he attempted to put the theories of Antonin Artaud into practice.

He founded the International Centre of Theatre Research in Paris (1970) and, like Barba, began experiments with **intercultural** theatre. He toured remote communities in Africa and Australia and through improvisation, the use of masks and the exploration of ancient texts created such productions as *Orghast in Persepolis* (1971), involving a lost Persian language, Avesta, *The Conference of the Birds* (1979) taken from a Sufi poem, and the Indian epic *The Mahabharata* (1985), which made a significant contribution to the debate on **interculturalism**. In all these experiments he focused on the interaction with 'non-theatre-going' audiences and the use of 'non-theatrical' venues wherever possible, while demanding high levels of focus and technical skill from his actors.

Figure 1.4 Peter Brook and Jerzy Grotowski in discussion
Source: © Adela Karszinia-Karpowicz

Jerzy Grotowski (1933–99)

The Polish director, Grotowski, recognized as one of the greatest of the twentieth century, left a considerable legacy of writings and theatre practice that continue to be studied and emulated today. The fact that he called his company, based first in Opole and subsequently in Breslau, the 'Polish Laboratory Theatre' indicates that he was constantly engaged in experimentation and research. His work falls roughly into three phases: (1) the 'production' phase, extending from 1959–70, in which he devised some internationally acclaimed productions using a range of literary and documentary sources; (2) his 'paratheatrical' phase in which he sought to 'eliminate the idea of theatre' and transform the spectators into participants in a 'meeting'; and (3) his 'Theatre of Sources' or 'Art as Vehicle' phase from 1986 onwards in which, heavily influenced by diverse ritual performances from around the world, he excluded audiences and concentrated on the work of the performer, leaving behind his work i n production.

Throughout his work, Grotowski has adhered to two main objectives:

1. to strip away the barriers which inhibit communication, including the theatrical paraphernalia of staging and the masks, 'the daily mask of lies', behind which both the actor and audience hide their sensitivity and vulnerability;

2. to take these exposed and receptive parties to a confrontation with their cultural myths in a communal 'trying out' of traditional values.

We shall discover many of Grotowski's ideas about acting in a later chapter but at this stage we must note that:

◆ He sought to put an end to the actor/ audience, stage/auditorium separation. His audiences were witnesses to his actors' nakedness; the confrontation was to be an 'osmosis' and the stage eliminated in favour of a 'chamber theatre'.

◆ Grotowski thought deeply about the kind of event and communication he desired in the theatre and developed an approach that drew on religious ritual to create a sense of 'communion'.

◆ Division in society, he believed, had led to a need to package and sell theatre in order to widen its potential audience. This compromise has led to the 'commercial' theatre and the obsession with making money. Grotowski opposed this kind of commercialism and referred to the conventional actor as the 'courtesan' who has accumulated skills to sell on behalf of the director/pimp.

◆ Grotowski recognized the difficulty in making profound communication across cultural barriers: 'the performance' he said, 'is national because it is a sincere and absolute search into our historical ego'.

Eugenio Barba (b. 1936)

The Italian-born director Eugenio Barba has made a very significant contribution to the study of the phenomenon of Theatre during the past 45 years and has probably done more than anyone to promote knowledge and understanding of the work of the Polish director and thinker, Jerzy Grotowski. Barba regards Grotowski as his 'master' and was his assistant director in Opole from 1960 to 1964.

Barba was also influenced by his encounter with the Kathakali theatre of India.

He took up residence in Norway and founded a theatre company, Odin Teatret, initially formed from students rejected at audition by the Oslo State Theatre School. Odin Teatret relocated to some farm buildings in Holstebro, Denmark, and have since mounted a large number of productions, often using and extending the principles advocated by Grotowski.

Barba edited and ensured the publication of Grotowski's seminal set of essays and conversations under the title *Towards a Poor Theatre*.

Barba's interest in Theatre practice in the universal sense led to his pioneering the study of **Theatre Anthropology**, an enquiry into what influenced performance techniques and styles from many different cultures. He established the International School of Theatre Anthropology and at its events has organized inter-cultural performances, of which perhaps the best known was *Theatrum Mundi* (1982).

His touring performances have visited many remote communities and these have often involved what he calls 'barters': exchanges of songs, stories, training exercises and other aspects of performance with the audience.

Barba is primarily concerned to develop rigorous methods of actor-training derived from multi-cultural sources and involving an awareness of what he terms 'pre-expressivity': that energy a performer senses before attempting any form of communication.

He has described the main thrust of his work as being the 'Third Theatre': companies that experiment widely, operate collectively and attempt to rediscover a ritual-like experience for the theatre event outside the mainstream of Western Theatre.

■ The text and the single performer

Playwrights and actors in the 'modern' theatre (i.e. since the end of the nineteenth century) from many countries have been quick to recognize the potency of the single performer relating directly to an audience. In our considerations so far we have focused on certain key elements of Theatre but we have yet to identify the importance of the text. For students of Theatre, the term 'text' has traditionally meant the words written or devised for live performance by a playwright or the actor. However, in recent Communications Theory and in some Performance Studies contexts, the term can embrace almost anything that can be studied for the meaning it creates: books, films, drawings may all be considered 'texts'. In the Theatre, it may be possible to refer to the lighting or sound effects as part of the text and, in order to differentiate from the printed words of the play, postmodernist scholars tend to refer to those printed words as 'the work'.

In this book we shall use the term 'text' to mean the words intended to be spoken by the performer and any printed stage-directions. In order to prevent confusion we shall sometimes refer to such a text as a 'dramatic text' or 'performance text'.

The monodrama and monologue

When a dramatic text for solo performances is written, it is often referred to as a **monodrama**, an extension of a **monologue** (which simply implies a single speaker but which might be part of a play containing many characters). The monodrama may be a playwright's text written for performance by an actor but in the modern theatre such texts are often **devised** by actors for their own performance. The phenomenon of actor-generated texts is frequently the result of the economics of theatre in which it is preferable to devise and present original material suitable for a wide variety of spaces and which can be portable and self-financing.

We are now going to consider some textual examples of monodramas or the use of monologues drawn from Indian, Syrian and American sources (all written in or subsequently translated into English) in order to further explore some of the issues about text and performance that we have introduced. Unlike the street performances we mentioned, the three texts we are introducing here were all intended to be presented in a designated theatre building but many of the risks of performance that we have identified still pertain. We suggest that, after reading our introduction to each play, you read the passage aloud several times and keep in mind a number of questions we pose at the outset of each passage.

The Journey Within by Usha Ganguli

We take our first example of a play for a single performer from the Indian sub-continent: Usha Ganguli's one-woman play, *The Journey Within*. This is an unusual play in substance and form because it takes as its theme the role of women in Bengali theatre but indirectly investigates the way in which drama approaches women's issues.

The play

The Journey Within was written in 2000 and has subsequently had many performances and has been translated into English. This is appropriate because Bengali drama shows strong European influences and has resonances of colonialism. The play is highly experimental and combines autobiographical material with thought-provoking enquiry into the nature of theatre and performance themselves. The single performer, simply referred to as 'she', is an actress who is also the playwright who has played many roles in the professional theatre. When 'she' speaks, the text is described as narration but these sections lead into a series of monologues spoken by the various characters the actress has created and inhabited during her career. These monologues are described in the text as 'performance' and the entire, very substantial play alternates between narrative and performance.

The play is staged in an overtly theatrical setting: the stage directions require that the *actress enters and stands by a huge triangle erected on the stage* accompanied by the sound of the *dhaak* (a kettle drum played during festivals). Thus the audience expects a 'theatrical' performance even though the language consists of direct address to them in the **'narrative'** sections. In the 'performance' sections, the 'characters' played by the actress address other, unseen characters as if in dialogue with them. We have, therefore, a play of two distinct modes. It is not uncommon in monodramas for a single performer to play multiple roles; this, however, usually occurs within the precise storyline of the play. In *The Journey Within*, the performer/writer/deviser herself inhabits roles that relate to many other texts: this is a good example of what we call **intertextuality** and you will find further instances in other examples of monodramas we shall provide. The desire of the writer herself to perform the play does not mean that it cannot be performed by anyone else. However, as we shall see when we consider David Hare's play *Via Dolorosa*, the decision to be the direct voice of the author has implications for the mode of presentation. The concept of **playwright as performer** infuses this play. If you have access to the internet you will be able to study **reviews** of the work of this playwright/performer and find some **critical responses** to the play we are considering.

The extract

The chosen extract is a complex blend of feminist writing and intertextuality. At this point in the play the actress recalls playing the role of Munia in the play *Guria Ghar* which is an adaptation of Ibsen's famous play *A Doll's House* written in 1879. Although Ibsen's play cannot be said to have had a specifically feminist agenda in the way that the term would now be understood, it was one of the most eloquent and shocking statements of the cause of women and Nora, its central **protagonist**, has become almost a theatrical icon for the independent spirit of women. Ibsen was writing in the context of a relatively repressive Lutheran Christian society.

In *The Journey Within*, the actress selects one of the key moments in the play *Guria* for her performance as Munia. Munia/Nora's husband has been promoted to the status of manager of his bank, a highly respected role in society. During his illness, his wife has created income independently and borrowed some money for a holiday for her husband's convalescence in collaboration with a former Bank employee: this has involved her forging her husband's signature. This is the moment of revelation in the play when, because her pleas to her husband to reinstate him have failed, the former employee reveals what she has done by means of a letter to her husband. Munia/Nora had hoped for understanding and even admiration for her independent actions: instead she is condemned by her husband for bringing him into disrepute. Munia/Nora's response is one of the most powerful moments in all of world theatre and it is fascinating to see it operating in a very different culture from its original.

This extract raises the much debated area of interculturalism (already encountered in our entries on Eugenio Barba, Peter Brook and Jerzy Grotowski).

The extract begins and ends with passages of 'Narration' and, in between, moves into the 'Performance' mode: as you read, we suggest you keep in mind the following questions:

◆ What do you understand by the statement 'Actually, theatre has no language'?
◆ How would you stage this play and how would you ensure that the audience remained engaged for the 75 minutes of the entire performance?
◆ What are the problems of transferring a play from one culture to another?
◆ What kind of actor/audience relationship is envisaged in this piece?

The Journey Within

Narration: Actually, theatre has no language. In theatre, it doesn't matter at all if it is Bengali, Hindi, Marthi, or another language that is spoken. Theatre creates its language through acting, narration and dialogue, movement and sound. Tripti *di* created that language for us in *Doll's House*. I acted as Munia. I had adapted *Doll's House*. Nora had become Munia. I was doing Munia's role. I was the actor and she was the character. We were joined with a thread. Munia loves her husband and to save his life she forges a signature. She is stunned at the way he insults her. How does she react? After all, there can be nothing more precious in life than self-respect. That's the reason why she changes her wedding dress for her daily wear, goes into her room and shuts the door.

Munia in Guria Ghar: (*Performance*) My first identity is that I'm a human being. And I must strive to become a complete human being. I know that most people will accept what you say as the truth because these things are written in good books. But I no longer believe what is written in the books nor what is spoken of by the people. But I must think of something to be able to live. I must think of the meaning of every word myself. I cannot use the words of others as my own. For instance, what do ethics, knowledge, and religion mean? I thought I knew the law but now I realize that these laws are different. These laws do not permit a daughter to release her dying father from his pain. These laws do not permit a wife to save the life of her husband. I have to examine whether such laws are right or wrong.

I thought that there would be a miracle tonight. But that didn't happen and I saw that you are not what I had thought you were. I had waited patiently for eight years because I knew that miracles did not happen every day! Instead, this is the result! Kundan's letter languished in the letterbox. I never imagined for a moment that you'd believe his story. I don't know why I always thought that you'd tell him one day, 'Go, publish it in all the papers.' I don't know why I imagined that you'd come forward to carry my mistakes on your shoulders. Though I wouldn't have let that happen – I wouldn't have accepted charity. But I couldn't have resisted you, could I? That's why whenever I thought of the day of revelation, I grew apprehensive. Had it happened the way I had imagined, my life would have been fulfilled! I had imagined that when you overcame your fear, you would draw me close and love me as if nothing had happened. I would again be your lovely doll, your beloved doll. Then, all was revealed. I saw that all these years I had been living with a stranger and had given birth to the child of a man I couldn't recognize. When I think of myself as the mother of your child, I want to cut myself to pieces!

Narration: Oh my goodness! I distinctly remember the absolute silence in the auditorium when I rubbed off the *sindoor* from the parting of my hair as I spoke these lines. Once an elderly gentleman remarked, 'This Usha Ganguli will spoil all the women with her drama.' I don't know how many women I have spoiled.

But after all these years when I see so many young girls joining our troupe, I feel that maybe a new path has opened for them.

Source: (Ganguli, 2005. Reproduced by permission of Oxford University Press India, New Delhi)

That's Life by Mamduh Udwan

For our second example of a monodrama, we take another play that investigates the role of women within marriage: in this case, through the eyes of a man in the context of a modern, predominantly Islamic culture. The play, *That's Life* (*Hal al-Dunya*) was written in Arabic in 1984 by the Syrian playwright, Mamduh Udwan and had its first performances in Jordan and Kuwait before being recognized as a major reintroduction of the monodrama into Syrian theatre through performances in Damascus.

There are marked differences in the staging envisaged by the writers of the various monodramas we are considering. In this play, there are precise details of a realistic, internal setting, including significant photographs and a telephone, together with coffee pot and cups. So, although we still have a single performer, we have travelled a great distance from the street performer who gathers an audience around. This play uses all the potential technology of theatre to create a fictional world into which the audience gazes and listens. In this monodrama far less of the dialogue is directly aimed at the audience; much of the dialogue takes place on the telephone and some of the language almost takes the form of a soliloquy in which we become aware of an inner dialogue on the part of the single character: Abu 'Adil. There are, however, some narrative sections in which the protagonist describes the events that frame the play.

The play begins with Abu 'Adil smoking, drinking coffee and sitting in silence. The silence is broken by a knocking on the door to which he does not respond. Abu 'Adil suddenly leaps up, plugs in his telephone and looks at the photograph of a woman.

We realize from the initial speeches that Abu 'Adil has just lost his wife and the entire solo action of the play is a reaction to this event. Here is a short extract from the play in which the protagonist recollects how his wife used to serve him; as you read, keep the following questions in mind:

◆ How does the protagonist's interaction with the telephone affect the dynamic of the performance?

◆ Does 'Adil acknowledge the presence of the audience?
◆ What is your reaction to Abu 'Adil's description of his wife's role?
◆ Is this an intercultural issue?

That's Life

A sitting room in an ordinary house, with a telephone, a desk and some chairs. On the wall, a photograph of a woman looking at the audience and a photograph of a man – Abu 'Adil, star of the stage – but the photographs date from their youth. There is another photograph of a group of children of various ages. Near the door there is a mirror. The house has a vaguely chaotic air. The chairs look as though they have been pulled from their places, suggesting that people were there and that the house has not yet been put in order after their departure. The lighting is dim, appropriate to just before sunset. There is some fruit on a tray in a corner of the room.

Abu 'Adil is aged fifty but still retains a fine healthy appearance. He enters by a side door [from the kitchen] holding a coffee pot and turns on the light. He sits on one of the chairs, pours himself some coffee, and lights a cigarette. He smokes calmly and drinks the coffee with evident enjoyment. He relaxes. Silence. Someone knocks at the door of the house. Abu 'Adil doesn't move, as if he hadn't heard. He carries on smoking and drinking coffee. The knocking on the door stops. He pours himself another cup and drinks.

Suddenly he gets up with an unexpected burst of energy as if he had remembered something important, and takes hold of the telephone wire to put the plug back in. He looks at the woman's photograph.

*He puts down the receiver, walks to and
fro, slowly and silently. He sits down,
drinks his coffee, then gets up and
walks to and fro.*

Whatever things were like, it's not easy
to forget thirty years of living together.
I can't sit still. This silence is stifling.
The house seems bigger or wider.
God, is this what the disappearance
of a single person can do? They leave
us, then the house becomes a void,
and the world becomes a void, a
wasteland. Is this why they say, 'Better
a bachelor for a lifetime than a widower
for a month'? I didn't think her passing
would be as painful and hurtful as this.
Her shadow's everywhere. She was
the one who organized this house as
painstakingly as an ant. Thirty years
she worked in this house. Only when
absolutely necessary did she ever go
out for a few hours. Then back to work
here. I always used to wonder: what
is this strange creature called woman
that can find constant occupation day
in day out for thirty years in one place?
She was the house and the house was
her. Now the house without her really
is a great void, as though it's become
a forest or a desert. It's become
deserted like damp, mouldering ruins.

*He sits down, stretching his legs over
the chair, speaking in a distracted
manner as he drinks the coffee.*

This was the time I used to wake
up from my siesta and she'd bring
me a cup of coffee (*He looks at the
photograph.*) I couldn't sleep this
afternoon because of you! (*He turns
away from the photograph.*) When I was
asleep her only care in the world was
for me to rest and not be disturbed.
No ringing the doorbell and no callers.
She'd turn off the electricity in the
house and disconnect the telephone.
'Adil would say to her, 'Mother, you
shouldn't disconnect the telephone.
There could be an emergency call.' And
she, God bless her soul, would say,
'What emergency can't wait until your
father wakes up?' Often we'd forget to
put the plug back in when I did wake up.
(*To the photograph*) We're a family that
unplugs the telephone. Every family has
its peculiarities, and you got us used
to this one. You began it for our sakes.
(*Addressing himself*) All her life she took
more care of me than she did of 'Adil.
After coffee, she'd sit alone, waiting until
my temper improved or until I'd finished
reading and went into the kitchen. I'd
get home from work and find her in the
kitchen, because she knew what time
I'd be back. I'd ask her, 'Umm 'Adil, how
do you know that when you can't tell the
time?' And she'd reply with that laugh of
hers that meant the whole world to me:
'My heart can tell the time.' If I didn't
speak to her, then she kept quiet. She
knew I was tired or tense because of
work or the traffic. No sooner did I ask
for food than it was put before me in
an instant. Fresh, hot, delicious food,
into which she'd put her heart and soul.
Yes, cooking's a gift, so they say. The
food was never the same in my family's
house, in my friends' houses, and even
in my son 'Adil's house; 'Adil, who all my
life I'd hoped would have a house of his
own. It's true that 'Adil's wife's young
and beautiful, but how could she ever
be as skilful as Umm 'Adil?

(Udwan, 1995. Reproduced by permission of Indiana University Press)

York by Bryan Harnetiaux and David Casteal

In order to deepen and extend your understanding
of the power and potency of a play for a single
performer we are going to consider an extract from
a play initially created for a specific place and
event. *York* was written by the white playwright,
Bryan Harnetiaux and performed and partly
devised by the black actor and drummer, David
Casteal, both of whom live and work in the city of
Spokane in the North-West of the United States.

The play and its context

York was written in 2005 to mark the bicentenary
of the 'Lewis and Clark Expedition'. Between
1803 and 1806, Meriwether Lewis and William

Clark and their Corps of Discovery completed an expedition commissioned by United States President Thomas Jefferson to explore the uncharted American west, in search of a practical route to the Pacific Ocean. Much of this historic and harrowing journey is chronicled in the journals of Lewis and Clark, and others who were members of the expeditionary force. However, very little is known about York, the only Black man on the expedition, who was William Clark's slave and manservant. This one-man play captures the slave York's life before, during and after the Lewis and Clark Expedition, focusing on his spiritual awakening as he first leaves the suffocating world of slavery behind, shares in the epic journey of the Corps of Discovery, and then returns home, once again to confront the slave culture. The storytelling in York is enriched by a West African *Djembe* drum score, and York's drum talk.

York was originally presented at the Firth. J. Chew Studio, part of the Civic Theatre in Spokane Washington (illustrated in Chapter 2). Because the play was concerned with an aspect of local history and had particular meaning for the people of Spokane, situated close to a key point in Lewis and Clark's journey, the piece could be said to be **site-sensitive**.

An integral part of Bryan Harnetiaux's text is the African drumming devised by the actor and drummer, David Casteal. This was largely performed by the actor himself but other sections of the play are underscored with recordings of more extensive ensembles of drummers and by traditional American Indian drumming. Here, then, we have an example of the **text** consisting of more than words and the blend of African drumming, heavy with significance for York's cultural and ethnic origins, and of Native American drumming, with its resonances of colonialism creating a rich and complex **interculturalism**.

The play shows a considerable contrast to those we have considered so far: it is largely narrative and, although York is the only seen character, he interacts with other unseen characters at times and occasionally takes on the roles of other characters. The text is divided in 31 short 'episodes', each of which represents a shift in time from the previous episode. The play involves both 'flashbacks' and sequential incidents. York sometimes 'acts out' aspects of the story and at other times narrates it, accompanying himself on the drums. Sometimes he is rowing, sometimes singing a slave song. Here is a short example from episode 14, of the integration of dialogue, role-play, live drumming and recorded music envisaged in the script of the play, you should note the point at which York takes on another 'voice'.

Figure 1.5   David Casteal as York
Source: © Steve Rodenbough

(YORK reveals the African drum he and Sheheke have made. As Sheheke:)

This is for York – a drum talk.

Thank you, Sheheke. Thank you.

(YORK drums the beginning rhythms of Sak Paka Set, which in Creole means 'That Which Cannot Be Done'. This is an original rhythm played in the spirit of traditional West African Djembe. His drumming is increasingly intense and complex. after some headway, he stops drumming. The Mandan singing and drumming are back and continue softly underneath.)

Our last night in the village Sheheke asks me about the tribes downriver, that live with the white man. About their life. I have the trader tell him he must ask the Captain about this. That I am not the one to say. This is true. it feels like a lie.

(Mandan singing and drumming fades out.)

At points in the play York reveals the extent of the racism prevalent among his white contemporaries and his extraordinary dignity and resilience throws these unacceptable attitudes into relief. Like the protagonist of any good play, York takes his audience on a personal journey as well as on a physical journey and he begins with the following speech, which plunges us immediately into the harsh reality of the expedition he has undertaken. Here is the opening speech of the play. You will notice that the various sections of the play are numbered.

York

(At rise: A makeshift tavern/livery stable in St. Louis, circa 1811, where Abolitionists and Freedmen gather. There is a hand-painted sign that says 'YORK TONITE'. A drummed heartbeat in the darkness slowly builds in tempo. Lights up on YORK, eyes closed, drumming. As the heartbeat nears a fevered pitch, his eyes snap open.)

[1] My heart tole me somethin' was wrong. Poundin' so hard, woke me up. Near five years ago – summer a '05. Only there's a foot a snow an' flakes comin' down big's flapjacks. And we're all buried in it 'round the camp pit, with a fire tha's dead out. Except Pryor, who's sittin' 'neath a tree on guard duty, rifle 'cross his lap – froze up. I'm thinkin' the Captain 'ill give him the lash for sure, if he ain't dead already. I climb outa my bag. It's a mean snow. *Summer* snow, Rocky Mountain kind. I go on over to Pryor, kinda protected under this tree. His face's all glazed over. I shake him, an' it sounds like fine China breakin' into pieces. Take my knife and go to chipping the ice away around his eyes an' mouth, 'til I hear this small sound inside him. Like it's coming from down aroun' his knees. He's in there, barely. I straighten him up an' lean him 'gainst a tree, dig around and find the axe an' flint. Cut underbrush 'neath every limb I can find. Then I clear out the pit an' flint it up and pretty soon it's roarin' good. Then I hurry an' cut a coupla strong yokes and drive 'em in on each side a the fire pit, find a limb and tie Pryor to it and lift him up on the yokes over the fire. So I can turn him some, thaw him out. 'Tween turns I dig up Captain Clark and Cap Lewis an' the others, an' stack 'em up next to the pit. I'm dusting the Captain off 'cause I figure he'll be next, bein' I'm responsible for him, when Pryor starts a hollerin' like a banshee. So I know he's done. I'm liftin' him off to get the Captain situated on the spit when there's a hellish roar and this she bear comes a bustin' outa the trees, headin' straight for Captain Clark. Now, this ain' no regular bear. Make a Kentuck black bear look like a house cat. Well, she sees me an' pulls up sudden like, not three feet away. Standin' on her haunches, 8–10 feet high, teeth long as icicles. An' as she'sa ponderin' this black creature, one hand brings my knife up through her middle an' the other reaches in an' yanks her heart out an' shows it to her – still beatin'. That old sow she just nods – almost smiles – an' drops like an oak. Shakes the ground so hard the Captain falls off the spit an' thrashes around in the fire, 'fore I drag him out.

(YORK spots an unseen CAPTAIN CLARK as he enters the tavern/livery.)

YORK.

(See CLARK.)

Speak a the devil.

(*Returning to his story.*)

His hair's a bit singed, but he's fine. I 'member Captain laying there, steam comin' off, staring up at me – lookin' one part mad, the other right grateful-like

(*YORK acknowledges the unseen Clark again*)

You 'member that Captain? Gentlemen, Captain William Clark, a the Lewis an'

Clark Expedition. Yessuh. Now that ain't the look I'm talkin' about.

(*Mimicking CLARK'S arms-folded military stance*)

Tha' your 'bes' come with me or else' look. Don' believe I will, Captain. Maybe you'd like ta tell these fellas one a your own stories 'bout the expedition an' all. Fine by me.

(*YORK exits the tavern/livery stable for another time and place, glancing back at CLARK as he leaves*)

(From *York*, an unpublished play. Reproduced by permission of the writers)

◼ The reflective practitioner and the monologue

Your response to reading the three substantial extracts from plays will, to some extent, depend on the bias of your course of study and your specific interests. You may be fascinated by the topics and issues raised, the playwrights' techniques or the performance considerations that are created. However, most recent university and college courses in Theatre Studies include as one of their stated aims the development of the 'reflective practitioner'. The idea that students engaged in practical exploration of Theatre and of the relevant skills involved should cultivate the habit of reflecting critically upon their practice is central to the convictions that underpin this book. We can, perhaps, best illustrate this by considering the experience of David Hare, a leading playwright in the contemporary British Theatre, who experimented with the creation and performance of a play for a single performer.

David Hare is a major exponent of **political theatre** and has written and continues to write plays dealing with many aspects of public life arising from his passionate convictions and detailed research. His plays have encompassed such subjects as the Chinese Revolution (*Fanshen*), the English judiciary (*Murmuring Judges*), the Church of England (*Racing Demon*), the railways in Britain (*The Permanent Way*) and the war in Iraq (*Stuff Happens*), and these are all full-length plays with substantial casts. However, when it came to creating his response to his visit to the Middle East in dramatic form he explained in an article that his visit: 'had left me despairing of any other means of conveying the vividness of my reactions except by direct address. I felt, for this one subject only, I had no alternative but to stand in a theatre in person and forgo the playwright's usual convenient cover of hiring a specialist who will do the speaking for him' (2002, pp. 192–3).

The result of Hare's conviction was the play *Via Dolorosa*. The Via Dolorosa (Way of Sorrows) is the street in the old city of Jerusalem along which Christ is traditionally said to have carried his cross. David Hare's play of the same name was written in 1997, following his visit to Israel and the occupied territories of Palestine.

◆ Hare allowed the director Stephen Daldry to direct him at London's Royal Court Theatre in a 90-minute monodrama, which was later staged both in the West End and on Broadway. The performance was also made into a film in 2000 and Hare's experiences of preparing and giving the performances were documented in detail in his published diary *Acting Up* (1999).

Following the invasion of Iraq, Hare also felt compelled to revive the play in London and provides a fascinating insight into his thinking in his article 'The Second Intifada' (2005b). The performances of the play were invariably highly controversial but Hare had attempted to remain even-handed in his treatment of the conflicting Palestinian and Israeli attitudes, arguing that an intelligent audience needed to step back from the immediate passions aroused and consider the issues carefully.

The play was also the subject of a lawsuit brought by the Los Angeles actor/writer, Steven Greenstein, who claimed that *Via Dolorosa* had plagiarized words, forms and ideas from his own one-man play *Voices from the Holy. . .and Not So Holy Land*, which he had sent to Daldry at the Royal Court. The judge, however, rejected all these claims.

Hare has never been tempted to repeat the experiment of writing a monodrama, and it is not clear if he would allow another actor to present his play.

Hare's working diary and his article 'The Second Intifada' (2005b) are excellent examples of the playwright as performer reflecting creatively and analytically on his practice. We shall be encouraging you to follow Hare's example in critically examining your practice as this book progresses.

Suggested activity

◆ Observe the relationships and dynamics between performer and spectators in a piece of street entertainment, stand-up comedy or public speaker.

◆ Devise a monologue based on a diary or similar personal document of a real or imagined character. Experiment with its performance.

◆ Read other plays containing monologues such as Chekhov's *On the Harmfulness of Tobacco*, Cabal's *Tejes Verdes* or Clare Luckham's *The Choice*.

◆ Identify examples of the use of the monologue or direct address to the audience in any plays for stage, TV or film.

◆ Compile a list of venues in which you have seen or been aware of live performances. What are their essential components?

◆ Begin your own log as your work as an actor.

■ Conclusion

In this chapter we have introduced the major, basic elements of studying Theatre in order to establish a foundation for your work. The concentration on plays with a single voice has enabled us to focus on the key relationship between performers, performance spaces and audiences. We have also considered the potency of direct address to the spectators. Moving from the immediacy and risk of a piece of street performance to the relative sophistication of the play with multiple characters, we have seen how the decisions concerning the staging, mode of language and the role of the spectator all intermingle to create what we call 'theatre'. Along the way we have introduced many of the significant terms we use to discuss performance.

As we have seen, the use of a single speaker is not confined to plays containing a single character. The interaction of characters on stage using language is a topic for later discussion and we have yet to deal with concepts such as *character*, **plot** or *dialogue* which are frequently introduced very early in a more literary orientated study of drama. We need, however, to be reminded that Theatre is a narrative art in which stories are told to the audience, enabling them to make sense of the past and the present. As an art-form, it must be alive to the needs and interests of potential audiences and the text, written by major playwrights or devised through workshops must relate to the language spoken in recognizable life situations.

Topics for discussion and reflection

◆ How would you now define an act of Theatre?
◆ How might a performance in a **found space** differ from that in a permanent theatre?
◆ In what ways is the relationship between performer and spectator affected by the form of staging chosen?
◆ What is the historical, social and theatrical **context** of each of the extracts provided?
◆ Provide an example from one of the play extracts of **intertextuality**.

◆ What performance issues are raised when the writer becomes the performer?
◆ Are there significant performance problems when the play is based on 'real' events and people? How does this differ from a play in which the entire work is a fiction?
◆ What are the differences between performing to an audience sitting at tables and one seated in theatre with 'stalls'? What other audience configurations have you been aware of?

◼ Further reading

Allain, P. and Harvie, J. (2006) *The Routledge Companion to Theatre and Performance*, London: Routledge. An accessible and comprehensive guide to terminology and fact which will be of use throughout your studies.

Barba, E. (1994) *The Paper Canoe: A Guide to Theatre Anthropology*, trans. R. Fowler, London: Routledge. A fascinating survey of many kinds of theatrical activity.

Hare, D. (1999) *Acting Up*, London: Faber and Faber. Provides a fascinating insight into the work of a playwright/performer which will serve as a model for your own reflective work.

Hare, D. (2005) *Obedience, Struggle and Revolt*, London: Faber and Faber. A series of challenging and provocative thoughts on the nature of Theatre.

Pavis, P. (2003) *Analyzing Performance*, Ann Arbor, MI: University of Michigan Press. This book will act as a constant support to your critical thinking about Theatre.

Pickering, K. (2005) *Key Concepts in Drama and Performance*, Basingtoke: Palgrave Macmillan. A source of reference which will support your work in each of the areas introduced in this chapter. See especially the entries under **monologue** and **analysis**.

◼ Website

For Playwright Profiles and extensive discussion of other monologues/monodramas, see our website: www.palgrave.com/foundations/pickering

Exploring Theatre Spaces

CHAPTER

2

An act of Theatre may take place in almost any space but, throughout history, there have been many attempts to create permanent theatre buildings. In this chapter, we shall introduce the study of theatre spaces and invite you to consider a number of examples very carefully. We shall emphasize the use of illustrations and personal observations and discuss the concept of inter-dependence between the nature of the theatre space or form and that of the performance.

Learning outcomes

By the conclusion of this chapter, you should be able to:

▶ look at Theatre spaces with understanding and perception;

▶ identify and describe a variety of types of acting 'space' or stage configuration drawn from practice both past and present;

▶ outline examples of factors influencing a performer's relationship with the audience in at least three of the above;

▶ indicate the means by which the 'location' of scenes may be conveyed in various forms of staging;

▶ describe a real 'found space' of your choosing and outline how it might be used for a performance 'event'.

■ The importance of exploration

The title of this chapter suggests an active engagement with the consideration of theatre spaces. Unless you are able to be physically present to witness, or personally experiment with, a space being used, you are unlikely to achieve the level of learning intended here. The exploration may well also involve studying photographs and other forms of illustration and, again, the emphasis must be on using such material as important sources for understanding rather than on seeing them as decorative aspects of this book. Looking at photographs of a space both when empty of performers and being used in a production requires perception and care: skills well worth developing in this context. Fortunately, recent years have also seen the development of an additional tool in the exploration of theatre spaces: computer aided design (CAD). This has been employed most impressively by Richard Beacham, a distinguished theatre historian leading the Theatron project. The results of his work are easily accessed via the internet and enable students to enter a whole range of historic theatre structures through virtual reality.

However, let us begin with a relatively straightforward, but none-the-less informative, example. Study the illustration of the Theatre Royal Margate in Figure 2.1 and note the following points:

◆ Margate is a coastal town in the South East of England and its Theatre Royal (one of many Theatres Royal in the UK) was originally built in 1787 but substantially remodelled by J.T. Robinson (who also designed the much more famous 'Old Vic' Theatre in London) in 1874.

◆ The Theatre Royal Margate dates from what is usually considered the 'heyday of provincial theatres'.

◆ This Theatre claims to have the oldest surviving stage in Britain and retains some of the pulleys and counterweights used for lowering and 'flying' scenery and a 'star trap'

The Theatre Royal · Margate
(CIRCA 1760)

Figure 2.1   The Theatre Royal, Margate
© Kenneth Pickering

in the floor of the stage that would have enabled characters to be almost catapulted up through the trap for a spectacular entrance.

◆ Towns and cities throughout Britain, mainland Europe and North America all once contained, or still do contain, a similar form of theatre building.

◆ For many people, the building shown here still constitutes what they expect a 'Theatre' to look like.

◆ The most obvious features of such buildings are the tiered *auditorium* and the picture-frame or *'proscenium* stage'.

Suggested activity

◆ Research the existence of a 'Theatre Royal' in your nearest town or city. Does it still function? Is it now a disused building or has it been demolished? What records of its repertoire and activity now remain?

▋ Proscenium staging

Such was the dominance achieved by the proscenium form by the end of the nineteenth century that it is still often referred to as the 'traditional' theatre form. This is misleading and inaccurate because the period during which the proscenium arch was used to create a complete separation between the acting area and the auditorium was a comparatively brief one. The proscenium arch itself is an ancient feature but it was only during the late eighteenth and nineteenth centuries that theatres were built in such a way as to ensure that the audience's view of the entire stage was framed by this arch. The dominance of the proscenium arch has coincided with the increased popularity of opera, ballet and various forms of musical Theatre and light entertainments, such as the British **panto-mime**, all of which delight in staging 'pictures' and spectacle.

A proscenium arch stage is ideal for the creation of illusion and pictorial effects. It is possible to hide from view a great deal of machinery, lighting equipment, construc-tional reinforcement and scenery in preparation for several transformations of the stage picture. By careful use of perspective, a designer can create the illusion of a larger space. Single, flat surfaces can be painted to resemble buildings or landscapes or create whatever environment is desired. By the cunning use of gauze and lighting, characters or entire scenes can appear and disappear at will. By the construction of a **box set** using canvas flats, a designer can create the appearance of a solid, three-dimensional interior and this feature contributed to the rise of many dramas with a domestic setting.

The invention of, first, gas and then electric stage lighting, together with the innova-tion of darkening the auditorium for a performance, both enhanced the new sense of the proscenium arch as a barrier dividing actors and audience. Audiences and theatre prac-titioners in the late nineteenth and early twentieth centuries came to think of the stage as just a room from which the fourth wall had been removed in order to allow the audi-ence to witness the action inside. To some extent this concept still exists. Variations on the proscenium from have been the subject of fairly recent experiment. For example, the illustration of the twentieth-century Civic Theatre in Spokane, Washington (Figure 2.2), shows a set constructed on a central proscenium stage that, unusually, is flanked on either side by two smaller prosceniums.

Figure 2.2   The Civic Theatre: Spokane, Washington
Source: © Michael B. Herzog

Alternative spaces

We have demonstrated in our opening chapter that an event or activity we might term 'Theatre' does not, necessarily, depend on the existence of a building called a theatre or playhouse. Indeed, such purpose-built **cultural spaces** are unknown in many theatrical traditions. For example, the editors of Udwan's play *That's Life* from which we took an opening speech in Chapter 1, point out that there is a long legacy of Arabic drama that presumes no theatre building and that the use of Western-style staging is a relatively new feature in Middle Eastern countries.

Theatre can take place almost anywhere and the history and study of the activity show that much of it has involved and continues to involve the finding of convenient sites for performance. We catch a glimpse of this in Shakespeare's play *A Midsummer Night's Dream* in which a group of amateur actors go into the woods in order to find a place for rehearsal and on finding it, their leader remarks: 'Here's a wondrous convenient spot for our rehearsal.'

We know, in fact, from surviving place names in England, that the 'playstool' was a location in a village or town where plays could be presented and a crowd gather round without any sense that this was permanent structure. The emphasis in all traditions of itinerant players was on the performers and their ability to engage an audience directly in virtually any suitable location.

The radical alternative to the permanent theatre building is the **found space**. Theatre practitioners have increasingly found the concept of permanent staging constricting and, like the itinerant troupes of players in previous generations, have sought to rediscover a sense of immediacy achieved by performing in a huge variety of non-theatrical venues. Added to the sense of liberation in this activity is the ability to shape a particular performance to exploit the unique qualities of the found space and of any **found objects** (*objets trouvés*) within it. Consequently many devised performances are labelled **site-specific** or **site-sensitive** because they derive their qualities, themes or ideas from the chosen venue and, accordingly, could not be presented elsewhere. This was largely true of the performances devised by Richard Schechner and his Performance Group in the New York of the 1970s where he originally termed his works **environmental theatre**. Schechner, whose writings have had a profound influence on the development of Performance Studies, was allowing the nature of found spaces to both inspire and shape the nature of performances.

This very creative use of space has provided the impetus for some of the most interesting experiments in modern theatre: here, for example, are significant statements by three influential twentieth-century practitioners:

> I propose abandoning the architecture of present-day theatres. We shall take some hangar or barn, which we shall have reconstructed according to the processes which have culminated in the architecture of certain churches or holy places, and of certain temples in Tibet.
>
> (Antonin Artaud, 1970, p. 74)

> The arbitrary conventions of our auditoriums and stages placed face to face still control us! Let us leave our theatres to their dying past, and let us construct elementary buildings, designed merely to cover the space in which we work.
>
> (Adolph Appia, quoted in Roose-Evans, 1988)

> The theatre must give the audience of today a new experience of space. It is as necessary for us to rediscover a relationship with space, the space around us as it is to explore outer space. We need to experience afresh the height and depth and breadth of space, its intimacy and immensity.
>
> (Roose Evans, 1988, p. 135)

There appear to be practical, aesthetic and ideological reasons why many theatre practitioners have chosen to move away from the confines of the proscenium stage and seek a sense of liberation in the found space or in some alternative structure. In recent years psychotherapists such as Lanyado (2004, p. 81) have used the term **transitional space** to define a space that is the exact opposite of a space in which individuals feel trapped, unable to breathe, think or play. Transitional spaces are those which are full of possibilities and new ideas. For the theatre practitioner these may be found spaces. Many found spaces have, of course, become permanent venues: basements, outdoor natural auditoria and a whole variety of halls and rooms have eventually been adopted by theatre companies as their chosen working and performance spaces. For example, our illustration of the Theatre of Convenience in Great Malvern, Worcestershire (Figure 2.3), shows what was once a public lavatory transformed into the smallest public theatre in Britain.

Figure 2.3 The found space becomes permanent venue: the Theatre of Convenience in Malvern Worcestershire, once a public lavatory and now the smallest public theatre in Britain
Source: © Kenneth Pickering

Peter Brook, writing in *The Shifting Point* (1988), attributes his move away from the proscenium theatre to a gradual realization that his original production style consisted of having a set of mental images that he wished to bring to life, framed as a picture would be. His subsequent work, and that of many recent practitioners, has tended to focus more on the human body in a space and on attempts to engage the audience by breaking down the physical barriers created by the proscenium and its comfortable seated audience.

As we have also seen, more democratic and less commercial forms of theatre organization have led to a constant search for new audiences and new performance locations. Much of this activity relates to efforts to re-discover the essence of Theatre as we began to define it in our first chapter.

The concept of the found space is by no means the only alternative to the erroneously labelled 'traditional' proscenium form. There has, in fact, been a considerable emphasis on the use and construction of many forms of flexible yet permanent theatre forms since the middle years of the last century. It would be relatively easy to illustrate this, and the continuing presence of the proscenium stage, with illustrations and descriptions of theatre buildings in, say, London, New York or other major cities. However, in order to emphasize the extent of diversity in theatre construction and design we are taking less well-known but equally important and informative examples: the theatre spaces to be found in the city of Spokane, in the North West of the USA.

◼ The studio theatre

Study Figure 2.4 carefully. The term '**studio**' implies a place in which a work of art is made. The studio theatre in Spokane, named after one of the major benefactors of theatre in the

Figure 2.4   The Firth J. Chew Studio at the Civic Theatre, Spokane, Washington
Source: © Michael B. Herzog

city, is fairly typical of the kind of space that now often exists as an alternative to the 'main house' auditorium in theatre complexes. In the case of Spokane, as in many theatres, this is the venue for more experimental theatre and for the development of new work, including the play *York* described in Chapter 1. Studio theatres are sometimes known as 'laboratory theatres' or 'theatre workshops' both of which suggest the process of experiment and 'making'. (Remember that the makers of plays are known as playwrights.)

The most important feature of any studio is its flexibility and its ability to be a place where work is both developed and shown. In this sense it differs from some other forms of theatre where work is often developed in rehearsal rooms and transferred to a 'stage' in another location some time later.

At its most basic, the studio theatre is simply a rectangular room that can accommodate a performer and some spectators: it may well be painted black or in some other neutral colour to enable the actor to be the major feature of any performance. In fact, a 'black box' theatre has become a familiar part of the provision for practical work and its move towards the 'white cube' reflects a fascinating development in the visual arts that you may wish to discuss.

A studio may be equipped with rostrum blocks to facilitate a variety of levels for the performer or spectator; there may be forms of seating and there may be structures to enable lighting and/or sound equipment to be used. The concept of the studio includes the idea that the performer and the audience may be placed virtually anywhere within the space and that a sense of intimacy is central to its use. Both performers and spectators may be static or mobile according to the demands of the particular piece of work being presented. In Europe, the form of Theatre that takes place in a small studio is sometimes known as 'Chamber Theatre'.

All this will be familiar to you if you are a student of Theatre because most Theatre or Drama courses include access to a studio as a basic facility. The proliferation of such courses since the middle of the twentieth century, together with the influence of such practitioners as Brecht and Grotowski, with their emphasis on experimentation and **workshop** approach, led to the construction of studios on campuses and in theatres throughout the Western world. It has been said that in the 1940s and 1950s some large campuses in the USA were built containing as wide a variety of theatre spaces as many entire British cities.

Using the studio

We can illustrate some of the many possibilities for the use of a simple rectangular space by considering some of Grotowski's productions.(At this point you should turn back to the 'Practitioner Profile' of Grotowski in Chapter 1 to refresh your memory on his ideas of staging.)

The characteristics of the type of theatrical event he aimed to create are that it permits the 'proper spectator/actor relationship for each type of performance' in which it is possible to 'embody the decision in physical arrangements'. Experiments with these principles led Grotowski to set *Kordian* (1962) in a psychiatric ward with the spectators sitting on and around two-tiered bunk beds as though they were patients. Then he set Marlowe's play *Dr. Faustus* (1963) as if it were a Last Supper. The spectator/ guests were welcomed by Faustus and seated at two long refectory tables while Faust himself finally sat at a small table at one end rather like the Prior presiding over his refectory.

For his production of the *Constant Prince* (1965), the 'spectator-peepers' looked down on the action from the walls of a wooden bear pit. The only staging element in the pit itself was a low oblong dais just long enough to take a man's body.

Describing Grotowski's next production *Akropolis*, his literary adviser wrote: 'it was decided that there would be no direct action between actors and spectators'. The actors were 'to be dead; the spectators represent those who are outside the circle of initiates . . . they are the living' (*Towards a Poor Theatre*, 1969, p. 63). The concept was that the separation, combined with the closeness, of the spectators gave the impression 'that the dead are born from a dream of the living' and the only material element present at the opening of the piece was a large box with metallic junk piled on top of it: 'stovepipes of various lengths and widths, a wheelbarrow, a bathtub, nails, hammers. Everything . . . old . . . rusty . . . picked up from a junkyard.' During the action all of these objects became elements in an evolving civilization for whom the ultimate metaphor was the gas chamber.

Grotowski's experimentation reached its final point in his production of *Apocalypsis Cum Figuris* in which the space occupied by spectators and performers was completely undifferentiated and actors and audience shared a large, empty hall.

Figure 2.5 Using the studio: Grotowski's production of Dziardy's *Forefather's Eve*
Source: © Grotowski Institute

■ Techniques using space

The effect of these productions by Grotowski on subsequent practitioners and approaches to theatre has been profound. Indeed, it is highly probable that work you have seen or been engaged in has been unconsciously influenced by the experiments Grotowski carried out 40 or more years ago. His techniques involved a far freer use of space than had been common in previous generations and we can learn from his work how a simple studio can be used. Here are some possibilities.

Promenade

The studio theatre is often an ideal situation for a production in which the audience moves from one part of the room to another, gathering round the action. This process may also be combined with the actors moving into and around the seated or standing audience. Such promenade productions have already been mentioned in Chapter 1 and very often they create a level of audience participation in the event that can be achieved in no other way. Promenade productions usually involve no permanent seating but may provide situations in which the audience sit in various pre-prepared areas or on some form of moveable stool or chair. Most frequently, the audience will either be standing or sitting on the floor.

The use of promenade is by no means confined to the studio situation: think back to the review of *Apocalypsis Cum Figuris* and consider some of the extended examples of the use of the found space in this and in later chapters.

Theatre in-the-round

Many studio performances are a variation on **arena** staging or what is known as '**theatre-in-the round**'. In this form, the audience entirely surrounds the performers and is obviously based on very ancient practice. 'Rounds' appear to have been common in Western Europe during the medieval period and involved a **central platea** or acting area with a number of raised structures around the edge. Records suggest that the audience crowded into the round with the actors and were kept in order by attendants, who would clear spaces for the actors and help direct the audience's attention.

In more recent times the impetus for the revival of theatre-in-the-round came from Margot Jones in the USA who was producing theatre-in-the-round in an old fair-ground building in Dallas, Texas, as early as 1945. In Britain, the cause was led by the director Stephen Joseph during the 1950s and 1960s. His book, *New Theatre Forms*, took on the force of a manifesto for all those practitioners who felt stifled by the dominance of the proscenium arch theatres. Joseph gathered round him actors, writers and directors who shared his beliefs and in the small Library Theatre in the northern English coastal town of Scarborough they carried out their experiments. One of the most successful contemporary British dramatists, Alan Ayckbourn, was a product of this experience and, as director of the new, permanent theatre built in Scarborough to Joseph's memory, he still crafts his plays to be performed initially 'in-the round'. Other permanent theatres of this kind include the Interplayers Theatre in Spokane, Washington (see Figure 2.6) and the New Vic Theatre in the English Midlands town of Newcastle-under-Lyne.

Figure 2.6 Theatre-in-the-round: Interplayers Theatre, Spokane
Source: © Michael B. Herzog

The central area of a theatre-in-the-round, which might be circular, square or many-sided, ensures that an audience, viewing from all sides, is always relatively close to the action. Entrances and exits must be created through the auditorium, and these, usually situated on opposite corners or sides, allow for great fluidity of movement across the acting area. The only background against which the performers are seen consists of the spectators themselves and actors have to find ways in which to address or relate to their audience. Rules applicable to the proscenium stage no longer have any validity: groupings of characters, sight lines or the apparent dominance of one part of a stage take on an entirely new dimension when the acting space must be virtually free of décor.

The transverse stage

The flexibility of any studio should allow the performers to opt for the use of a **transverse stage** where the audience watches from either side of a central space or elevated 'catwalk'. Some would argue that the event of a fashion show is an act of Theatre: it is certainly a performance. The advantages of a transverse arrangement will be discovered in your own experiments but will include the ability to create processions, carnivals and situations where the audience is aware of the reactions of those sitting or standing opposite. In dramas where characters need to be close to the audience yet have a point from which they enter at some distance from the bulk of the spectators, the transverse arrangement can produce a sense of immediacy and intimacy. A succession of short scenes following quickly upon each other can often benefit from the qualities created by this particular use of space and there are many studio spaces that can be and have been adapted to exploit this form.

The open stage

Most studio spaces enable action to take place at one end of the room while the audience, possibly seated on 'bleachers' or some form of tiered seating, watch from the opposite end. In this arrangement audience members are all facing in the same direction and the acting area is a simple, **open space** with a rear wall or **cyclorama**. Because the stage is not framed by a proscenium and because the acting area usually does not have **wings** or borders of any kind other than the walls of the studio, there is a sense of 'shared space' between actors and audience and access to the stage can be achieved from almost any direction. Actors can invade the audience space and, if necessary, the audience can invade the actors' space with ease. It is, however, possible to erect three-dimensional structures on the stage area and provide facilities for disappearances, entrances and variations of level.

Finding studio spaces

Studio theatre spaces have been created from many different starting-points. Even when they constitute a facility on a college campus or as part of the assets of a permanent theatre company, they may well not be purpose-built. Theatre studios have been created from disused chapels and churches and farm buildings, warehouses, halls of various kinds, factories, coach-houses or rooms in houses and basements. Where it is possible to build a studio theatre, the needs of performance, experiment and study must all be taken into consideration.

Suggested activity

◆ Look for studio theatre spaces in your own location and discover what activity goes on there.

◆ Look for potential studio theatre spaces in your location and form you own company to create theatre there.

◆ Decide the essential qualities and features for the design of a purpose-built studio.

◆ Visit as many performances in studio theatre spaces as possible. Far too many students of Theatre fail to support their study with wide experience of current practice.

◆ Select one of the following options using a central pathway in your studio: (1) audience seated on two sides on a level with the acting area; (2) acting area raised like catwalk with

audience on two sides; or (3) audience raised in tiers on both sides of a ground-level acting area. Present the same scene in all three arrangements and critically examine the effect on performers and audience. Log your findings.

◆ Use your studio to create a number of variations on arena staging, including having the audience on three sides or in a semi-circle. Discuss the results and the advantages of any particular physical arrangement.

◆ Using the various options mentioned above, analyse the acting process involved in presenting a monologue to an audience. Log your findings.

The thrust stage

The Bing Crosby Theatre (Figure 2.7) has a proscenium arch, far more semi-circular than is often the case, but also a section of the stage projecting into the auditorium as a form of forestage, which, were it to project further and have seating audience seating around it,

Figure 2.7   The Bing Crosby Theatre, Spokane
Source: © Michael B. Herzog

would be termed a **thrust**. This theatre, named after one of the most famous residents of the city, is a particularly good example of the conjunction of two major theatre traditions.

In the history of theatre forms from the English-speaking world, two periods stand out as having been marked by the predominance of a particular theatre form: (1) the Elizabethan age, when a thrust stage was common, jutting out into an audience that surrounded it on three sides; and (2) the Victorian age, when the theatre was virtually divided into two distinct rooms, stage and auditorium, separated by a proscenium arch.

The main difference between a thrust stage and a proscenium arch stage lies in the relationship established between actors and their audience and it would seem that the Bing Crosby Theatre attempts to provide elements of both kinds. On a thrust stage, as is the case with most uses of a studio space, the actors inhabit the same space as their audience. They may therefore find it easy to address the audience directly: an actor wishing to do this in the Bing Crosby would probably come down to the **apron**, the area projecting into the auditorium.

It is often maintained that the use of the soliloquy in Elizabethan drama was particularly suited to the kind of thrust stage shown in Figure 2.8 of the Swan Theatre. This is probably

The Swan Theatre Stage, c. 1596

Johanne de Witt's sketch copied by Arend van Buchell. The only contemporary pictorial evidence of the interior of an Elizabethan playhouse.

Figure 2.8 The Swan Theatre, c. 1596

the best-known illustration of any theatre and you are almost certainly familiar with it: however, you should now study it in greater detail than usual and, hopefully, with new insights. Many scholars have argued that this type of theatre building evolved from the found spaces of inn courtyards and you might like to consider what evidence there might be for this idea.

Figure 2.8 shows the Swan Theatre in London in about 1596. The original sketch was made by Johanne de Witt on a visit to London from Holland but the only surviving version is a copy made by Arend van Buchell. This is the only contemporary pictorial evidence of the interior of an Elizabethan playhouse. All recent reconstructions of Elizabethan Theatres (such as The Globe on London's 'South Bank') have been partly based on this illustration.

Suggested activity

Find illustrations of the exteriors of Elizabethan theatres or visit one of the conjectural reconstructions of such a theatre, such as The Globe in London or Stratford, Ontario.

◆ Using Shakespeare's *Macbeth* or *A Midsummer Night's Dream* as an example, describe how you imagine the following parts of the theatre were used: (1) the doors at the rear of the stage; (2) the balcony-like structure above the doors; (3) the upper level from which a flag is flying; (4) the front part of the

stage area; and (5) the area at the rear of the stage underneath a roof.

◆ Imaginatively reconstruct the relationship between audience (including the groundlings) and actors as suggested by the drawing, particularly remembering that performances took place in daylight.

◆ Consider what effect the open-air nature of the theatre and the fact that many of the audience stood in the area surrounding the stage might have had on the style of performance.

■ Transitions

In the **masques** that became popular at the English court during the first part of the seventeenth century, new Italian methods of providing spectacular backgrounds came into use, involving elaborate machinery for **flying** scenery in and out. Following the restoration of the monarchy in 1660, new theatres were built to facilitate the use of perspective scenery, painted on backcloths and on flats placed at intervals on each side of the stage. But the scale of such theatres was much more intimate than the Elizabethan theatre had been. Part of the stage remained thrust out into the auditorium and a door at the front of the stage on each side allowed for entrances and exits in close proximity with the audience. This was theatre form in transition between the Elizabethan thrust stage and the proscenium arch that was to dominate the eighteenth and nineteenth centuries. However, you should remember that the idea of darkening the auditorium and confining the lighting to the stage is a relatively recent innovation. In the seventeenth, eighteenth and early nineteenth centuries both the stage and the auditorium were lit by candles or oil lamps, thus creating the sense of a shared room. It was only with the introduction of gas from about 1817 onwards, and subsequently electric lighting in the 1880s, that the division of the acting area and the watching area was made complete by the use of light.

The situation today is that no one single theatre form is predominant. Because of this we can draw parallels with the medieval period when a variety of different theatre forms were also in use. As modern staging methods have become more flexible and adventurous, so interest in medieval staging has grown and it is significant that some of the most fascinating uses of the found space, promenade and small platforms around which audiences gather, has been in the various revivals of the medieval **cycles** of **Mystery Plays**. The great English cycles appear originally to have been performed on a number of different mobile stages or **pageants**, each one representing a particular location in the course of the cycle. This technique remains part of **carnivals** in many countries to this day. Other plays were performed in **rounds**, and we have noted how that influenced the work of some directors in the twentieth century. A simpler and very common form of staging was the **booth** stage, consisting of boards on a trestle with a curtain behind which the actors could change costumes and from which they could make surprise entrances. We see this form perpetuated in many puppet theatres and in the peculiarly British tradition of Punch and Judy. Finally, many plays, like the Valenciennes passion play, of 1547, were performed on a long stage or a town square, forming a central plateau while behind it were ranges a sequence of **mansions** or small, separate stage sets, representing different locations, from heaven (at the left) to hell's mouth (at the extreme right). Such **multi-focus** settings are frequently employed by theatre companies today as they utilize the variety of levels, niches, entrances and surfaces of a whole variety of different buildings and locations.

◼ Conclusion

In this chapter we have seen that Theatre can be created in a wide range of possible venues and that these, in turn, may affect the very nature of a performance. Beginning with what, mistakenly, has come be thought of as a 'traditional' theatre building we have emphasized the importance of close observation in exploring theatre forms through visits, illustrations or computer aided design. We have noted that many modern practitioners have rebelled against what has seemed to be restricting and deadening in permanent theatre buildings based on a proscenium arch design and have explored some of the variations that have emanated from the rise of the 'studio' theatre. In order to achieve a sense of liberation from the proscenium many thinkers have turned to a rediscovery of ancient theatre forms that created a different dymanic between performers and audience.

We have also discussed how some practitioners have abandoned the concept of permanent, purpose-built theatre structures altogether and encouraged you to think how this practice relates to our earlier considerations as to the nature of Theatre as a human activity. The examples drawn from a broad spectrum of situations have encouraged you to be aware of diversity in theatre spaces and the ways in which the buildings or locations may both determine and be determined by the shaping of the dramatic text. In order to understand plays and performance styles of all kinds, it is necessary to acquire a familiarity with both current and historic theatre spaces and staging forms.

Topics for discussion and reflection

◆ What types of play were written to exploit the particular qualities and properties of the proscenium stage or Theatre-in–the-round? Give examples.

◆ What effect did the invention of gas and electric lighting have on play production in the nineteenth and twentieth centuries?

◆ How was 'flying' achieved in relation to: (1) scenery; (2) people?

◆ The terms 'waiting in the wings', 'facing the final curtain', and 'curtain line' are clearly drawn from the theatre. What is their precise meaning and what other such terms can you list and define?

◆ What was the effect of the distancing of the audience from the performers and the gradual retreat and eventual loss of the apron or fore-stage?

◆ Which form of staging, from the many considered in this chapter, would you employ for a production of any of the texts included in Chapter 1?

Further reading

Artaud, A. (1970) *The Theatre and its Double*, trans. V. Corti, London: Calder and Boyars. One of the most influential approaches to Theatre of modern times.

Brook, P. (1988) *The Shifting Point: Forty Years of Theatrical Exploration*, London: Methuen. A wide-ranging consideration of many of the topics dealt with in this book.

Grotowski, J. (1969) *Towards a Poor Theatre*, London: Methuen. An essential text for understanding the profound influence and continuing relevance of Grotowski.

McAuley, G. (2000) *Space in Performance: Making Meaning in the Theatre*, Ann Arbor, MI: University of Michigan Press. A very clear treatment of the relationship between space and performance.

Mudford, P. (2000) *Making Theatre: From Text to Performance*, London: The Athlone Press. An engaging discussion of various kinds of theatrical performance and of their shaping by their environment.

Schechner, R. (1994) *Environmental Theatre*, New York: Applause Books. An excellent introduction to the work of one of the most significant scholars and practitioners of recent years.

Website

For information on Theatres Royal, extended examples of exploring provincial theatres and discussion of the use of theatre spaces, see our website: www.palgrave.com/foundations/pickering

CHAPTER 3

Developing Theatre Skills

This chapter aims to provide you with the necessary basic skills and approaches that will enable you to respond to a variety of performance tasks and understand the process of acting from a critical stance. It is the most interactive of our chapters and we would encourage you to respond practically wherever possible. The material presented should help you to be sensitive to the needs of dramatic texts and to explore ways of recording your experience.

Learning outcomes

By the conclusion of this chapter, you should be able to:

▶ identify the skills needed by an actor;

▶ discuss the responsibilities of an actor;

▶ debate to what extent acting can be learnt;

▶ maintain an acting journal;

▶ develop the skill of story-telling in theatre;

▶ use a text as an indicator for performance;

▶ understand the process of researching a role;

▶ utilize the concept of 'purpose-driven' behaviour as the basis for a role.

■ The primacy of the actor

> A man walks across this empty space while someone else is watching him, and this is all that is needed for an act of theatre to be engaged.

> (Peter Brook, *The Empty Space*, 1968, p. 9)

In what is almost certainly the best-known statement in Theatre Studies, Peter Brook establishes the absolute primacy of the actor as the key element of Theatre. The man or

Figure 3.1 The potency of the single performer; Victoria Szebesta in *The Dance Project*, the Oakwood Centre, Woodley. Set and lighting design by John Forth, photography: Mathew Foster
Source: © Thames Valley University

woman who 'walks across this empty space' creates the initial act of Theatre from which everything else in the art form proceeds. For Brook and for many modern theatre practitioners who have followed him, the space needs no embellishment and the 'audience' may be few or many, seated, standing or gathered around in a variety of ways, but it is the focus of attention on the actor that constitutes the event. Modern Theatre Studies has tended to reflect this fact and, although there continues to be scholarly work on the design, technical and textual aspects of Theatre, a study of the role, function and skills of the actor, often shaped by the director, has become central to our understanding of the nature of our subject.

Can acting be learnt?

Recent autobiographies by such actors as Rupert Everett seem to suggest that nothing very useful can be learnt at a Drama School, university or college and there are plenty of examples of successful actors who had little or no formal training. Others have indicated that they found their studies restricting and often confined to preparation for a particular kind of Theatre tradition so that they felt unable to respond to the constantly shifting nature of acting. These attitudes are by no means confined to acting: similar feelings have been expressed by musicians and dancers, many recalling only the eccentricities and egos of their teachers!

Perhaps, therefore, the real question for students of Theatre Studies is 'Can acting be taught or studied?' Clearly, there is a general consensus that it can and this is reflected in the considerable number of undergraduate courses in aspects of Theatre that include one or more modules or courses in acting and practical theatre skills. We can set alongside the comments of those actors who claim to have learnt little from their courses of study the fact that the greatest English actor of the nineteenth century, Sir Henry Irving, and one of the greatest of the twentieth, Sir John Gielgud, both maintained they continued to learn to the very end of their respective careers. Such learning is *experiential* and a great deal of theatre learning is: very often, the best that a gifted tutor can do is to provide a situation in which such learning takes place. Students need to recognize this important aspect of their work.

However, if acting is to be studied and theatre skills developed, it is now recognized that the various processes involved must be analysed and understood *systematically*. This entails breaking down acting into its constituent elements and identifying those aspects of acting that can be developed through practice, observation, reflection and reading.

Practitioner profile

Denis Diderot (1713–84)

A number of ancient texts giving instruction for highly complex modes of performance have survived from the Indian sub-continent and these have been of increasing interest to practitioners in the West seeking to explore aspects of multi-culturalism through performance. However, the first significant writing on acting in Europe was an article by the eighteenth-century writer and philosopher, Denis Diderot, entitled *The Paradox of Acting* which is included in Lee Strasberg's (1957) book *The Paradox of Acting and Masks and Faces*. It is well worth dwelling on Diderot's thinking to see an example of the development of critical thinking in relation to the acting process.

We can summarize Diderot's main ideas as follows:

◆ The paradox of acting is that, in order to move an audience, the actor must remain unmoved. In analysing this paradox, Diderot concluded that an actor must acquire personal discipline and techniques to control involvement in a role.
◆ He stated: 'An actor who has only sense and judgement is cold' (1957, p. 11). He balanced this by saying:

> One who has only verve and sensibility is crazy. It is a peculiar combination of good sense and warmth which creates the sublime person; and on stage as in life he who shows more than he feels makes one laugh instead of affecting one. Therefore

never try to go beyond the feeling that you have; try to find the true point

(1957, p. 11)

His concern was to analyse the actor/character dualism that is the basis of all discussion about acting.

He found the exaggerated acting style of actors trained for classical drama incompatible with the demands of his own plays.

He was concerned with the source and behavioural logic of emotion: his main objection was to allowing actors to give their own emotions full rein. He opposed the use of emotionalism for its own sake.

He thought that the actor must not perform some being that is neither the character nor him or her self but who appears to have an independent emotional life whose rationale is the manipulation of the audience's emotion through exploitation of their gullibility.

For modern audiences, Diderot's ideas have a remarkably familiar ring because it seems that all the most creative and perceptive analysts of the acting process have been reacting against a style of performance they regarded as deadly and over-blown. Successive generations have often found the style of their predecessors artificial and have gone in search of a new naturalism and sincerity. We may be reminded of Hamlet's plea in Shakespeare's play for the actors who are to present the piece he has written to 'acquire and beget a temperance' (Act III Sc. ii).

◼ Performance skills

Diderot and Shakespeare identified several necessary skills for the actor – physical, vocal and mental – and it is important to investigate these areas of activity in order to understand the ways in which acting can be developed. One of the problems with a lot of actor education is that these three facets of acting are studied in isolation. While it is perfectly logical to work on the voice or body in a specialized way, it is vital to remember that acting is a holistic activity and never utilizes one aspect of personal resources without drawing on others. Recognizing and appreciating your own personal resources will be the first step in learning about acting.

The actor's physical resources

If you study Figure 3.2 showing some actors working with Grotowski, you will be struck by the sheer physical dexterity of the performers. An actor needs to be able to respond physically to the demands of any role or task created by a director or play and must be free from any tensions that might inhibit the freedom to direct energy or carry out the imperatives of a task.

Figure 3.2   Actor-training with Grotowski
Source: © The Grotowski Institute

For many people, freeing the body in this way is a very difficult process. The food we eat, the clothes we wear, the personality and the attitudes we adopt, the tasks we perform, the attitudes we bring or the pressures we experience all contribute to destroying natural good posture and relaxation. For example, spinal specialists have now identified how stress or sports accidents can cause the spine to become misaligned. This 'subluxation' can interfere with the nervous system and create severe movement and postural problems unless adjusted by a skilled chiropractor.

Many systems have been devised for the freeing of the body, voice and imagination and we shall be looking at some of these in the next chapter. At this point, you should understand how the physical and vocal work you may undertake as part of your course will contribute to creating a responsive and multi-skilled actor.

A great deal of recent work in acting has derived from the ancient practices of T'ai Chi and Yoga and we shall be employing some of the terminology from these forms in subsequent discussions. The fundamental ideas of T'ai Chi is that the body has an energy, the Chi, which is centred on the Tan T'ien, a point just below the navel. Both Yoga and T'ai Chi encourage methods of deep breathing and these have been found to be very beneficial in voice production as well as in sustaining the other physical demands of performance.

Centring

If the Tan T'ien is the energy centre of the body, it is also the centre of gravity and the approximate point to which the diaphragm contracts when we breathe in. It is the point around which the body balances and it acts as the source of breath and voice control. The term '**centring**' describes the process whereby an actor eases away tension from the centre and then uses that centre to originate and energize speech and movement. It becomes a point of concentration, a centre for balance and for relaxation. A moment spent 'centring' before embarking on any activity is a most important habit to develop.

Posture

Our centre is both an energy and a physical centre so the actor's posture must reflect these facts by avoiding unnecessary tension in the muscles and nerves which will inhibit the free flow of energy and movement. The purpose of good, balanced and upright posture is to enable the skeleton to fulfil its function of holding us together in such a way that the force of gravity acts vertically downwards. Most of us destroy the alignment that makes this possible through such habits as wearing high-heeled shoes, reading with the head down, staring at a computer screen or driving. As a result, we develop tensions or use energy inefficiently and, as actors, are unable to respond to the demands of flexibility and agility in a performance or lope across the stage drawing attention to ourselves rather than to the character we are attempting to portray.

The voice

In the Western tradition of actor education and particularly in the context of the British Theatre, there has been a great emphasis on the voice, very often to the exclusion of other, equally important aspects of the craft. With the growing awareness of the organic nature of the actor's work there has been a realization that the body, intellect and imagination must harmonize in response to the demands created by the playwright, director or improvised material in order to make a joint communication with the audience. The actor's voice and speech are part of this unity, they must not be thought of as separate from other aspects of an actor's resources. Centring of the voice is akin to centring the body: both contribute to the concept of a deep centre for the imagination and emotions. The tensions we have already noted are just as likely to inhibit vocal communication, and emotional inhibition will reveal itself vocally as well as physically. In the same way that much of your physical work will be aimed at achieving a sense of 'release', this will also be the case for work on the voice.

Because we speak every day and use our voices in multifarious ways we rarely analyse the process in order to improve and refine it. So, for a moment, you should consider what actually happens when you speak:

- An impulse is sent from the motor cortex of the brain, stimulating our body to allow air to enter and leave it.
- This air (breath) plays on the vocal folds, which are situated in the larynx (voice box), creating oscillations.
- The oscillations cause the breath to vibrate.
- These vibrations are amplified in the resonating cavities of the pharynx, mouth and nose.
- The resultant sounds are articulated by the lips and tongue in conjunction with the teeth and hard **palate** to create words.
- Additional **resonance** (carrying power) is available through all the hollow areas of the upper body, including the skull and chest. This resonance is achieved by the conduction of sound through the skeleton and by sound waves from one surface setting up vibrations on another.
- The resonators provide the **tone** of the voice while the pitch is determined by the rate of vibration of the vocal folds.

Breath

As we have seen, the breath initiates the production of sound. But breath is far more fundamental to acting skill than this. Breath is the primary life force: in all ancient traditions and creation myths it is the Divine Spirit or Breath that initiates life. We preserve that link between breath and spirit in the word **inspiration**: literally 'taking in the breath'. Breath underpins all your work in acting, whether as a support to your voice and movement or as a source of physical and mental energy.

Breathing is initiated by a signal from the brain to the diaphragm to contract. The diaphragm is a muscular membrane which separates the chest from the abdomen. In response to the signal from the brain, the diaphragm lowers and flattens and the result is that the area around the lungs is increased and the density of air in this region decreased. Now that the air inside the lungs is denser than that around them, it expands, pushing the lungs out in order to equalize the pressure. By this time the pressure inside the body is less than that outside, so air enters the lungs via the trachea (windpipe) to restore the pressure balance. This process is known as **inhalation**.

In order to achieve **exhalation** (breathing out), the diaphragm expands and moves up, increasing the density of the air in the body and the whole process is reversed.

Notice that the emphasis of the process we have described is in the abdominal and lower chest areas. In order for the lungs to be filled to their maximum capacity, the abdominal muscles and the muscles which control the lower, 'floating' ribs (the intercostal muscles) must be toned and relaxed.

When we breathe *in*, the view from outside the body is of the stomach coming *out* and the lower chest coming *up*. When we breathe *out*, the reverse is the case.

In spite of the certainty of the statement we have just made, many people do exactly the opposite: they pull their stomachs in as they inhale and push it out as they exhale! The effect of this very common faulty breathing is that they only use the upper part of their lungs and, in order to compensate for the lack of movement in the comparatively rigid upper chest they raise their shoulders in a desperate attempt to increase lung capacity. The result is catastrophic for an actor: there is no control over the voice and the tone is thin and inadequate; there is serious tension in the upper body and a lack of dynamic energy.

In order to develop your breathing to provide the sound foundation for work as an actor, you should:

◆ encourage yourself to be aware of the *possibility* of correct breathing;

◆ discover a *sense memory* of the process so that it eventually become an unconscious reaction;

◆ release *all muscular and postural* inhibiting factors.

Speech and language

While a great deal of an actor's communication will take place through movement, body language and sound, a substantial element of Theatre is the use of language and **text**. Indeed, many teachers of acting would maintain that the ability to respond to the quality and content of a text remains the actor's single most important task. Spoken language is created by the shaping of the voice into the specific sounds that constitute language and an actor must be able to free the sound so that it fills the performance space and celebrates the complex patterns of the text.

Vocal sound does not literally emanate from the belly or centre but an actor should sense that it is happening in order to create a relaxed and focused stream of sound that culminates in the mouth for further shaping and resonance. Unfortunately, the most inhibiting factor at the mouth is the face itself.

The face

Nineteenth-century textbooks on acting showed dozens of illustrations of human faces in a huge range of expressions that students were expected to study and reproduce in an attempt to produce 'truthful' emotions. We can now see that such an approach produced precisely the opposite of what was intended but it does remind us of the sheer expressiveness of the human face and the way in which it may inhibit vocal communication. When, in Shakespeare's *Macbeth*, King Duncan remarks:

> There's no art
> To find the mind's construction in the face.
>
> (Act I Sc. iv)

and a little later Lady Macbeth tells her husband:

> Your face, my Thane, is a book where men
> May read strange matters.
>
> (Act I. Sc. v)

We are reminded powerfully of the paradox of non-verbal communication through the face. The face is, after all, the most readily perceivable area for human communication, a fact that actors using 'close-ups' for the camera must constantly remember. The face is potentially the most revealing part of our body: pain, anguish, love, the whole range of emotions are likely to show themselves there and, paradoxically, it becomes the most tightly defended part of the body for the very same reasons. In order to inhibit emotional 'leaks' we find ways of clamping the complex muscles groups into single states, permitting a few controlled communicatory variations. We employ a 'stiff upper lip', a firm or tightly set jaw, eyes of steel and manufacture special compositions of laughter or anger or whatever other emotion we are prepared to show to the world. Regional loyalties, shyness, anxiety, tension, desire for control or superiority and severe introverted patterns of behaviour all contribute towards making the tongue, jaw, soft palate and throat inflexible so that vocal sound becomes inhibited. Thus, ironically, one of our main means of communication – the face – may well destroy our ability to communicate verbally. By freeing the face, an actor is enabled also to move towards achieving the flexibility of the jaws, tongue, lips and soft palate, all of which contribute to clear and dynamic utterance.

Suggested activity

An exercise that explores some of these ideas further was devised by Jerzy Grotowski, whose ideas on acting we shall investigate more fully in Chapter 4:

◆ Stand with a good, balanced posture, checking that your head and neck are in relaxed and centred positions.
◆ Hold the chin with your hand and open the mouth by lifting the top jaw as far as possible.
◆ Close the mouth by pushing your lower jaw up.

◆ Open your mouth again upwards and again push your bottom jaw to close your mouth. At this stage your head should be as far back as it can go. Complete the exercise by reversing the process and then repeat it until you are fully aware of the movement of the lower jaw.
◆ Help the jaws by opening and closing the mouth with the help of your hands on either side.
◆ Complete the exercise by vocalizing the sound 'ah' on an exhalation while opening the jaws upwards.

Personal resources

The actor is continually required to strip away the barriers and defences with which we mask ourselves. Before we can even begin this process, however, we need to understand ourselves and recognize those inner qualities and aspects of our personal history that we bring to the acting task. Many Theatre/Drama courses now require students to devise autobiographical pieces in order to help them to understand, recognize and acknowledge why and how they have arrived at the point in their lives when they wish to engage in work involving acting and other aspects of performance.

We all bring with us a huge backlog of personal experience which feeds into our work as actors. We also need to recognize that Theatre is essentially an experiential medium and its meanings are dependent on the interplay of the actor's body, mind and imagination which, in turn, affect the minds, bodies and imaginations of our audiences.

The theatre communicates largely through behavioural images rather than intellectual content and one of the actor's principal tasks is to release these images. Making images of your own lives is a helpful preparation. You must also realize the importance of recalling emotional experience through what we term 'sense-memory' and a total commitment to the art of acting if you are to have any success.

Your personal qualities

Learn to recognize yourself so that, eventually, you can lose yourself in the task of acting and presenting a role. Consider:

- your own strengths and weaknesses;
- how your upbringing has shaped you;
- your cultural, ethnic and religious origins and their effect on your attitudes;
- how some of your attitudes may have changed;
- the various 'characters' that make up your inner life;
- how your inner life and outer persona adapt according to the company you are in;
- how what you now think of as your 'self' has developed to its present stage and where it is going;
- which things you love, hate, or mistrust;
- what constitutes your 'identity';
- what motivates you at present.

We do not wish to give the impression that, in order to become a competent actor, you must subject yourself to psychological analysis or psychotherapy, both of which may probe some of these questions. However, it is vital that you acquire the reflective approach we have outlined if you are to inhabit another character convincingly.

Purpose-driven behaviour

Virtually all human behaviour is driven by a purpose, which may be conscious or unconscious. Even inactivity is driven by a purpose. We can often gain insights into our own or other people's characters by considering the underlying purpose. Consider these examples and think how they might apply to you or to a fictional character.

- concealing the truth;
- personal ambition;
- dislike of another person;
- basic insecurity;
- greed;
- sexual ambition or frustration;
- enjoyment of power;

◆ avoidance of responsibility;

◆ delaying the inevitable;

◆ an aspect of a relationship;

◆ unease with body image.

You can see that any one of these factors may affect communication between two or more people. If we consider what happens when several people have conflicting purposes, we are moving towards the very centre of the dilemmas of acting.

An actor's responsibilities

There is, of course, a great danger with some of the more personal and introspective aspects of preparation for acting recommended here that actors will become so obsessed with themselves and their lives that they lose sight of the boundaries between 'being', 'behaving' and 'performing'. We shall need to return to this basic dilemma frequently.

However, as Peter Brook (1988) recognized, our lives can be thought of as being represented by two circles: the inner circle contains our drives and impulses, our secret thoughts and emotions, none of which are visible on the outside. The outer circle is our social circle; our relations with others, our work and our recreations. Theatre tends to represent the outer circle: the visible, known world. However, the personal research in which an actor engages is like an intermediate circle which attempts to bring aspects of the inner circle to a point where they are visible and able to be comprehended in the Theatre.

As an actor, therefore, you have *three* responsibilities that you must address in all your work:

1. Responsibility to the integrity of the *text*, be it written, devised or improvised.

An actor must be able to express the content and respond to the quality of the text. This involves meticulous study and learning so that any words spoken and any dramatic situations, relationships and insights presented will be seen as sincere and rooted in profound familiarity with what has been written or created.

2. Responsibility to the *other actors*.

This will be dependent on not being so wrapped up in personal research and motivation that the needs of other cast members are neglected. As an absolute minimum, actors should *listen* to the other actors, be *aware* of their physical positions on the stage in relation to themselves and recognize when they must *give* the central playing of a scene to another or *take* it from them for a while. Every actor must feel and contribute to a sense of mutual support and establish an atmosphere of *trust*.

3. Responsibility to the *audience*.

When actors are working together or they have convinced themselves of the 'reality' of what they are showing, there is a tendency for them to behave as they would in life: they grow to be too comfortable in their private, fictional world. Accordingly they become inaudible, inward in their focus and self-indulgent. In short, they have *forgotten the audience*, without whom there is no Theatre. Brook (1988, p. 234) maintains that it is this relationship with the audience that 'gives Theatre its fundamental meaning'.

Achieving a balance between all three areas of responsibility is the main task of the actor and the single, most important skill to be acquired through study and practice.

■ Acting as story-telling

Throughout this book we have been constantly challenging you to consider what constitutes an act of Theatre and we have given examples of where the existence of a performer, a space and an audience appear to provide the basis of what we understand by that term. This, however, does little to capture the essence or excitement of Theatre or provide a satisfactory reason for studying this phenomenon. We obviously need to move to a further stage and ask what actually *happens* in the course of an event we call Theatre. At its simplest yet most profound we *relate and share stories*. If this statement surprises you, then consider the comment made by Richard Eyre (2000, p. 377), the distinguished director of Britain's National Theatre: 'The theatre has to tell us stories about ourselves: then we will listen to them.'

All societies relate stories that express their beliefs, attitudes, history and value systems or encapsulate an attempt to explain the world or make sense of an aspect of existence. Where such stories utilize the skills and conventions of Theatre, we may label the mode *drama* and the form, *a play*. However it is equally possible to see stories told through re-enactment of myths and events, through songs and poems or through elaborate rituals, ceremonies or carnivals. You may wish to consider the particular relationship between 'performers' and 'spectators' in some of these situations and compare this with the situation in Theatre.

A single story-teller in front of an audience works on the assumption that a relationship of direct communication with that audience is an absolute and basic necessity. The entire attention of the story-teller is focused on the audience and sensitivity to its response is a fundamental aspect of the process and craft. Actors also need to be able to work in this way while simultaneously remembering their responsibilities to the text and other actors. If, however, the actor has never experienced the role of story-teller, the work presented will be incomplete and ineffectual. A story is a good example of what is often termed a **performative text**: a text that has potential performance embedded within it. We suggest that the following are the main qualities of a successful story-teller, qualities that should be held in common with all actors:

◇ total mastery of the text;

◇ constant, active awareness of the audience and of their reactions;

◇ response to the quality of the writing;

◇ an ability to engage and maintain the interest of listeners/spectators;

◇ a free, clear and uninhibited voice: consistently audible;

◇ relaxed, controlled and expressive physicality;

◇ the ability to employ changes in pitch, pace, pause and emphasis to establish meanings and convey mood, suspense, excitement or any appropriate emotional state;

◇ an ability to use multiple 'voices' or adopt accents;

◆ awareness of the form of the text: prose, verse, song, etc.;

◆ ability to create verbal and visual images;

◆ a sense of energy, focus and vital communication skills.

■ Acting as character

The majority of Theatre students enter their courses thinking that acting is largely concerned with the creation of characters. They will often speak of the characters in a play or devised piece as if they were living people with whom it is possible to have a close acquaintance and consider that the process of acting simply involves representing those people on stage. This is an entirely understandable error because much modern discussion about acting is derived from those who like to speak of getting 'inside' their characters or of 'finding' their characters. Furthermore, many literature-based drama courses culminate in the writing of essays about the behaviour, attitudes or beliefs of the characters in plays as if these characters could be interviewed tomorrow.

In fact, the only clues to character that an actor has are the words of the text: what a character says, what is said about them, what a character does and any other information that a playwright may choose to offer. It is the actor's *imagination* that brings together the various elements provided in order to create a character about whose destiny an audience may have a concern and it is the actor's primary task to *tell that character's story*.

Plays vary enormously in the amount of information they provide about the characters: the story may be allegorical and the 'characters' may be representative types rather than fictional human beings capable of psychological analysis. A character named Beauty or Strength in a medieval morality play requires a very different approach from the actor to a character named Mrs Alving in a play by Ibsen. If we consider the stage directions provided by George Bernard Shaw in his play *Candida*, written in 1895, we find that, after a full-page description of the room in which the main character is sitting, including details of the books on the desk and in the bookcase, the pictures on the wall and the décor of the house, we are given a lengthy and very detailed portrait of the man himself. Both Shaw and the American dramatist, Arthur Miller tended to follow Ibsen in providing extensive information about the characters and their environments in their stage directions and these provide a particular problem for actors who are more accustomed to texts with no such features. Shaw, certainly, had a reputation for seeking 'truth' as a director of his own plays but actors must be prepared to find their own truth in response to texts.

■ Using the text

It is important to establish from the outset that there is *no substitute* for a close scrutiny of any **performative text**. In addition to what we might term **performance indicators**, such as obvious pauses or linked lines of verse, an initial careful reading should reveal:

◆ any distinctive patterns of speech and utterance;

◆ any tendency towards long or minimal statements;

◆ any regional or class-related speech or attitudes;

qualities as a listener;

tendencies to say one thing but mean another;

characteristics like flattery, smooth talking, blunt or rude comments, clichés, formal or informal utterance;

use of images, poetry or evocative language;

language that changes in tone according to situation and context.

At a second level of reading/study, you ought to be able to recognize:

the use of language as a tool for manipulation and intimidation;

the motives, desires and strategies that lie below the surface of the language to form what is often known as the **sub-text**;

the use of language to distort or evade the truth;

structure of any verse form that may be employed, e.g. rhymed, end-stopped, blank verse;

language used to probe another character for information or response;

soliloquies, monologues, argument, passionate outbursts.

■ The life of a character

Once you have carefully examined the text, both the words spoken and the stage directions, you can begin to give your character and fuller life. The text will have provided you with clues as to what Aristotle in his *Poetics* called **functional traits**. These are aspects of character that determine behaviour and must be recognized by an actor preparing to take on a role. You will already have considered your own traits and that personal work should enable you to think perceptively about the traits of others. Two great American acting teachers and thinkers, Oscar Brockett (1994) and Robert Benedetti (1994), have categorized the traits that combine to create a character and we use their ideas here to enable you to systematize your thinking.

Physical

Many actors like to work from physical traits in order to give a concrete sense of creating their character. These traits include basic facts of gender, age, size and ethnic origin, but will also extend to the kind of detailed information supplied in the stage directions in plays like *Candida*. We often employ posture, attitude, gait or gesture to indicate an aspect of a character's inner life but, at times, we are supplied with so little information by the playwright that we must imagine the likely impact of emotions, situations or activities on physical behaviour. Some famous actors have liked to work from the feet upwards to establish their character, others have worked from the voice. Whatever system you employ, it is important to give your character a believable physical presence that is consistent with the information supplied in the text. This is the simplest level of characterization because only external traits are revealed. However, they may well be indicative of many less obvious factors.

Social

These are the traits that derive from a character's social situation but will include such factors as economic situation, education, profession, social class, religion, trade and, above all, relationships. Actors must always relate to and be supremely conscious of the other actors who may share a scene with them. Accordingly, the characteristics of the way in which relationships are handled are crucial: does the character listen sympathetically, look at people when talking to them, treat people with disdain or kindness? How does the character see him or her self? As a leader? A follower? A success? A failure? Is the character shy, confident, assertive, manipulative, witty, over-serious or optimistic? Is the character popular and easy to be with or difficult to relate to and regarded as an outsider? The answers to these and similar questions will form an essential level of an actor's research.

Psychological

The most important aspect of understanding the psychological traits of a character is that thought precedes action. In order to understand the **motivation** and justification that lie behind any behaviour and action of our character, we must develop an understanding of the way in which he or she thinks. Windows into the minds of characters were provided in the Elizabethan Theatre through the device of the soliloquy in which the audience could hear their inner dialogues and thought-processes. Not all plays provide such insights but, if you recall your own traits, they will have included some reflections on the way in which you think and you will also be aware of the thought-processes of others.

Moral

These traits refer to a character's set of values that will determine courses of action, choice and inner conflicts. One of the best indicators as to how a character will behave will be his or her set of values. Most people hold some things to be sacred and others to be of little value and it is an indication of this scale of values when we know how hard they will fight for something. This, in turn, will provide insights into the emotional life of a character and the strategies that they will employ in order to achieve their ends. Where a character is confronted with a moral dilemma or is tempted to act out of expediency rather than principle, there will be conflict. Moral stance may be influenced by religious, political or philosophical beliefs and characters may well be affected by a perceived erosion of spiritual values. Modern materialism often intrudes heavily into the moral lives of characters in plays written since the late nineteenth century and we can find many examples of characters who wrestle with their consciences over the right course of action. Active expressions of a character's value systems will sometimes include what seems like irrational behaviour.

As you consider all these issues from the perspective of a student of acting, you should be acutely aware that you are entering one of the great philosophical debates of the past two hundred years: the tension between human nature and environment as determining factors for behaviour. Plays and novels from the late nineteenth century form a very significant part of our literary and theatre heritage and frequently explore this debate. They were written at a time when ideas of heredity and evolution were also increasingly being postulated as potential determinants.

One of the characters in Dostoyevsky's great novel *Crime and Punishment* (1866) captures an aspect of this dialectic that was later to be taken up by Ibsen, Strindberg, Shaw and Chekhov in their plays:

> It all began with the point of view of the socialists. Their point of view is well known: crime is a protest against bad and abnormal social conditions and nothing more. No other causes are admitted. Nothing! … I can show you their books: they reduce everything to a common cause-environment. Environment is the root of all evil and nothing else. Human nature isn't taken into account at all. Human nature is banished. Human nature isn't supposed to exist.

(Dostoyevsky, [1866] 1951, pp. 272–3)

In our study of the character traits we have admitted the existence of some pre-determining factors in our natures that might profoundly affect our actions but the exploration of character also needs to take into account some environmental factors. Stanislavsky, whose work we shall consider in much more detail in Chapter 4, called these factors in relation to acting in a play the **given circumstances**.

■ Understanding the given circumstances

There are two elements to the given circumstances as they affect an actor. The first is the theatrical context in which the play is being performed: this will include the space, the form of staging, the lighting and other such factors. The second element relates to the fictional content of the play's action and it is to this that we must look first to develop our character research.

There are so many factors that are capable of influencing human behaviour that it would be virtually impossible to list all the potential given circumstances. However, the following checklist will provide a substantial foundation.

The material environment

◇ Does the scene take place outside or inside?

◇ Is the environment familiar or unfamiliar to the character?

◇ Does this environment induce feelings of security or insecurity in the character?

◇ Are the physical conditions in which the character lives squalid, comfortable or luxurious and are these represented on stage?

◇ Where and what are the objects on stage?

◇ What is the climate, time of day, quality of light?

◆ Are there any totemic or taboo objects that have particular resonance for the character?

◇ What is the immediate 'off-stage' world? How is it accessed and is there a sense of freedom, restraint, fulfilment or deprivation associated with it?

The character's psychological world

What has just happened to the character?

What do we know of the character's family or ancestors: are there mentions of any inherited traits or issues?

Where has s/he just been?

What was the nature of the character's previous experience in the material environment?

Is s/he in a hurry?

How obvious and near the surface are the character's intentions?

Is there a threat to the character's attempts to achieve certain goals?

Is the character anticipating a future event?

The social and interactional world

How do the other characters impact on the achievement of the character's goals and purpose?

What is the nature of the character's relationship with each of the other characters and what was the result of their previous encounters?

What does the character know about the other characters?

Does the character wish to be perceived in a particular way by the other characters and what qualities do they perceive in him/her?

How comfortable is the character in the presence of other characters?

What events/meetings are taking place simultaneously with the action of the scene?

What events have taken place between the various scenes in which we see the character?

■ A personal system and a working journal

Much of the material we have offered so far will enable you to devise your own system of preparation and approach to the challenges of acting. In the following chapter we shall be considering some of the most frequently used systems for actors but we have deliberately delayed introducing these until we have established the need for students to be selective and active in their personal work on performance skills, eventually using those aspects of their exploration that they find helpful and realistic.

To assist in this process and to fulfil the requirements of many Theatre Studies and similar courses, we suggest that an invaluable process and resource is the maintenance of an *actor's working journal*.

Your approach

An actor's journal is like an artist's notebook: it is an objective record of your work and of your learning. It is an essential opportunity for reflection upon and analysis of your experience and a resource for you to draw upon. The process of recalling, recording and clearly expressing your perceptions will reinforce your learning and make it more real and personal. Initially your journal will serve to do the following:

- Develop your ability to observe human behaviour and retain this in your memory.
- Record important sources of information, activity and learning.
- Undertake research into character.
- Recognize aspects of personal work that need development and particular attention.
- Develop and record discussion and discourse on the topic of acting.

You are likely to maintain your journal in two main contexts: first, as a result of daily classes, lectures and exercises and, second, in response to productions or work on plays for performance.

Classes

In this context you may be reminded of Stanislavsky's book *An Actor Prepares* ([1937] 2008), written in the form of a working diary kept by an acting student. This is largely anecdotal but it reveals a growing level of understanding and perception on the part of the student. This is the balance you should be aiming for: a simple record of what happened or a collection of your personal feelings about individuals are of little value but the insights you gain and the activities and research you may wish to remember and record are an essential tool for your work. Students on courses with a strong practical bias are likely to be taught by a large range of practitioners and, in this situation, it is even more important to use the journal as a unifying strand in what can be disparate and contrasting learning experiences.

Use your journal to do the following:

- *Make connections* between the various strands of your course, taking particular care to note when teachers are complementing each other's work and when they are making similar points in differing ways.
- *Note questions* to be asked or that you wish to pursue and leaving time for answers to emerge from your work and study.
- *Maintain your own reflective commentary* on the long march towards your own system of acting, remembering that the road goes on for ever and is not confined to your time in initial training and study. Critique what you hear and see in the media; foster your curiosity, delve into areas unknown to you previously and diversify beyond the confines of a syllabus.
- *Note your research needs* and any work that you need to do in following information trails.
- *Note references* from lectures, workshops, practical classes and tutorials. Follow up on news of productions, publications and broadcasts.
- *Set your goals* in vocal and physical work: perhaps a voice capable of communicating the whole range of human emotions or experience and a body that is supple, strong, balanced and responsive. Note how you hope to achieve such goals. Reflect on your progress towards your goals.

Make a checklist of personal do's and don'ts for the future, to include warm-ups and cool-downs (both vocal and physical) and concentration exercises.

Collect articles, interviews, details of books about actors and records of any conversations you may have had with actors. Assemble information about auditions, rehearsal processes and your pacing of them, agents, directors and how much you really need to know about microphones and cameras before facing them.

Productions

Use your journal to maintain a record of your research and thought processes in approaching a role and in participating in rehearsal. Use the concepts we have introduced in this chapter to form the basis of your character research, and, if necessary, create checklists of given circumstances, etc.

As you progress in your study of acting, employ a system of thinking about your role and your close reading of the text. Note the following:

Questions such as 'What does my character want?, How do I achieve or aim to achieve it?, What are the obstacles to my attaining this?' When you have been introduced to one or more 'systems' (e.g. Stanislavsky, Meisner, Grotowski), use the vocabulary you find useful to form the basis of your questions.

Features such as sub-text, **through line**, **beats**, **units** and even punctuation. Notice small words at the start of sentences, and what a character might have intended to say when s/he began to speak. Examine the playwright's stage directions.

Evidence from your character's words and actions, evidence from other characters, the use of time and of time jumps, place and shifting locations, weather conditions or quality of light, the age, health and stories from the past that the character brings with them. Record 'hot seating' or improvisations, exercises and discoveries.

Thoughts on properties and costumes as they arise.

Rehearsal spaces and the eventual performance space and adaptations to your performance that the move from one to the other might necessitate.

Likely effects of promenade or site-specific performance.

Reflections from peers, colleagues or directors. Discoveries made and problems needing to be solved in rehearsal.

Personal debriefing once a project is completed, notes for next time, observations on spaces, audiences and what was learned by touring or using several spaces.

■ Conclusion

In this chapter we have established the fundamentals of the vocal, physical and imaginative skills necessary for an understanding of the acting process. We have provided you with the raw materials to enable you to devise your own 'warm-up' sequence which is an essential tool for your work as a student of acting.. We hope that you now have some understanding of the mechanics of voice and of the physical aspects of performance skills. The exercises we have suggested are not an end in themselves. Acting involves opening yourself to your own feelings and responding to those of others and, as Grotowski (1969, p. 46) once remarked: 'If this body restricts itself to demonstrating what it is, then it is not an obedient instrument capable of a performing act.'

The most important aspect of this chapter, however, is the emphasis on the approaches to the text and on reflection and experiential learning. In order to study acting as an aspect of Theatre Studies you need to develop the skills and habits of observation and critical thinking implicit in maintaining an acting log book. We have taken our lead from a number of recent practitioners and teachers who believe that it is not sufficient to have vocal and physical skills but that an actor must reveal something of their entire person in the service of the text.

Topics for discussion and reflection

◆ What do you understand by the paradox of acting as described by Diderot? Is this analysis still valid?

◆ How would you hope to ensure your vocal and physical resources serve you as an actor?

◆ Discuss the following statement by Peter Brook (1988, p. 107):

> The purpose is to be instruments that transmit truths which otherwise would remain out of sight. These truths can appear from sources deep inside ourselves or far outside ourselves. Any preparation we do is only part of the complete preparation. The body must be ready and sensitive, but that isn't all. The voice has to be open and free. The emotions have to be open and free. The intelligence has to be quick. All these have to be prepared. There are crude vibrations that can come through very easily and fine ones that come through only with difficulty. In each case the life we are looking for means breaking open a series of habits. A habit of speaking; maybe a habit made by an entire language. A mixture of people with lots of habits and without even a common language, have come to together to work.

◆ Consider these typical remarks by actors: 'Don't worry, it will all come up when we move into the theatre.'

◆ Or consider this imaginary exchange between two actors:

> 'We didn't rehearse it like that!'
>
> 'Yes, we did, I am simply conveying what we discovered to those sitting in Row D of the Upper Circle.'
>
> 'For goodness sake, why don't they pull these old theatres down: they've got nothing to do with modern acting!

◆ Do these comments arise from constant work in 'studios' surrounded by walls, lack of regular and varied stage experience, directors unaware of problems and actors saying in interviews that they now prefer rehearsal to performance?

◆ Is this why there are complaints about inaudibility or is it because we often use old proscenium theatres without 'box sets' so that the sound simply goes up the fly tower or because so much modern theatre building is acoustically inadequate.?

◆ How do we play 'asides' from Restoration plays when the audience sits far away in a high circle or how do we use 'curtain lines' if there is no curtain?

■ Further reading

Alfreds, M. (2008) *Different Every Night: Freeing the Actor*, London: Nick Hern. The views of a very experienced director with a tried and tested methodical way of working with actors.

Benedetti, J. (2005) *The Art of the Actor*, London: Methuen. A profound and helpful approach to the task of acting.

Eyre, R. (2000) *Changing Stages*, London: Bloomsbury. A comprehensive exploration of the modern theatre by a former director of the Royal National Theatre in Britain.

Houseman, B. (2008) *Tackling Text and Subtext*, London: Nick Hern. A refreshingly clear guide to the use of the text.

Keefe, J. and Murray, S. (eds) (2007) *Physical Theatre: A Critical Reader*, London: Routledge. Provides many important insights into recent developments in practice.

Stanislavsky, K. (2008) *An Actor Prepares*, in *An Actor's Work*, trans. J. Benedetti, London: Routledge. One of the great classics of the literature of acting.

▇ Website

For vocal exercises and an extensive example of the actor as story-teller/troubadour, see our website: www.palgrave.com/foundations/pickering

4 | Approaches to Acting

Continuing our study of performance skills, we now turn to examine four of the most influential approaches to acting of modern times. As we consider the theories and principles of leading practitioners, we shall see that, although their methods are very distinctive and frequently used as the basis for courses of study and training, they are, to some extent, complementary.

Learning outcomes

By the conclusion of this chapter, you should be able to:

▶ understand the basic principles of four major systems of acting;

▶ describe in detail the content and application of at least two of these systems;

▶ adapt or incorporate material from systems of acting into your own practice;

▶ develop a substantial discourse on the topic of acting in various contexts;

▶ have further insights into approaches to a text;

▶ develop criteria for the evaluation of performance.

■ What system shall we use?

Acting theories and systems appear to be confusingly diverse, especially when it comes to the concept of creating a character. The nineteenth-century critic A.C. Bradley saw Shakespeare's tragic characters as real people with a pre- and post-play existence and an overriding passion. F.R. Leavis maintained that Shakespeare did not invent people but simply 'put words together'. Stanislavsky insisted that characters must have consistent objectives and the playwright Strindberg that they must vacillate, be 'out of joint, torn between old and new … conglomerates, made up of past and present stages of civilisation'. Some actors like to work from physical externals such as gait or gesture; others borrow behavioural traits from people they know. Some prefer to dig deep into their own personalities in the belief that they have number of different people inside them. Brecht asked that his actors should reveal their contradictions; Grotowski (1968) insisted that his actors use **inductive technique** to eliminate external effects in the search for their own 'psycho-analytical language of sounds and gestures', Meisner demands that actors stay 'in the moment'.

How are you, as a student of acting, to make sense of all these varying approaches? In this chapter, we shall be providing an overview of four 'systems' for the study and analysis of acting, all of which were developed by theatre practitioners in varying contexts. Between them, these systems should provide the basis for the development of your own approach, although there are some courses and colleges almost entirely devoted to the work of one practitioner or set of principles. We would urge you to take insights from a range of systems and to find contexts in which it is appropriate to apply them. No one system is likely to equip you for every situation that arises in the modern theatre: that field has become too diverse for narrow thinking or practice. Facts about the various directors/practitioners whose work we are about to consider are of less importance that the principles that lie behind their practice and, unless you can imagine how you might incorporate aspects of the systems into your own work, you have learned little of value. However, some basic facts establishing the original conditions in which particular principles were developed will enable you to understand the kind of play or acting problem to which such principles might be practically applied. We begin with the most frequently studied and misunderstood figure in the field of actor education: Stanislavsky.

■ Konstantin Stanislavsky

Probably no-one has had a greater influence on acting as we perceive it today than Stanislavsky. His system and various interpretations of it have become the single most powerful factor in determining the nature of performance on stage or screen. This far-reaching effect of the work of one man is the result of his being the first person to create a recognizable and documented 'system' and curriculum for the analysis and teaching of the art of acting and it is still possible to find institutions or training establishments where his ideas alone are considered all that is necessary to acquire sound acting technique.

However, a great deal of nonsense is talked about Stanislavsky. We have heard students claim that he invented Naturalism, improvisation or hot-seating: it is often assumed that he established the 'method' and that he retained the same ideas throughout his life. All such errors result from a failure to understand the precise context in which Stanislavsky developed his thinking and the situations in which his thinking might be applied today.

Practitioner profile

Konstantin Sergeievich Alexeiev Stanislavsky (1863–1938)

Stanislavsky was born (and later died) in Moscow. His life was suffused with theatre from the start because his family members were passionate enough about the art to have constructed small theatres in both their homes. In adulthood, Stanislavsky worked as both an actor and producer (we would now say 'director') in the amateur theatre but eventually an 18-hour meeting with the acting teacher Nemirovich-Danchenko in 1897 led to the formation of the Moscow Art Theatre where Stanislavsky was to carry out his most innovative work. It was a sense of dissatisfaction with what actors and audiences rated as 'success' that made Stanislavsky realize that there was no sound foundation on which to base the teaching of acting. Producers, he observed, were adept at telling actors what *not* to do but seemed incapable of explaining *how* they might achieve desired ends. He felt that the future of the theatre lay in the hands of actors but, after some time at the Art Theatre, admitted that he had, to that point, behaved as the typical 'producer-autocrat' and simply treated his actors like 'mannequins'. His determination to discover the 'elementary psychophysical and psychological laws of acting' was reinforced during a holiday to Finland in 1906 when he attempted for the first time to reflect upon and analyse his experience as actor and producer in order to establish the laws for the technique of acting. This process followed a number of very significant events:

◆ The founding of the Society of Art and Literature in 1888 which provided him with his first semi-professional acting experience and brought him into contact with the director Fedotov. Stanislavsky's experience with this company reinforced his sense of dissatisfaction with a style of directing that relied on demonstration and imitation and strengthened his belief in the importance of minute detail.

◆ Stanislavsky's production of Shakespeare's *Othello* in 1895, in which he both directed and played the leading role. Prepared by careful research, including a trip to Venice for observation and the purchase of fabrics, the production centred on intense realistic detail and profound psychological insights into character.

◆ Stanislavsky's production of Chekhov's *The Seagull* at the Art Theatre in 1898 (Figure 4.1) which established Chekhov as a leading dramatist and as a lifelong collaborator. This production is still studied as an icon of theatrical realism and Stanislavsky's approach to the direction of the play demonstrated the emergence of the ideas that he was to codify into his 'system'.

Stanislavsky's thinking was set out during a long career in a substantial body of writing. The experiences preceding his 'teaching books' on acting are documented in his *My Life in Art* and there are also copious articles and notebooks relating to his productions. However, most actors use Stanislavsky's three great teaching books as the major source for their inspiration and the titles of these are most commonly translated as *An Actor Prepares*, *Building a Character* and *Creating a Role*.

Figure 4.1 Chekhov (centre) reads *The Seagull* to Stanislavsky (on his right) and actors from the Moscow Art Theatre

■ Stanislavsky's underlying principles

Throughout his long career, Stanislavsky's prime concern was with what he termed *truthfulness* in the theatre: typical of his thinking was what he wrote in 1905:

> What does it really mean to be truthful on the stage? ... Does it mean that you conduct yourself as you do in ordinary life? Not at all. Truthfulness in those terms would be sheer triviality. There is the same difference between artistic and inartistic truth as exists between a painting and a photograph: the latter reproduces everything, the former only what is essential; to put the essential on canvas requires the talent of a painter.
>
> (1968, p. 20)

Now we might well ask with Pontius Pilate in the Bible and the Mystery Plays 'What is truth?' Stanislavsky clearly means 'something in which you can believe' and all his work was focused on achieving this sense of sincerity and verisimilitude. You should notice that the creation of this 'truthfulness' actually requires a high level of selectivity in acting. It is not simply a reproduction of everyday behaviour, although it must be firmly rooted in that.

As Magarshak (1950) pointed out, what Stanislavsky found he hated most was 'falsehood on the stage', especially what he termed 'theatrical falsehood', and he determined to replace this with 'genuine life, not ordinary life, of course, but artistic life'. This, he believed, would lead towards 'truth' and he felt that external reality might lead towards inner artistic reality. Accordingly, he became known for the immaculate detail and accuracy of the **mise-en-scènes** he insisted on.

As he reflected on his practice, Stanislavsky (1968) noted various discoveries:

◆ that he must concentrate ultimately on the inner conception of a character rather than the external;

◆ that the feelings with which he imbued a role were drawn from his own memory;

◆ that acting must involve total relaxation of the muscles if it is to be truthful;

◆ that characteristics he employed as an actor were developed as a result of close observation of other people.;

◆ that 'the greatest joy an actor can ever experience' is to develop 'the ability of speaking the thoughts of another man on the stage, of putting yourself entirely at the service of someone else's passions, and reproducing someone else's actions as if they were your own'.

Working from these findings, he came to the conclusion that what the actor needed most was a creative state of mind and he set about trying to establish the constituent elements and nature of such a state.

His research led him to believe that only the fullest possible concentration of the actor's spiritual and physical being could establish the creative state and that all five senses, together with the entire body, mind, memory and imagination must be involved if the actor is to enter into the soul of the person being represented on stage.

Such beliefs resulted in Stanislavsky's insistence that actors must arrive several hours before a performance in order to prepare themselves physically and spiritually for their work.

◆ One of his major concepts was that of the **magic 'if'**. He argued that an actor's work began when that magic 'if' appeared in his or her imagination or soul. The real actor, he maintained, knows that all the theatrical trappings of scenery, lighting or costumes are actually a lie but s/he must behave as 'if' they were true.

◆ Using the magic 'if', the falsehood of the stage must become truth in order to be a work of art.

◆ The actor must develop the *feeling for truth* as the best possible antidote to the potential falsehood of the stage.

Towards a 'system'

Following his long period of reflection and analysis, Stanislavsky came to the conclusion that the qualities he would strive for in an actor could be developed through exercises and eventually become a habit. No doubt this would be the claim of all subsequent systems of training and development but Stanislavsky pioneered this idea in the West:

◆ Stanislavsky began to refer to his **psycho-technique** and claimed that everything he used as the basis for his system was the result of his own, direct experience.

◆ His system was divided into two main parts: (1) the inner and outer work of the actor on his or her self; and (2) the inner or outer work on his or her part.

We must remember that all Stanislavsky's teaching presumed that the work of an actor centred on the creation of roles in scripted plays presented in a proscenium theatre with 'realistic' settings.

Significantly, the title of the book that Stanislavsky wrote at this point in his career is literally translated as *An Actor's Work on Himself*, a concept that is somewhat lost in the more common translation of the title as *An Actor Prepares*.

Before elucidating his system, Stanislavsky drew a distinction between the three main types of actor found in the theatre: the creative actor, the imitative actor and the stage hack (this latter category included the ham actor).

In trying to develop the skill of the creative actor, Stanislavsky maintained that s/he would be able to draw on powers from the subconscious mind that were beyond explanation and this mysterious force is best described as Nature.

Towards the end of his career, in April 1936, Stanislavsky wrote:

> There is really no question of my method or your method. There is only one method, which is of organic, creative Nature ... and I am willing to state in writing that if any student entering our theatre has anything to contribute towards a means of reaching the laws of that nature, I should be only too happy to learn from him.

From the outset, he considered that the main task of the creative actor is to re-create on stage the inner life of a character by drawing on his/her own feelings and soul. An imitative actor would probably only do this in rehearsal but, in performance, would simply imitate the previous experience.

The system to emerge from the initial thinking was based on ten aspects of the psycho-technique:

1. The magic 'if'
2. Given circumstances (see Chapter 3)

3. Imagination
4. Attention
5. Relaxation
6. Pieces and problems
7. Truth and belief
8. Emotional memory
9. Communication
10. Extraneous aids.

■ Working in the theatre

We can explore the significance of the various aspects of the 'system' by considering how they might apply to working both in performance and on the text of a play. You will already have studied the concept of given circumstances in the previous chapter and, hopefully, you have mastered the idea of the magic 'if'. These are both aspects of Stanislavsky's concern for action, and many students make the mistake of thinking that he was only concerned with psychology and an inner life. In fact, his work as a director led him to realize that it is essential to give an actor something to do and this is one of the reasons why he liked to fill the stage with objects that the actors must use or circumnavigate during the course of a scene. Although the given circumstances are really another 'if', they are the foundation for the action of the play: its plot, events, time, place, etc. and they all require the use of the actor's imagination which can only be developed by a finely tuned and well-trained level of attention.

The circle of attention

Stanislavsky insisted that an actor must devise exercises to focus attention on the stage rather than allowing it to stray into the auditorium. By focusing attention on some object or person on stage, the actor will naturally want to relate to it or him/her and truthful action will result. Audiences will soon notice if an actor's attention has strayed, whereas the actor can focus the attention of the audience by personal concentration of gaze and focus.

In order to develop these ideas Stanislavsky postulated the concept of the **circle of attention**. This is the small circle of intense attention in which the actor should operate. Like a small and intense circle of light, this enables the actor to examine everything in minute detail but this is also observed by the audience who are outside the actor's circle. In this state of what he termed **public solitude**, Stanislavsky maintained that an actor could consciously widen the circle while remaining fully focused and in control and that an actor must continually be aware of the circumference and boundaries within which s/he is working. In order to develop such powers of attention, actors must engage in exercises that sharpen their observation and give close attention to works of art, appreciating their qualities of beauty, and cultivate the habit of examining the material world in great detail. They must ultimately turn their attention on the emotions they receive from their communications with people in order to find the creative material that will support their acting.

Other contributory factors in creating a believable role include the need to get rid of all muscular tensions which inhibit the actor's inner work and hamper attempts to discover and enter into the feelings of the part.

Approaching the text

Stanislavsky tended to think of acting in terms of a series of problems to be solved: many of these would arise from the text of the play itself and he argued that this must be divided into **pieces** or **units** to enable close study and identification of the successive creative problems that the play poses. Those problems that he considered relevant to the actor included:

◆ those relating to the stage rather than the auditorium (remember that, unlike Grotowski, for instance, Stanislavsky considered these to be two entirely separate entities);

◆ the actor as human being in relation to the part being played;

◆ communicating the 'life of the human spirit of the part';

◆ human action that keeps the part alive and in a state of continuous motion;

◆ the ability of the actors and audience to believe in the truth of the performance;

◆ exciting problems that stimulate creativity;

◆ those relating to the main idea of the play;

◆ those relating to the inner nature of the part rather than superficially related to it.

In order to facilitate the study of the play for performance Stanislavsky suggested that the play be divided into units (pieces) and each of these units be given a name in the form of a verb. This process would enable the actor to identify the relevant problem and, because a play is primarily concerned with action, the recommended verb for the label of each piece is 'I want to'.

Once an actor understands what the character that sh/e is representing on stage 'wants', s/he can bring truth to the performance.

Recognizing the super-objective

Stanislavsky used to refer to a character's intention as the **super-objective**, which he defined as 'the logic' of a character's behaviour. Each element of behaviour, he argued, fits into a causal pattern related to a character's principles and goals. Therefore, each character has a long-term objective to which his or her behaviour is directed and which gives it coherence. The context in which these goals are pursued provides a number of obstacles that might inhibit their realization or attainment: the material world, the circumstances or the ambitions or goals of others may all stand in the way. Thus, a character will be obliged to employ strategies in order to destroy, circumvent or overcome such obstacles and will develop short-term objectives that are designed to overcome specific blocks in the progress towards the long-term super-objective.

Understanding the wants of a character depends on the use of the actor's **emotional memory** as a motivating factor in performance. Stanislavksy illustrated the idea of emotional memory by asking his actors to imagine a house full of rooms, cupboards, drawers and boxes inside which are stored smaller and smaller containers. In the smallest box of all is a tiny bead that may be found and disappear again. So with the actor's memory: it stores so much but will only occasionally reveal that 'flash of memory and insight' that must be treasured. Bringing to life the 'soul' of a character will involve aspects of the actor's own soul and emotional memory.

First readings

The first reading of the text will usually produce a feeling of sympathy for the characters and this must be transformed into the actor's more specific feelings for the inner life of his or her part. In studying the text, the actor must use *reason* to understand the part, *will* to provide the courage to proceed with the work and *feeling* to enable the transformation of general sympathy into actual experience. These three elements will constitute the motive force of the inner life of the characters and the balance between them will shape the character's behaviour.

At first, an actor may not be able to make any sense of the text and may have to rely on others' opinions to make any meanings. Gradually, however, an inner meaning will emerge, although this may initially be a vague perception of the main idea. The vital stage is to perceive the character's main aim and the more familiar the actor becomes with a part the more s/he will see the lines of direction (usually termed the **through-line**) that govern the character's conduct.

In rehearsal

The playwright, Stanislavsky pointed out, only provided sections of that 'line', often leaving gaps that the actor's imagination must fill. For example, the actor needs to know what happens to a character off stage as well as in a scene on stage. The actor's duty is to discover the playwright's **ruling idea**, the reason why the play was written, and to give it embodiment in the theatre. Only by playing the through-line will the actor be able to present the ruling idea of the play and avoid the introduction of tendentious material that will destroy the clarity of the work.

Much of the actor's work on the text, as s/he becomes more familiar with the play will involve an exploration of the **sub-text**, that level of understanding that lies beneath the surface of the spoken word to reveal the true motives and wants of the characters. These may be in direct contradiction to what is said and may often emerge during rehearsal. At that stage an actor must be very conscious of his or her responsibility to other actors, first, by refraining from introducing any distracting elements of their private lives into the rehearsal space, and then by ensuring that they communicate the thoughts and feelings of their character to their acting partners.

To ensure that those thoughts and feeling have entered the mind and heart of the other actors, it may be necessary to pause and use eye contact rather than words to express them. Conversely, actors must cultivate the habit of concentration and listening so that they absorb the words of their partners on stage differently and freshly every time they hear them, as if they are hearing them for the first time.

◼ Bertolt Brecht and the 'A' effect

In some regards, the teachings of the German director and dramatist, Bertolt Brecht, seem to be at odds with those of Stanislavsky and his legacy remains a powerful influence in the modern theatre. During the 1960s and 1970s, the plays and approaches of Brecht were widely produced and studied, particularly in college Theatre departments, but, in recent years, there has been a tendency to neglect his work. Although his ideas on acting are still of great value and relevance, Brecht's influence can be more clearly seen in styles of production that have moved away from the photographic realism of Stanislavsky's theatre and have embraced story-telling techniques and the more blatant theatricality of direct address to the audience, extreme physicality and episodic structures. Playwrights as diverse as Edward Bond, Caryl Churchill, John Godber or David Hare have employed what are often termed 'Brechtian techniques' in their writing and any attempt to bring theatre to an audience outside the confines of conventional middle-class entertainment or to employ theatre for political purposes is seen as owing something to Brecht. No study of acting today, however, would be complete without re-examining Brecht's practice and its underlying theory.

Practitioner profile

Bertolt Brecht (1898–1956)

Bertolt Brecht was born in Augsburg in Germany and died in Berlin. It was in the world of Berlin cafés and nightclubs of the 1920s and 1930s (so graphically portrayed in the musical and movie *Cabaret*) that Brecht matured as a playwright with such plays as *The Threepenny Opera*, written in collaboration with the composer Kurt Weill, *The Mother* and *Saint Joan of the Stockyards*. Significantly, *The Threepenny Opera* contained the song 'Mack the Knife' that was to enter the British 'charts' at a much later date and typified the kind of **'popular theatre'** deriving from the tradition of variety and cabaret that Brecht was looking to create.

Brecht was a committed Marxist and his early political plays were often termed *Lehrstücke* ('teaching' or 'learning pieces'). These take the form of stories that pose a moral dilemma for the actors and audience and also seek to instruct them in aesthetics and ways of thinking.

In 1933, when Hitler came to power, Brecht, keenly aware of his vulnerability as a Marxist, fled Germany, and after a time in Europe went into exile in North America in 1941. During this period away from Germany he began work on some of the plays on which his fame now largely rests, his 'parables for theatre', *The Caucasian Chalk* Circle and *The Good Person of Sezuan*, together with the historical plays *Mother Courage and Her Children* (set in the Thirty Years' War) and *The Life of Galileo*.

In 1948, he returned to Communist East Germany and, together with his wife, the actress Helene Weigel, founded the Berliner Ensemble, a theatre company that pioneered a more democratic process and enabled Brecht to develop his techniques of playwriting, production and acting in a highly experimental ethos. The style of production developed by Brecht aimed to reform much of twentieth-century theatre practice and he used the term **Epic theatre,** originally coined by the director Erwin Piscator (1893–1966), to describe the techniques involved.

Brecht wanted his audience to behave more like the audiences who attend sporting events (applauding the action and the performance and even smoking, eating and drinking) than those that patronized the bourgeois theatre (see Chapter 9 on Audiences).

Brecht defined Theatre as 'the production of living representations of recorded or invented happenings among people, and its aim is entertainment'.

The concept most frequently associated with Brecht is probably also the most frequently misunderstood: this is *Verfremdung* that has often been translated as '**alienation**' or the '**A**' **effect**. The term 'distancing' might be a less misleading translation.

The Berliner Ensemble visited London in 1956 with productions of *Mother Courage* and *The Caucasian Chalk Circle* (both in German) a few weeks after the playwright's death. The acting of Helene Weigel as Mother Courage and the style of playwriting and production had a profound influence on a generation of actors, new theatre companies, directors and playwrights that can still be felt. Perhaps the pre-eminent directors to promote a 'Brechtian' approach were Joan Littlewood and her Theatre Workshop at the Theatre Royal, Stratford, East London, George Devine at the English Stage Company based at the Royal Court Theatre, and William Gaskill who directed what is generally considered to have been the first successful production of a Brecht play in English: *The Caucasian Chalk Circle* for the Royal Shakespeare Company in 1962.

Brecht's ideas on acting and production are most clearly preserved in his many articles and publics statements. Many of these are collected as *Brecht on Theatre* (1964) by John Willet, but Brecht's clearest statements on acting are contained in his *Messingkauf Dialogues* ([1965] 1974), written in the form of an imaginary conversation between an actor, a **dramaturg** and a philosopher.

The post-modernist critic and philosopher Roland Barthes once wrote 'Brecht's theatre is a moral theatre which asks itself and the spectator: what must be done in a given situation?'

Brecht's non-prescriptive approach is best summed up in his suggested epitaph:

I require no tombstone, but
If you require one for me
I wish it to be inscribed:
He made suggestions. We
Accepted them.
By such inscription we should
All be honoured.

Brecht's acting process

Like Stanislavsky, Brecht evolved his ideas on acting during a lifetime's working towards a vision of what the theatre could and should be. Both men developed their systems through research and practice with a particular group of actors and challenged the accepted conventions of their day. Although Brecht did not propose a specific progression for the training of students, nevertheless he expounded his methodology and engaged his actors in constant evaluations of their work. While Stanislavsky sought for truth by employing psychological naturalism to simulate reality, Brecht focused on the reality of the theatre itself to represent the fictional reality of a play on stage.

There may appear to be a greater legacy from Stanislavsky in today's approaches to acting, particularly because his followers were eventually to establish 'the method' in New York, but wherever you see a small group of actors playing multiple roles arising from some contemporary issues, belief or ideologies or a democratically operated theatre company presenting a play in a workplace or public space, directly confronting their audience and employing virtually no scenic devices, you are almost certainly witnessing the influence of Bertolt Brecht.

Working with Brecht

According to Wolfgang Wolf (1973) who had worked as a designer with Brecht since 1929, he 'hated discussions, but loved arguing'. Brecht would say 'Don't talk so much, don't give me a reason, show me what you want to do.' This is how he would work with actors because he liked to think of the relationship as master and pupil. 'Then,' he said, 'pupils learn as masters and masters become pupils.' To the designers, Brecht would say:

> Don't try to put everything into something where it does not belong. You only do that to cover up your inability. You substitute things for the essence. The performers should be the greatest part of our scenery: when the setting becomes a comfortable place for the actors to walk around in, only then is it meaningful. No effects. They're not necessary. No false moods.

(Wolf, 1973, p. 15)

You may wish to reflect upon and discuss these statements at this point as they are crucial to understanding the reforming nature of Brecht's theatre.

Brecht took as his models the Elizabethan theatre of Marlowe and Shakespeare and the comedians and cabaret acts of the nightclubs. In the Elizabethan theatres, he argued, the actors worked in daylight, seeing, and directly relating to, their audiences, not relying on 'scenery' but using the building to create the desired locations. Their text was in blank verse of ten syllables a line and the parts of women were played by boys. They acted with real 'objects' as props and cut and shaped the text to suit the event. He cited a play of 1601 containing a note from the author suggesting alternative readings of the text and this advice to the actor 'Choose whichever reading seems best to you', and 'If this way of putting it is difficult to understand or unsuited to the audience, then use another' ([1965] 1974, p. 57). This same spirit of adaptability and direct approach to audiences led Brecht to admire and seek to employ and emulate the skills of entertainers working in the cabarets and nightclubs of Berlin.

He worked in direct contradiction to the cult of celebrity that has come to dominate the performing arts in our time. In a fascinating article written in 1978 for the (now sadly defunct) journal *Theatre Quarterly*, Peter Holland reflects on the impact made by Brecht's Berliner Ensemble when it came to England:

> George Devine had commented on his surprise at the appearance of Angela Gurwicz who played Grusche in *The Caucasian Chalk Circle* for the Ensemble: 'The heroine was a girl who would never be employed in any theatre in England, at least not as a heroine. She was plain, she had thick legs and was completely unglamorous.' Tynan made similar comments after seeing the play in 1956 'By contrast with the blinding sincerity of the Berliner Ensemble, we all seemed unreal and stagey. Many of us must have felt cheated. Brecht's actors do not behave like Western actors; they neither bludgeon us with personality or woo us with charm; they look shockingly like people – real potato-faced people such as one might meet in a bus queue.' Kenneth Tynan, who was widely regarded as the leading theatre critic of his day reiterated this sensation a few year's later:' When the Ensemble arrived in London in 1956 the press photographers flocked around the make-up girls and completely ignored the leading performers, who looked too much like ordinary human beings to be acceptable as celebrities.

Brecht was acutely aware of the differences between his theatre and that of the commercial West and, although he died before the visit of the Ensemble to Britain, he gave his cast this warning:

> For our London season we need to bear two things in mind. First ,we shall be offering most of the audience a pure pantomime [by this, he means what we would now term' mime'], a kind of silent film on the stage for they know no German ... Second, there is in England a long-standing fear that German art, literature, painting, music, must be terribly heavy, slow, laborious and pedestrian. So our playing needs to be quick, light, strong.

It is now recognized that the visit of the Berliner Ensemble affected every aspect of the theatre in Britain, including approaches to acting, and we must explore the reasons for this.

Understanding *Verfremdung* or the *Verfremdungseffekt*

The translation of *Verfremdung* as **alienation** or 'estrangement' has negative connotations, but for Brecht the concept was entirely positive. He wished to establish a dialectic in his theatre whereby audiences engaged in a critical attitude to human affairs. He explained (1965, p.104) that, 'An estranging representation is one which allows the object to be recognised, but at the same time makes it appear strange.' These estrangements or aspects of the 'A effect' can be of many kinds and are not confined to acting, they can extend to the whole *mise-en-scène* and may involve varying techniques. Put simply, they enable the audience to see things with detachment and judge for themselves.

The implication for Brecht's actors was that he encouraged a 'distance' method through which the actor attempts to demonstrate rather than impersonate his or her role, commenting on the character being portrayed and revealing the relationship between motives and restraints to action. At the same time, Brecht was developing new staging techniques, also devoted to highlighting the material causes and effects of human action. He often achieved this by means of a striking but contradictory central image. A good example of such an image is that of Mother Courage at the end of the play, alone between the shafts of her cart on an otherwise empty stage. The entire action of the play has been building up to the significance of this stark image with which the audience leaves the theatre.

Explaining how the 'alienating' style of acting might be achieved, Brecht (1965) indicated that:

◆ The story line must be a broken one (this would often be achieved by very short episodes and the action punctuated by songs).

◆ The style of acting must draw all its force from comparisons with reality and continually draw attention to the causes of the incidents reproduced.

◆ The actor must give up the sense of *complete conversion* into the stage character.

◆ The actor *shows* the character, *quotes* the character's lines and *repeats* a real-life incident.

However, Brecht also considered his 'A' effect to refer to the critical perspective employed by an audience in response to what it was witnessing. He hoped that an audience would not be entirely 'carried away' and would, instead, feel free to imagine different courses of events or try to imagine one. We shall return to this topic in Chapter 9 on audiences.

Brecht derived his 'new' acting style from a number of sources but he was particularly influenced by the strongly narrative but highly stylized nature of the Beijing Opera. In an attempt to have his actors stand, as it were, outside their parts, he would rehearse them speaking their lines in character but with the addition or prefix of 'he said' or 'she said'. In *The Caucasian Chalk Circle*, one of the characters employs this technique in a 'narrator' role and, as a means of separating actors from their text, which they could then view objectively. Brecht created several parts for story-tellers and narrators, sometimes employing half-spoken, half-sung text known as **Sprechgesang**.

Brecht, acting and reality

In certain respects, Brecht eschewed the physical and psychological realism created through the naturalistic approach of a director like Stanislavsky working on a play by Chekhov. Rather than have the audience eavesdropping on the lives of 'real' characters in their 'real' environments, Brecht insisted that there must be no attempt at disguising the theatre. The qualities and texture of the theatrical environment must be observed, the event must be pleasurable and there must be a projection screen for commentary and illustrations. His approach was invariably simple and direct. In another respect, however, Brecht's concern with a level of reality was intensely complex and detailed: this was particularly revealed in his use of properties. For him, a character's relationship with any object was revealed by the way in s/he used it. Willet explains:

> the jobs done by his characters, whether plucking a chicken or mending a motor tyre or scrubbing a man's back in the bath, always had to be done properly, as if the actor had had a life-time's practice behind them. They could never be allowed to degenerate into 'business'; a botched up imitation of activities which to Brecht were at once beautiful and socially important.

(1964, p. 159)

Working as Brecht might have done still involves certain principles that a contemporary student of acting should find stimulating. For example, in the *Messingkauf Dialogues*, Brecht suggests:

◆ A character is built up from its relationships with other characters and this means that the actor must be interested in the playing of the other actors rather than concentrating on his/her own part.

◆ There are several operations involved in building a character: you start with what you can get from the text you have to speak and by imagining the people you want to imitate. You must then try to get inside the person you are representing by understanding the situation, physical characteristics and modes of thought. Then you must know how to get out of the character again!

◆ He rejects the audience's demand that the actor should be wholly absorbed in the part When he filmed Helene Weigel applying her make-up, he cut the film into frames and used this to illustrate the detail and potency of gesture and facial expression: 'Each gesture can be analysed into as many gestures as you like, and all of them are perfect. Everything is there for the sake of something else, and at the same time for its own' ([1965] 1974, p. 75).

You should carefully consider the implications of Brecht's ideas for your own practice because his approach eradicates much that is shoddy and unnecessary in performance and provides a solid base for the exploration of a very wide range of theatrical styles and situations. Before we leave Brecht we must, however, encounter one of the concepts that has traditionally been found 'difficult' that of the **gestus**.

Understanding the *gestus*

Brecht considered it to be the actor's responsibility to perceive the *gestus* of a play or an incident/episode. The *gestus* comprises actions that have socio-political significance or implications: it is really a combination of understanding the **gist** of a scene and finding the gestures that might convey it. Actors might discover the *gestus* of a scene through improvisation or experiment: for example, suppose the gist of a scene you are working on is that one of the characters is, in some way, subservient to the other, then the scene may well involve bowing, averting the gaze or doffing the hat. Pickering puts it as follows:

> In Epic theatre the actor must discover and develop the *gest* that encodes the social relationships in which the character operates. A *gest* may involve a single movement, gesture or tone of voice or may extend to entire modes of behaviour that reflect the play's depiction of a world of social pressures and relationships: the play's *Grundgestus*.

(2005, p. 88)

In the *Messingkauf Dialogues*, Brecht describes how an actor will gradually move from 'something general' that might illustrate the *gest* towards something more specific and detailed and all accounts we have of Brecht's rehearsal techniques emphasize the experimental nature of the work. Little seems have been prescribed except the underlying beliefs: actors were encouraged to try out movements, tones of voice, activities and actions until the *gest* of a scene was achieved.

All Brecht's approach was carried out in the context of his development of his particular concept of **Epic theatre**. Now that you have become familiar with his way of working, you will be able to benefit from a close scrutiny of the table he drew up to illustrate the difference between what he termed **Dramatic Theatre** and his own Epic Theatre (Table 4.1).

Table 4.1 Comparison between Dramatic Theatre and Epic Theatre

Dramatic Theatre	Epic Theatre
Plot	Narrative
Implicates the spectator in a stage situation	Turns the spectator into an observer
Wears down his capacity for action	Arouses his capacity for action
Provides him with sensations	Forces him to take decisions
Experience	Picture of the world
The spectator is involved in something	He is made to face something
Suggestion	Argument
Instinctive feelings are preserved	Brought to the point of recognition
The spectator is in the thick of it, shares the experience	The spectator stands outside, studies
The human being is taken for granted	The human being is the object of inquiry
He is unalterable	He is alterable and able to alter
Eyes on the finish	Eyes on the course
One scene makes another	Each scene for itself
Growth	Montage
Linear development	In curves
Evolutionary determinism	Jumps
Man as a fixed point	Man as a process
Thought determines beings	Social being determines thought
Feeling	Reason

■ Jerzy Grotowski

We have already introduced you to some of the ideas of Grotowski in Chapter 1 (see Practitioner profile, p. 9) but now we must consider specifically his contribution to the development of acting. Grotowski's approaches have always provoked considerable controversy: some greet him as a genius and others with great hostility. For example, Peter Brook says:

> Grotowski is unique. Why? Because no one else in the world, to my knowledge, no one since Stanislavsky, has investigated the nature of acting, its phenomenon, its meaning, the nature and science of its mental-physical-emotional processes as deeply and completely as Grotowski.

> (1988, p. 37)

But when Eric Bentley, who worked with Brecht and translated many of his plays, was asked about Grotowski, he replied:

> Well, what about him? What is it he is up to now – American group therapy given the seal of European super-snobbery? What is Grotowski but another highbrow hoax? Not that I underrate hoaxes. Look at the history of Christianity – of which the Grotowski movement may well be an offshoot.

> (*Theatre Quarterly*, 21: 11)

This reference to religion is significant and apposite because the images Grotowski used to describe his work were religious. Although he himself was an atheist, he liked to speak of the **holy actor** who 'sacrifices his body'. In his *Towards a Poor Theatre*, he wrote:

> If the actor by setting himself a challenge publicly challenges others and through excess, profanation and outrageous sacrilege reveals himself by casting off his everyday mask, he makes it possible for the spectator to undertake a similar process of self-penetration. If he does not exhibit his body, but annihilates it, burns it, frees it from every resistance to any psychic impulse, then he does not sell his body, but sacrifices it. He repeats the atonement, he is close to holiness.

> (1968, p. 34)

The concept of the holy actor could only be realized through rigorous training of the body and voice so that they became available to any demands made upon them. This process involved:

◆ eradicating blocks that inhibited response;

◆ removing habits;

◆ working in a laboratory situation rather than developing skills for their own sake;

◆ achieving the 'total act' where an actor offers him or herself to the audience in complete honesty and vulnerability in order to provoke an open response.

It is not difficult to understand the sort of event and communication that Grotowski was hoping to achieve. He seems to have resented the spiritual monopoly achieved by the church and aimed to replace its moribund 'services' with his own penetrating and dynamic 'confrontations' or 'meetings'. That 'total act' to which he urged his actors was, in his opinion and in that of many critics, fulfilled by his leading actor Ryszard Cieslak, in his production of *The Constant Prince* so, like Brecht, he liked to draw attention to instances where his ambitions were achieved.

The holy actor

It is probably unhelpful to think of Grotowski as having established a 'system': it is better thought of as a 'way of working' that changed and developed over many years and may provide material for your own practice.

Participation in Grotowski's 'laboratory' for actor training was invariably a challenging, if not always comfortable, experience. He worked with great seriousness and intensity, insisting that the 'research' be carried out in silence except when an exercise required vocalization. Observers and participants were forbidden to whisper or laugh, even if the activity being explored resembled a circus act. Actors were required to be bare-foot in order to ensure direct contact with the ground and expected to be as near to naked as possible to prevent any kind of physical inhibition of movement and invoke a sense of openness and vulnerability. Grotowski would work alongside his students, often devoting 30 minutes or more to an exercise carried out by one of them. He discouraged analytical thinking during the process, aiming to develop the body's innate intelligence in response to the various tasks. Text was mainly used simply as a source of sound and for extensive exercises in aspects of vocalization. The physical exercises pushed the flexibility and control of the body to the extreme and demanded total commitment and concentration. Only by this approach could an actor 'overstep every conceivable limit'. These activities were all designed to produce what Grotowski termed an **inductive technique** (i.e. a technique of elimination) as opposed to the **deductive technique**, a mere accumulation of skills that characterized the '**courtesan actor**'.

Figure 4.2 Grotowski's actors at work
Source: @ © Grotowski Institute

When asked to explain the conditions essential to the art of acting which should be made the object of methodical investigation, Grotowski (1968, p. 96) listed the following:

 to stimulate a process of self-revelation, going back as far as the subconscious, yet channelling this stimulus in order to obtain the required reaction;

 to be able to articulate this process, discipline it and convert it into signs. In concrete terms, this means to construct a score whose notes are tiny elements of contact, reactions to the stimuli of the outside world: what we call 'give and take'.

 to eliminate from the creative process the resistances and obstacles caused by one's own organism, both physical and psychic (the two forming a whole)

From the many actors' accounts of working with Grotowski, it would seem that a typical session facilitated by him might have begun with his reiteration of the first principle: 'The essence of Theatre is the actor, his (her) actions and what s/he can achieve.'

A series of vocal and physical exercises would then follow, one of which we have used in the section on voice in Chapter 3, and Grotowski would move among his students, feeling their heads, backs, chests or abdomens for movement, resonance or distortion. Some exercises would be based on animal movements or sounds, others, such as shoulder stands, would be more directly and demandingly physical. In his famous 'tiger exercise', the teacher was aiming to make all students 'let themselves go' completely and lose all sense of self-consciousness while exercising the guttural resonator. Grotowski himself would play the tiger attacking his prey while the student, as prey, responded, roaring and following the 'tiger's' shouted instructions. Some exercises demanded singing or the use of associations of ideas to create images, others aimed for total flexibility of the spine. At the end of a session, Grotowski might survey the most important elements of his approach, emphasizing that 'the body must work first. Afterwards comes the voice.'

For students studying acting today, the ideas of Grotowski seem familiar. Many Theatre courses are situated in studios based on his ideas and many of the exercises he employed, or some like them, are employed by teachers of voice, movement or physical theatre. However, when Grotowski first visited Britain to work with the Royal Shakespeare Company, his approach was received with varying degrees of enthusiasm: some found that he brought about miraculous changes while others were bored. For Peter Brook (1988), Grotowski administered a series of shocks and it is important for your understanding that he continues to do so:

 the shock of confronting yourself;

 the shock of realizing your own evasions, tricks and clichés;

 the shock of sensing your own, vast, untapped resources;

 the shock of being forced to ask why you are an actor;

 the shock of realizing that that question exists;

 the shock of realizing that somewhere in the world of acting there is absolute and total dedication;

 the shock of understanding that the theatre is not so much a way of life as a way to life.

The influence of Stanislavsky and Brecht can still be seen in the mainstream theatre but the work of Grotowski has tended to promote new approaches in universities and in 'fringe' or 'alternative' theatre, partly because his work never envisaged any major financial expenditure. The development of non-text-based and physical theatre draws heavily, though sometimes indirectly, on the work of Grotowski and his experiments and methods are still explored and practised by dedicated followers. His re-establishment of the actor as the central factor of Theatre has been crucial and far-reaching.

▉ Sanford Meisner

During an interview conducted in 1958 (Emmet, 1975, p. 21), the popular British actor, Alec McCowen, who was later to hold West End audiences spellbound with his solo performance of the entire *Gospel of St. Mark*, attributed his success to the teaching of Sanford Meisner, highlighting especially the importance of recognizing and playing a 'moment' in a play with understanding. Other leading figures from the modern stage and screen, including the playwrights Arthur Miller and David Mamet, have paid generous tributes to the work of Meisner and his teaching is now perpetuated by a Center in the USA.

The Meisner 'technique' became increasingly popular in actor education during the latter part of the twentieth century and is now firmly established in colleges and universities as a system on which students may build their practice. Meisner 'classes' are also very popular among professional actors in the USA as a means of refreshment and refinement.

Practitioner profile

Sanford Meisner (1905–97)

Meisner was born in New York into a Hungarian Jewish family and his first artistic ambition was to become a concert pianist. He entered what is now the Juilliard School for this purpose but abandoned his studies to enter the theatre as an actor. His initial experience of professional acting was with the Theater Guild where he renewed his acquaintance with Lee Strasberg who was to prove instrumental in establishing the 'Method' school of acting.

◆ In 1931, a group, including Meisner, Strasberg, Stella Adler and Harold Clurman, established the Group Theatre, an experimental company that sought ways of achieving 'truthful' acting. Many of the participants had studied Stanislavky's work and had been particularly influenced by interpretations of it by Richard Boleslavski at the Laboratory Theatre.

The guiding principle of the Group Theatre in its early days was the concept of affective (emotional) memory and its ability to help an actor establish a role. This was to become the basis of **the Method**.

In 1933–34, Meisner became dissatisfied with the reliance on emotional memory, arguing that actors were not 'guinea pigs to be manipulated, dissected'. He believed that the approach being adopted was not 'organic' or 'healthy'.

Meisner's feelings were confirmed when one of the group, Stella Adler, returned from Europe where she had studied under Stanislavsky. She reported that his system was not based on **affective memory** but on the use of the actor's imagination in connecting with a character and the given circumstances together with a truthful playing of the character's objectives.

Although Meisner remained with the Group until 1941 he also worked with the Neighborhood Playhouse from 1935 and it was here that he was free to establish his own methods. Meanwhile, Strasberg left the Group Theatre in 1937 to establish his 'Method' school and the rift between him and Meisner became permanent.

Meisner was Head of the Drama Department at the Neighborhood from 1935–58 and then again from 1964–90. From 1958–64 he was director of the New Talent Division of Twentieth Century Fox and developed his career as a successful film actor.

In 1985 Meisner and James Carville founded the Meisner/Carville School of Acting on the Island of Bequia in the West Indies and later extended the school to North Hollywood. In 1995, the Sanford Meisner Center for the Arts was established and later combined with the school to form the Sanford Meisner Center that continues to teach Meisner's system.

Meisner's underlying principles

Meisner's most frequently quoted assertion is that he wanted to enable actors to 'live truthfully under imaginary circumstances'. This emphasis on 'truthfulness' resulted in actors finding something simple and real to do rather than playing an emotion or imitating an action. Arthur Miller's enthusiasm for Meisner's work was based on the fact that actors trained by him were' honest and simple and don't lay on complications that aren't necessary' (Emmet, 1975). Actors were encouraged to respond to each other in the moment and the ability to stay 'in the moment' was seen as their fundamental task rather than playing solely for a series of objectives, Meisner insisted that it was only through concentrating on and listening to (what he called 'reading and responding') to each other that actors could create something real that had a genuinely organic relationship with what was happening in the space. To some extent, Meisner was encouraging his students not to act but to find the truth in their response to each other and to delve into their own selves to find their real emotions and how those, when exposed, affected 'performance'.

With these principles, Meisner moved away from the idea of portraying a character into a situation where he required actors to effect a **transformation** of themselves into another personality. This process involved the creation of a complete fictional autobiography for the character.The 'self' was to be lost and another being created. This new being depended on such an intimate knowledge of the script that the actions, words, movements and silences all arose from natural impulses and from a reaction to the other characters. All this had to be achieved simultaneously and with spontaneity. The **authenticity** of what was achieved might result in performances changing from night to night because the roles were being lived by the actors. Meisner worked extensively with the idea of silence because it revealed the potential for deep meaning. 'Silence,' he said, 'has a myriad of meanings. In the theatre, silence is the absence of words, but never an absence of meaning.'

Working with Meisner

Studying with Meisner or one of his follwers was and remains a demanding experience. The intensity of the work and the personal exposure of fears and emotions, designed to strip away all artifice, are often met with initial resistance and it is not uncommon for students to drop out after a few sessions. However, for those that remain, the work is both stimulating and creative. Meisner left no extensive body of published work and his approach is continued by practitioners who studied with him or with one of his immediate students, rather as the teachings of great ballet masters are passed on.

From the observations we have made we can assert that a typical Meisner class might have the following qualities and elements:

An initial practice of spontaneous repetition in which actors stand opposite each other in pairs and look each other fixedly in the eye. One actor comments on a physical feature of the other and begins an exchange that might begin 'you have very red lips'. The actors repeat this phrase back and forth but might make a variation 'I have *very* red lips?', 'Yes, you have very *red* lips.' The statement retains reality, however often it is repeated, because it is based on a genuine physical reality. No physical contact is permitted although, in feeding of the emotions off each other, the exchange may end in an explosion of frustration or rage.

The actors undertake a similar exercise except that they must now have lost all self-consciousness and now have been given circumstances involving another actor. They begin a similar 'repetition' process but this may change as they sense a need arising from a change in the emotional state of the other.

Actors enter a space having previously been given specific roles. They have not been given specific lines and may begin with the 'repetitions' until they feel the need to change. The plot of the improvisation is created entirely from the surroundings and the dialogue is determined by one actor sensing the other's emotional state but each must remain 'in character' throughout.

A similar extension of the above in which one of the actors selects a relationship and creates difficult circumstances involving them both. They enter the scene without knowing the precise situation and interact as they attempt to convey their feelings, motives and idea through inflections and physical cues. This technique involves moment-to-moment spontaneity.

Students are given a single line of dialogue and told not to speak it until something happens to provoke those words. The teacher then creates a situation (such as pinching a student) that provokes the uttering of the line with total truth.

When memorizing lines, students are asked to repeat them without inflection or expression until they are known so thoroughly that it is possible to do almost anything with them vocally.

Actors are challenged to move beyond the script to discover the underlying emotional or philosophical themes and ideas of the play.

The intrinsic motivation of actions is explored together with the nature of interaction.

You should be able to see from this brief account of Meisner's work how he adapted the teachings of Stanislavsky to the situation in American theatre, as he saw it. This is an important aspect of your understanding of studying and developing the acting process. No one 'system' is likely to provide the entire key to acting in every kind of theatre situation: for example, the approach advocated by Meisner, developed in the context of the intensely psychological plays and movies in which he was involved, may not be helpful in undertaking or rehearsing the role of God in a medieval allegorical play or the methods of Stanislavsky, deeply rooted in the Russian theatre of his day, may be totally inappropriate for the 'characters' in an Absurdist play by Ionesco. American students tend to be more comfortable with introspection or talking about themselves than do some

European or British students and, thus, the approaches of the various practitioners we have considered may appeal to some more than others.

Suggested activity

By selecting only a few of the many 'systems' of actors' training and practice,k we are invariably in danger of omitting some very important practitioners and approaches whose work you will, no doubt, encounter either directly as the basis of the teaching you receive or indirectly as an influence on productions or actors you may observe. All great acting teachers have, to some extent, reacted against the limitations of the theatre practice of their day and situation and most have borrowed freely from insights gained by observing a wide variety of performance and style, often from very different cultures from their own. We would advise you to continue a lifelong investigation of the phenomenon of acting by exploring some of the ideas of:

◆ the Alexander Technique: a re-education of the body devised by an actor who frequently lost his voice;

◆ Arthur Lessac, whose work on the voice has laid the foundations for a more dynamic and holistic approach to what was once 'speech training';

◆ Kristin Linklater, Patsy Rodenburg and Cicely Berry, who have refined vocal work with actors and recorded their findings in accessible handbooks;

◆ Rudolph Laban, whose observations and analysis of human movement have provided the foundation for much actor/dancer training;

◆ Jaques Lecoq, whose physically exaggerated and comic styles of performance have influenced those who believe that an actor must know how to 'play';

◆ Peter Barkworth, the English actor, who produced some of the most practical and useful handbooks of acting ever written;

◆ Tadashi Suzuki, the Japanese director, who created a sense of 'stillness' in acting and continued the ideas of Stanislavsky and Grotowski on the integrated psycho-physical approach to the training of actors.

All these practitioners left a body of published work or set up institutions to promote their ideas for new generations of students and all these, together with substantial material on the Internet, are now accessible.

■ Conclusion

In our study of the systems evolved by Stanislavsky, Brecht, Grotowski and Meisner, we noted that their work was developed by substantial analysis and for a specific situation. It is, therefore, dangerous to consider the ideas of these practitioners to constitute fixed 'methods'. They are, rather, a source of guidance and insights into the task of acting and may be adapted to enable you to devise your own approach to performance in a play or theatrical event. We hope, also, that this chapter will have equipped you to experiment with variable means of exploring a dramatic text and to understand many of the developments in the theatre that have become obvious in recent years.

The ideas of the four practitioners we have considered have permeated the techniques and styles of most modern actors, both on the stage and in the recorded media, and it should now be possible for you to identify and more fully comprehend what you see and hear in these contexts. Most importantly, you will have seen that the study of acting, as an aspect of Theatre Studies, requires extensive concentration, persistence, honesty and imagination and demands an ability to reflect upon personal actitivity, progress and experience.

Topics for discussion and reflection

◆ The way in which Stanislavsky reflected upon and analysed his own practice can act as a model for your own critical thinking about acting. Furthermore, his ideas provide a checklist for considering your own skills. Using the knowledge and understanding you have gained from our brief survey of Stanislavsky's work respond to the following questions:

◆ Which of the three main kinds of actor that Stanislavsky describes do you consider yourself to be?

◆ What do you think is the value of the concept of the magic 'if'?

◆ What constitutes 'truthfulness' in acting for you?

◆ As with all the other systems and approaches dealt with in this chapter, the brief survey of the work of Brecht should inform your own work as a student actor. Knowing *about* Brecht is of little use unless you can see how his ideas might be applied in practice and we have emphasized that this can only be achieved through experiment:

◆ Do you agree with Brecht's definition of Theatre (see p. 64) and how does that compare with other definitions you have encountered in this book?

◆ What aspects of Brecht's thinking have you been aware of in theatre visits, your own practical work or any other aspect of Theatre Studies?

◆ What do you understand by the terms 'popular theatre' and 'political theatre'? How might your acting style reflect being involved in such a genre?

◆ Grotoswski demanded absolute concentration and commitment from his students: do you see this as vital for your own work in acting?

◆ Discuss Grotowski's use of religious terminology to analyse the acting process.

◆ What do you understand by the 'holy actor'?

◆ Do you consider yourself to be a 'courtesan' or 'holy' actor?

◆ What do you understand by the concept of 'poor theatre'?

◆ Meisner demanded intense concentration from his actors. Give examples from your own practice or observation of:

◆ Remaining '**in the moment**'.

◆ The use of silence.

Further reading

Bartow, A. (ed.) (2008) *Handbook of Acting Techniques*, London: Nick Hern. A most useful development of the topics of this chapter.

Brecht, B. (1979) *The Messingkauf Dialogues*, trans. J. Willet, London: Methuen. Provocative and, at times, complex statements of Brecht's influential ideas.

Hodgson, A. (ed.) (2000) *Twentieth Century Actor Training*, London: Routledge. Provides a very useful overview of current approaches and will enable you to see where your experience relates to that of others.

Meisner, S. and Longwell, D. (1987) *Sanford Meisner on Acting*, New York: Vintage. One of the few written sources of Meisner's work.

Stanislavsky, K. (2008a) *My Life in Art*, trans. J. Bendetti, London: Routledge. Excellent new translations of Stanislavsky's seminal thinking.

Stanislavsky, K. (2008b) *Building a Character and Creating a Role*, in *An Actor's Work*, trans. J. Benedetti, London: Routledge.

Website

For a discussion of acting for the recorded media, see our website: www.palgrave.com/foundations/pickering

5 Varieties of Theatre Performance

In this chapter we discuss examples from the vast range of performances which can be seen in the contemporary theatre in all its forms. We suggest a number of headings under which such performances might be categorized and studied, and encourage you to undertake substantial enquiries into the types of performances available in your own location. The chapter outlines the contributions of a number of key thinkers to the debates about the nature of Theatre.

Learning outcomes

By the conclusion of this chapter, you should be able to:

▶ develop a sense of curiosity and investigation into the variety of theatre available to you;

▶ understand and reflect upon a wide range of theatre genres and styles;

▶ devise your own categories to describe and discuss various forms of theatre;

▶ recognize and analyse efforts to extend the boundaries of theatre;

▶ discuss the work of a number of key practitioners and thinkers in the field of performance;

▶ discuss integration, fusion and inter-culturalism in theatre.

■ Performance varieties

One of the problems of Theatre Studies as a subject discipline is that it has frequently ignored large sections of the very subject it purports to study. Indeed, it has sometimes seemed that it inhabited a parallel universe consisting of a limited number of famous practitioners and theorists when, in fact, the real world of the contemporary theatre consists of something entirely different. There has also been a tacit belief that there exists a hierarchy of theatre, some of which is worth studying and some of which is not. No doubt this, to some extent, accounts for the rise in popularity of Performance Studies where performances are seen as part of a continuum, changing in style and nature but not in aesthetic, cultural or moral value.

Theatre is a far wider subject than is sometimes realized and, just as we have encouraged you to visit and investigate theatre spaces, we would also recommend that you take time to discover precisely what theatrical activity is available to you.

As an example, we might take the programme of events offered by three theatres situated in the same fairly small university city in England over a period of three months. The largest of the three theatres is a converted cinema in the City centre with an audience capacity of nearly 1,000, and named after the sixteenth-century dramatist Christopher Marlowe, who was born in the city. This theatre once occupied a smaller building and had its own company staging productions but now receives only largely professional tours and some local amateur productions. It is owned by the local council and the season began with a ballet version of Shakespeare's play *Hamlet* followed by an amateur production of the musical *My Fair Lady*, which, like the ballet, ran from Tuesday to Saturday. A pattern of productions that run for five or six nights, with some matinées, is continued with the children's play *Treasure Island*, the Ukrainian National Opera in *Madame Butterfly* by Puccini and *La Traviata* by Verdi and a new stage version of the orchestral piece *Peter and the Wolf* by Prokofiev. The first 'straight play' of the season was *The Deep Blue Sea* by the mid-twentieth-century British dramatist Terence Rattigan, followed by *Yamato*, a performance by drummers from Japan, and a stage version of a 'hit movie' *The Wedding Singer*, prior to its London run. A second play, *The Clean House*, was by the contemporary dramatist Sarah Ruhl and was succeeded by the Lloyd-Webber musical *Cats*. The remaining productions are a comedy version of *The 39 Steps* (featuring four actors playing 139 roles in 100 minutes), a play entitled *Secrets*, presented by a dedicated children's theatre company, a further children's play *The Emperor's New Kilt*, and the Russian State Opera of Siberia in the operas *Madame Butterfly*, *La Traviata* and *La Bohème*. During the same period the theatre also offered 14 one-night performances, including a play about Laurel and Hardy, a Shakespeare presentation aimed at school students, a large number of diverse concerts including jazz, classical and rock/pop and several comedians.

Now we can compare this programme with what was offered at the university theatre (endowed by and named after the Gulbenkian Foundation) in the same city at the same period. This 350-seater theatre is situated some distance from the city centre (where the previously mentioned theatre is positioned) on the university campus and is, at times, used by the university's own Theatre Department. However, the funding of the theatre obliges it to serve the whole community and it relies largely on visiting companies and performers to maintain a full programme of events. The theatre has also recently developed an attractive cinema and restaurant, open all day and providing a focal point and social centre for the university.

The season consisted of 42 one-night events together with one production of a devised play that ran for three nights and a period of six days in which student directors showed their work in a series of short plays. In addition, a 'comedy club' of 'top acts from the London circuit' operates in the theatre bar on a regular basis. (This is a university that offers a course/module in Stand-up comedy.) Of the 42 one-performance productions, nine were solo performances, including stand-up comedy, shows described as having had a successful run on 'the fringe' and even a one-man version of Shakespeare's *Henry V*. Nine of the productions are by children's or story-telling companies, all with very small casts. Eighteen of the performances are of music, ranging from classical orchestral, through Celtic and World music to ukulele orchestras, jazz singers and salsa There were three dance productions including a performance by the Beijing Modern Dance

UNIVERSITY OF WINCHESTER
LIBRARY

Company and the few remaining productions were of plays, most of which were devised pieces for small casts using physical theatre techniques, multi-media and/or puppets. Oscar Wilde's *The Picture of Dorian Gray* was the only piece not by a living writer/deviser.

The third theatre we shall consider is a playhouse converted from a former church, owned and administered by an amateur company and, occasionally hired out to other amateur performing groups. It is situated in a small seaside town a few miles from the city but recognized administratively as being part of it. The programme for the same period included three main productions by the 'parent 'company: the late twentieth-century play *Terra Nova*, based on the journals found on the body of the Antarctic explorer, Captain Scott, the nineteenth-century play, *London Assurance* by Dion Boucicault, both of them running from Tuesday to Saturday, and a two weeks' run of Ken Campbell's eccentric play *Old King Cole*, during the school vacation time. Additionally other local amateur companies provided productions of Noel Coward's *Fallen Angels* and the thriller *Black Widow* by Paul Thain. Performances by local dance schools and music theatre/ operatic societies completed the programme. Some of the productions were listed as having been entered for a competitive festival and subject to adjudication. There are literally thousands of similar theatres and playhouses across Britain and North America. Indeed, it is quite possible that you acquired your interest in Theatre from one such organization. Community or amateur theatre seems to be indelibly woven into the fabric of our societies and now often provides the only opportunity to see productions of substantial plays outside very large cities.

It has been necessary to enter into a considerable amount of detail in order to present an outline picture of the provision for Theatre in one modestly sized city. There is, of course, other theatrical activity happening at events and venues throughout the year but we have provided a basis for some serious consideration of the variety and balance of performance that we collectively label Theatre, the subject you are currently studying.

You might wish to reflect on:

◆ the balance between various forms of Musical Theatre, Dance and Drama;

◆ the relative number of performances targeted at children or for educational purposes;

◆ the absence of any major productions of sixteenth- or seventeenth-century plays in spite of the theatre's name;

◆ the playwrights whose work is represented;

◆ the fact that several of the productions had been seen in or were destined for London.

Suggested activity

◆ Carry out a similar survey and analysis of theatre provision in the town/area in which you are currently studying or where you live.

◆ How do your findings compare with the situation we have described?

◆ What trends and patterns of activity/provision do you detect?

◆ Now compare what you find with the productions currently running in the West End or on Broadway and in the 'fringe' theatres of London or other major cities or '**Off-Off Broadway**'. What is the balance between various forms of performance in these places? Which playwrights are currently

popular and what evidence of new writing can you find?
◆ Look at ticket prices for the various kinds of Theatre event you have discovered and draw some conclusions about the pricing policy.
◆ What evidence can you find of forms of subsidy and grant aid?

Now that you have considered the local and national 'scene' in some detail it is helpful to examine the various aspects of contemporary Theatre individually.

■ The predictable theatre

Imagine the following scenario. You are somewhere in Europe or the English-speaking world among a rather well-dressed audience comprising of all age groups including quite young children, watching a performance of the ballet *Swan Lake* with music by the Russian composer Tchaikovsky. This production is by the Siberian State Ballet Company, but it might easily be a company from Denmark, Australia, the Netherlands, London or New York, and it takes place in a proscenium arch theatre. The setting is created by large painted backdrops and alternates between a court and a woodland lake shrouded in mist. You have reached Act III, which takes place at the court. You have learned from the programme note that the principal male character is Prince Siegfried, who objects to being told how he is to choose who he will marry and has previously visited the lake where he has fallen in love with the beautiful Odette, a 'swan maiden' who, because of a spell, is a swan by day and a woman by night. During the current Act, at what appears to be a climax, the same female dancer who has played the role of Odette, dressed in white to resemble a swan, appears dressed in black as Odile, the daughter of the 'evil genius' Von Rothbart, who has constantly made menacing appearances throughout the action dressed in a black cloak.

The story-line of the ballet is constantly interrupted by formal 'set piece' dances and the audience behaves rather like the spectators at a ball game, applauding and appreciating the technical achievements of the dancers, and a generation of dance teachers and their students in the audience realize not only the discipline that must be followed in order to achieve such a level of technical mastery but also know the French terms that are used to describe the various movements.

You are watching what is confusingly termed one of the great 'classical' ballets, clearly written at the height of the Romantic movement .You may be able to follow the 'plot' line from the highly stylized actions but this is most unlikely because the progress of the story so often gives way to set dance numbers, some from differing cultures and all sumptuously costumed. There is no spoken dialogue and speech is simulated by a series of coded gestures: communication is entirely through physical movement in response to an elaborate orchestral score.

If you are a ballet enthusiast, you will know that the choreography being used is almost certainly that by Petipa and Ivanov devised for the revival of *Swan Lake* in 1895, shortly after Tchaikovsky's death and that this choreography, first seen at the Maryinsky Theatre in St. Petersburg in the same year as Stanislavsky's production of *Othello* in

Moscow, has been passed on from one generation of ballet performers to the next with little reference to a notated text.

You probably feel that the whole performance only makes sense if you accept that you are taking part in a tradition in which the meal in the 'pre-show supper' and the pre-ordered drinks or 'ritual' ice-creams patiently queued for in at the intervals are part of the event and that the entire process is only comprehensible if you understand the conventions that operate. This is the **predictable theatre**.

Other examples of the 'predictable theatre' would be Grand Opera, many forms of the stage musical, the Kabuki Theatre of Japan or some productions of the plays of Shakespeare or other plays thought of as 'classics'. Like classical ballet, opera is often the preserve of a particular elite: its conventions are equally preserved and only meaningful to an audience 'in the know'. Heroines die while singing impossibly high notes, dialogue is entirely sung and even the most expertly written programme notes sometimes admit that the plot lines are virtually unfathomable. Applause follows spectacularly sung duets or solos and the performance, like ballet, shows a clear division between the principal performers and the chorus. Some of the same characteristics are evident in stage musicals or operettas. An extreme example of the predictable theatre were productions of the very popular operettas of Gilbert and Sullivan until very recent times. For many years the thousands of productions of these stage works were controlled by a copyright ruling that the moves and gestures imposed by the original director, Gilbert himself, must be used. It was only when this restriction expired that directors and performers were free to follow their own creative ideas. Remarkably, however, the fact that audiences knew that they were to witness Gilbert's own choreography and stagecraft and that any two productions of the same work would be remarkably similar seems to have enhanced, rather than to have diminished, the popularity of such works as *The Mikado* or *The Pirates of Penzance*.

In the West, productions of Shakespeare's plays may have elements of the predictable because their texts will be familiar to audiences and the event shown will be expected; similarly, productions of 'thrillers' or 'situation comedies' may well take a form that audiences expect and may attract a certain kind of spectator in search of a 'good evening out'. In various forms of Oriental Theatre, audiences may be familiar with the plot and expect to see the performers conform to precise codes and styles.

The whole point of the predictable theatre is that audiences attend to see and enjoy *how* the production operates as the familiar re-telling of a much-loved story rather than *what* the work may have to say that might be new or challenging. In some cases it is difficult to say if the work is actually *about* anything significant except within a broad theme such as love or betrayal; it is the *execution* of the work that holds the fascination. With the current popularity and success of the stage musical as a genre, the predictable theatre has become almost global in its appeal and you are now as likely to see a production of *Cabaret* or *Cats* in Tokyo, Sydney, Mumbai or any major city in the world.

Efforts to make the predictable unpredictable are invariably interesting but do not necessarily alter the course of the genre. In the case of *Swan Lake*, for example, Matthew Bourne's production, that substituted male swans for the traditional female, was undoubtedly popular but more 'traditional' versions of the ballet remain in great demand. Similarly the rock or modernized versions of Gilbert and Sullivan have brought new audiences to see such shows as *The Mikado* but are rarely undertaken by the numerous operatic and dramatic societies, though they may intersperse their repertoire with the equally popular and familiar musicals of Rodgers and Hammerstein. Even though Peter Brook's production of *A Midsummer Night's Dream* was probably a reaction against the predictability of years of Old Vic and Royal Shakespeare Company work, it did not entirely prevent generations of theatre-goers expecting the lavish settings and performance styles they had come to expect, and opera productions which deliberately relocate works to settings and contexts not envisaged in the original, have not markedly increased the appeal of opera to 'new' audiences.

The predictable theatre in the West has tended to be the preserve of the European proscenium tradition. For some, this has been tiresome and is often rejected by those who seek a revolution in the theatre. For example, in his play *Some Americans Abroad* (1989), the American dramatist Richard Nelson shows a group of students from his own country trying to make sense of compulsory theatre trips in London and Stratford and exposes their bafflement and perplexity when confronting a series of traditions and conventions. Returning from fighting in Vietnam, another American playwright, David Rabe, found that the theatre: 'seemed lightweight, all fluff and metaphor, spangle, posture, and glitter crammed into a form as rigid as any machine geared to reproduce the shape of itself endlessly' (quoted in Cohn, 1991, p. 32).

Another American dramatist, John Guare, after some success and one total failure on Broadway, expressed his frustration in *Rich and Famous* (1977), a play about a Broadway playwright with the absurd name of Bing Ringling, who has written 843 plays. In a series of flashbacks we see how Bing comes to be wearing cuff-links initialled with 'R' and 'F' (for Rich and Famous). Even when we have seen the predictable and formulaic process of creating a Broadway show and Bing tries to throw away his cuff-links, he simply cannot remove the final one.

Looking at the predictable theatre today we are not suggesting that it is any less valid than any other form of theatre. Indeed, it remains the sole interest of huge numbers of theatregoers and performers. It requires considerable income to sustain it and audiences tend to expect, and demand lavish settings and high levels of spectacle. Their appetites may now have been influenced by television shows that conduct auditions for leading roles or seek to find potential 'stars'.

This may lead us to consider a uniquely British version of the predictable theatre: the traditional **pantomime**. For many producing theatres, this event spanning the Christmas period used to be the most lucrative period of the year and would partly subsidize less predictable work for the rest of the year: it may well be also the only theatrical event attended by large sections of the audience in any one year. The history of pantomime, with traditions dating back to the seventeenth century, is rich and complex and rewards further study but here we can note that it is the epitome of formulaic theatre, an extreme form of the predictable. Well-known fairy stories are transformed into stage plays: the characters invariably include those obviously considered 'good' and those deemed 'evil', together with young lovers and comic 'dames' (usually played by men). Until recently the leading man, usually a handsome prince or someone of similar status, was played by a young woman in what was traditionally known as a 'breeches' part. The origin of this tradition was that it provided the only opportunity for women's legs to be on display in more prudish periods of history. More recently, the leading male has more often been a 'rock' star or television personality and the leading female a well-known 'soap' actor. As foil to the main characters, the production might include a comedian and a sympathetic character who frequently relates directly to the audience, encouraging them to participate in singing.

Action ranges from scenes with dancing to comic routines involving ghosts or slapstick. Duets and solos sung by the lead characters are set to pre-existing 'pop' music and the entire *mise-en-scène* is colourful, elaborate and vibrant. Settings are changed by the use of 'flown' backdrops or swivelled flats and may be enhanced by the appearance of animals, actors in animal costume or lighting effects. The settings are evocative of a world of fantasy, often including gothic castles or medieval courts.

The text is sometimes written in verse and there may be passages where comics are expected to improvise. The end is invariably happy and the discomfort of the wicked is considered as enjoyable for the audience as the happiness of the young lovers.

This extraordinary theatrical tradition provides employment for many performers and appears to be fairly undiminished in popularity. It is undertaken by the professional and amateur Theatre alike and is unapologetically escapist, stereotypical and hierarchical. Like all productions that we have termed 'the predictable theatre', pantomime can be considered totally absurd or magical, or both according to your view point.

We might sum up some of the qualities and characteristics of the predictable theatre as follows:

◇ the complex plot or story line is either known or explained in a programme note;

◇ the 'text' may be familiar to the audience;

◇ understanding what is happening depends on understanding certain conventions;

◇ audiences may express their appreciation of the performances in the course of the action;

◇ there is an obvious division between the leading performers and the rest of the cast;

◇ productions tend to involve large numbers and considerable expense;

◇ staging probably depends on a proscenium theatre and may well be elaborate;

◇ audiences will hold strong opinions on, and have specific expectations of, performance styles.

■ The unpredictable theatre

An article in a recent London newspaper began with the statement 'Forget anything as boring as a stage. This, ladies and gentlemen, is the era of site specific performance.' It then went on to describe several current productions and began with a 'Hitchcockian' thriller entitled 'Contains Violence', which was to take place in an office block. The audience, it asserted, 'will become voyeurs, donning binoculars and headsets to witness the action through the office windows' from the terrace of the producing theatre opposite. The director was quoted as saying:

> I'm interested in expanding the idea of stages and how creating an apparent distance from the main action can actually make the experience more intimate. The plot plays with mystery and suspense but there are lots of stories in there. The audience sees a man and a woman working late and discover they have a personal connection that overlaps from the past. But the narrative is also part of the audience's fantasy of what they imagine is happening. We, as urban dwellers,

Figure 5.1   The unpredictable theatre: Lizzie Chittenden and Amy Flight rehearse a site-specific devised piece in Canterbury Cathedral: an art installation constructed from willow is in position
Source: © David Willis

often do precisely that – overhear a conversation and make up our own interpretation of these people's lives.

Clearly, we have here a totally different approach to the concept of Theatre from the ideas we grouped under the label 'predictable'. Details of similar challenges to the predictable emerge almost every week. In London, for example, a company known as The Factory mounts spontaneous performances of *Hamlet* every Sunday in a secret location. The audience is asked to bring along an object that may be used as a 'prop' and the actors change roles depending on whom the audience selects to play each part. The director explained that the company would perform anywhere that did not provide the same 'auditorium experience' that he believed everyone was 'bored with' and that, if a theatre was used, it was likely that they would put the audience on the stage or even play some of the action in the street outside.

In the Soho area of London, another company presented a Peking Opera style version of the Chinese fable *Slippery Mountain*. The 'theatre' was a Chinese restaurant and the director, Paddy Cunneen, remarked:

Traditionally, Chinese opera was performed in tea rooms. The shrill sounds it is famous for originated from trying to cover the noise there. What excites me is that it's a communal activity – the audience eats dim sum while being entertained.

Plays and productions which cheat the expectations of audiences are by no means confined to the early twenty-first century or to the work of directors. In 1973, for example, Lanford Wilson wrote his play *HotL Baltimore* in which the **protagonists** consist of an entire group: three prostitutes, an old man who is a health freak, a spiritualist who was once a waitress, a lesbian health freak and her very frail brother. These characters are meeting mysteriously in a condemned hotel. Speaking of the play which comprises the intertwining strands of the characters' biographies, Wilson said: 'The theatre, evanescent itself, and, for all we do, perhaps itself disappearing here, seems the ideal place for the presentation of the impermanence of our architecture.'

That sense of impermanence is a contributor to the creation of a theatre of the unpredictable and may reveal itself in both the text and the *mise-en-scène*. Plays from what has been called the **Theatre of the Absurd** frustrate and defy the expectations of an audience accustomed to predictability in the nature of the theatrical event. Such plays range from the world's longest-running play: Ionesco's *The Bald Prima Donna*, that has been playing at the same theatre in Paris since the 1950s, to Samuel Beckett's *Waiting for Godot* which shows a universe devoid of certainty or permanence in a form that mocks the usual conventions of a stage play. Although established as one of the seminal plays of the twentieth century, the experience of watching *Waiting for Godot* in performance still has the capacity to provoke feelings of discomfort and bafflement.

Profoundly influenced by directing both the plays of Brecht and Beckett, the American founder of the Mabou Mines Company, Lee Breur (b. 1937) embraced both Brecht's sense of distancing (see Chapter 4) and Beckett's world of unanswered and unanswerable questions. His play for three actors, *Red Horse Animation* (1970), begins with three printed columns that the playwright calls 'tracks'. These are Outline, Lifeline and Storyline. About a third of the way through the play, Lifeline and Storyline merge and the resultant performance includes cinematic and highly technological techniques in which such questions as 'why make art?' or 'why pretend?' are posed but not answered. Such bold experiments with the process of creating a text have led to a situation in which no aspect of the theatre can be wholly predictable.

Whereas the predictable theatre assumes an ordered and moral world, the unpredictable tends to embrace that set of attitudes and philosophical ideas we now term **postmodernism**. However 'unreal' the world of classical ballet, grand opera, operetta, or classic plays, there is usually an assumption of ultimate meaning and some workings of Providence. For the postmodernist there is no **meta-narrative**: language is deeply mistrusted and the existence of pre-ordained order rejected. We can see this is in the repeated attempts to reject the order of the theatre itself and a growing emphasis on insisting that audiences make their own meanings from their experience

■ The Theatre of Images

The programme note of a recent theatre performance contained the following challenge to the audience:

> why are you here? do you know? should we care? what are your ulterior motives? what, you don't have any? you're not here to assess, to test, to pass judgement, to condemn, to gauge your life next to mine, to say 'I told you so', to feel proud, to laugh, to support, to show willing? have you honestly just come to sit, to hear, to see and to leave? so be it ... but I have my motives, my reasons to show, to share, to compel you to view, to assess, to test, to pass judgement, to dare you to condemn, to gauge your life next to mine, to say 'I told you so', to feel proud, to laugh, to support, to show willing ... but do you care, if I share these with you?

Figure 5.2   *Return Journey*: Tina Carter performs an aerial piece
Source: © ExFeat

The audience were about to witness an '**aerial**' production that consisted of two performers climbing large ropes, suspended some distance apart from the roof of the stage in a studio theatre. Both performers were expert aerialists who had acquired their circus skills over some years and now, under the guidance of the devising performer, Tina Carter, were presenting a theatre piece inspired by her recent visit to her Palestinian family in their deeply troubled homeland. The performance, entitled *Peace Process*, explored aspects of the hopes and struggle for peace between Israelis and Palestinians but this was only made initially evident in a number of programme notes and publicity. What the audience actually witnessed was two aerialists climbing, twisting and suspending themselves in what appeared to be a long feat of endurance. (The company name is ExFeat!) At one time both performers would be climbing at differing rates and levels, at another one might rest on the ground looking up at the other. When they were both at the same level one sensed a brief moment of possible resolution but such moments passed and the uneven process began again. As the two performers were flown into the space the audience were aware of their breathing and of the physical effort involved in their activity. At some points a long cloth was intertwined with one or both of the climbers and the unravelling might have suggested engagement with an apparently intractable problem. The precise point at which the 'performance' ended appeared to be agreed between the two performers and it was impossible to judge if that moment of ending was pre-ordained or spontaneous. Throughout the performance no word was spoken and yet the intention was to raise and discuss an issue. What the audience saw was a series of images that formed the basis of this non-verbal piece of physical theatre. The idea of an Image Theatre was postulated by the director Augusto Boal (1979) as an aspect of what he called *Theatre of the Oppressed*. In **Image** Theatre, text is replaced by gestures and symbolic action and thus there is a strong emphasis on the physical rather than the verbal: we discuss Boal's work more fully in our section on celebratory Theatre. Marranca ([1977] 1996) also explores the concept in her book *The Theatre of Images* and this repays close study.

The inclusion of circus skills as an ingredient of theatre has extended the range of performance and production styles beyond clowning into more complex forms of visual and physical imagery. However, these have developed alongside actors' improvisations and other forms of 'play'.

Much of the pioneering work in this field was carried out in the context of the Open Theatre founded in New York in the 1950s by Joseph Chaikin. Established to explore non-naturalistic styles of performance in a laboratory situation and open the skills of acting directly to audiences, the theatre was instrumental in encouraging a generation of experimental playwrights like Megan Terry, sometimes called the 'mother of American feminist theatre'. Terry described her 1966 play *Comings and Goings* as a 'trampoline for actors and director' and requires the variable cast to portray electric plugs, pencils, a list and galaxies. All her plays demand that strong images are created, very often borrowing techniques from the cinema.

Strong visual images that ensure the engagement of the eye as much as the ear were created by several influential American practitioners: Peter Schuman with the Bread and Puppet Theatre: Robert Wilson, originally with the Byrd Hoffman Foundation, Richard Schechner with the Performance Group, who pioneered the concept of Environmental Theatre (discussed in Chapter 2) and Richard Foreman of the Ontological Hysterical Theatre: all their work rewards investigation.

In more recent years the work of Théâtre de Complicité, in such productions as *Street of Crocodiles* with its ropes and planks, has not only relied on physical acting skills but has blurred the boundaries with contemporary dance. Tina Carter's pieces, *Peace Process* and *Return Journey*, which she described as 'experimental aerial politics' involved 'exploring the creative potential of aerial: investigating why and how to generate aerial choreography, focussing in particular on the potential meaning behind the movement'. And, she concluded, 'will we always be condemned by critics as doing nothing more than tricks?'

Often the contemporary world seems to be obsessed by the idea of 'image': university departments restyle 'Drama' or 'Film Studies' as 'Image Studies' and there is a growing enthusiasm for various forms of dance performance which rely entirely upon visual images. Some would argue that 'image' has replaced substantial content, both as a way of life and in the theatre but others point to the potency of images and the failures of verbal language highlighted by such playwrights as Pinter. His citation for the Nobel Prize for Literature included the statement that he had revealed the 'precipice under the prattle of everyday speech' and it may be that the constant search for new forms of theatre 'language' is as alive as ever, as new stage productions extend their vocabulary to include Street Dance and Hip Hop.

The popular theatre

During 2008, Chalkfoot Theatre Company toured a production of Tom McGrath's play *Laurel and Hardy* to village halls and other small-scale venues throughout a large rural and coastal area of England. The cast consisted of two actors and the simple staging was based on two large trunks, a step ladder, two chairs and a table set in front of large screens of apparently stained glass, evoking the wating room of an 'art deco' railway station.

Figure 5.3   Popular theatre: Chalkfoot Theatre, directed by Philip Dart, perform Tom McGrath's play
Laurel and Hardy at the Theatre Royal, Margate
Source: © Patrice Pavis

The play was one of biographical action and the story of the two famous comics was
told through a series of narratives and acted scenes which incorporated some of their
familiar routines and lines. The remarkable 'hat routine', that was later employed by
both Beckett and Pinter in their plays, together with other sequences taken from some of
Laurel and Hardy's best-known films, not only provoked laughter from the audience but
also had some members of the audience, who were obviously enthusiasts for early film,
anticipating the next line of dialogue out loud.

Even though the two actors achieved a remarkable likeness to the physical and vocal
characteristics of their two main characters, they were equally at home in impersonating
other figures from the story by a quick change of posture, voice and headgear.

During the course of the play, the two characters traced their early experience as performers back to the popular Vaudeville theatre of their day, Laurel to his work in the
working-class theatres of Scotland as a child comedian with his own comic songs and
routines, and Hardy to touring parts of America as a juvenile minstrel. They both made
it clear that building upon the skills and techniques acquired in these initial contexts later
enabled them to develop their very successful film partnership.

The performances of the play in village halls were designed to attract audiences who
might not have the opportunity or inclination to attend a conventional theatre production. Many of the performances had an interval during which refreshments prepared by
local people were served and a raffle drawn. Dressing-room facilities were often minimal
and the audience met the theatre company as friends on a welcome visit. In every respect
the company was attempting to provide 'a good night out' for all concerned and that was
the impression given by the entire event.

When John McGrath wrote his book *A Good Night Out* in the 1980s he described
the experience of working-class audiences in clubs with their vitality, participation and

variable attention .His experience of touring small-scale venues in Scotland had affected his view as to how **popular theatre** might draw on the conventions of the 'working men's clubs', using comic routines, songs and 'acts' that related directly to the audience. McGrath, like Brecht before him, hoped to harness the style of popular entertainments for the political purposes of his plays, seeking to engage and draw reaction from the audiences in a way that the 'theatre-going' middle classes would find impossible. The playwright Dario Fo, in such pieces as *Accidental Death of an Anarchist*, draws heavily on slapstick, physical comedy and jokes to break down the reserve of his audiences and to make his plays accessible to those for whom theatre-going is seen as a middle-class function.

During the 1970s and 1980s, there was a widespread belief that it was through the techniques of popular theatre, as it was then understood, that a vibrant political theatre could be created. Companies devoted to issues of sexual politics, the power of big business, the exploitation of local resources or various forms of social injustice proliferated and sought to bring their work to non-theatrical venues and sections of the population ignored by mainstream theatre. In many cases they aimed to empower local communities and raise consciousness concerning the richness of local human and documentary resources that were in danger of disappearing.

A definition of what constitutes popular theatre today is more problematic and may well depend on your cultural and ethnic background. For an increasing number of people, it may be the extensive revival of stand-up comedy and of the comedy clubs, for others it may be forms of the **variety theatre** seen on cruise liners or in hotels. For some audiences it may be the revival of **music hall** or another performance of the seemingly indestructible *Joseph and his Amazing Technicolor Dreamcoat* and for others the visit of a puppet theatre, a children's theatre company or a piece of street theatre. Some people may find their popular theatre in **tribute shows**, others in **cabaret** or the entertainment provided in nightclubs or lap-dancing clubs.

Assigning popular theatre to a particular class or stratum of society now seems strangely outmoded. The audiences which attended the performances of *Laurel and Hardy* came from a wide variety of backgrounds, including those who came because of a special interest in the topic of the play. What they witnessed, however, was part of a very long tradition in which performers set up temporary stages, whether it be in fairground booths or in inn courtyards, and provided entertainment for a small community before moving on. In this particular case they saw performance skills that date back to **vaudeville** and, just as Laurel and Hardy transferred these skills to film, so we now see comedians and 'variety' performers using the skills they may have developed in the live theatre to act as hosts or comperes on television shows.

The production of *Laurel and Hardy* employs many of the historic characteristics of genuinely popular theatre, both through its references and the nature of the event:

◆ frequent direct address to the audience;

◆ a portable staging enabling relatively quick 'get ins' and 'strikes';

◆ use of circus or vaudeville skills;

◆ comic routines;

◆ the use of non-theatrical venues;

◆ integration of song and dance routines into the action;

◆ slick timing and verbal and visual jokes;

◆ absurd situations in which the protagonists are often in an uncomfortable position.

■ Fringe theatre

During a single week in 2008, a London free newspaper advertised performances at 36 theatres described as 'other' after its listing of West End productions. Of these theatres, 30 were presenting new plays by living playwrights covering such topics as cloning, the war in Iraq, attitudes to homosexuality, child abuse and abduction and relationships within 'mixed marriages'. Performances were to take place in pubs, halls, basements, disused libraries, former churches, cafés and a variety of other '**found spaces**' and the majority of the plays had casts of no more than five and a performance run of between five and ten days. Although it was not immediately evident from the publicity, it was likely that the venues were fairly small and the indications were that the plays were generally quite short.

This description of what we normally term **fringe** theatre, or in the USA, **off-Broadway** or even **off-off-Broadway** will be familiar to anyone who has attended the Edinburgh Festival or similar event, where every available space appears to have been taken over by a theatre company presenting new writing or an adaptation of another work. The terms 'fringe' or 'off' indicate that this kind of theatre is on the margins of something larger and more powerful but, by being on the edge, it is frequently in a position to experiment, take risks and pursue dreams that would be entirely unrealistic in the mainstream theatre. The fringe is rarely subsidized, except when venues are provided in some festivals, and the investment in the piece presented relies on the income from audiences for a return. It is one of the only remaining situations where new writing is crucial and where controversial issues can be debated fearlessly.

The off-off-Broadway movement in America had its greatest impetus in the 1960s when Joseph Chaikin's Open Theatre inspired hundreds of new plays by unknown playwrights in unorthodox spaces. The sheer creative energy is captured by one actor's description of his involvement:

> At eight o'clock, I was the left thumb in a group sensitivity demonstration called 'Hands off' in Merrymount Episcopal Community Center, and then at ten I played a movie projector with a twinkle bulb in my mouth in a drag production of 'Bonnie and Clyde' at the Mass Dramatists Experimental Tavern, and at the stroke of midnight I was the cathectic focus of a rather tedious theatre event in the basement of the Yoga Institute. I try to keep busy.

> (Cohn, 1991, p. 131)

Since that time, the deep distrust of the mainstream theatre and its perceived conservatism has led to the creation of innumerable 'alternative' theatres that have been particularly vocal and effective in the fields of gay rights, issues of war, peace and social justice. Free to offend, assault, seduce or infuriate audiences, the fringe has always been an actors' theatre and invariably organized as a collective, or at least with a nucleus of regular members. The fringe rarely, if ever, tours: it waits for audiences to come to it. The move towards the writing of shorter plays by major playwrights has enabled fringe companies to mix new writers' work with that of more established writers; it is not unusual now to see the plays of Pinter or Strindberg included in a season that may also introduce a devised piece or play by a previously unknown author.

The health of the fringe is often an indication of the apparent monopoly of the mainstream theatre by a small number of production companies but it tends to rely on areas of high population to attract sufficient audiences for survival. At one time, the fringe in Britain was the one theatrical arena where key international political issues could be aired. This has rarely been the case in the USA where theatre audiences have shied away from such debate. Now, however, we are increasingly finding that mainstream theatre is rediscovering the power of plays to influence political opinion and with writers such as David Hare the theatre 'establishment' has taken risks not contemplated previously. In Britain, a sequence of governments who have done little to encourage the Arts and who convey an impression of cultural illiteracy, may well have contributed to the more strident tone of the once rather acquiescent remaining subsidized theatre.

Figure 5.4   The London Fringe: Tom Green's play *The Death of Margaret Thatcher* directed by June Abbott, at the Courtyard Theatre
Source: © Peter Simpkin

One form of fringe theatre that has achieved some permanence in recent years has been children's theatre. As we observed during our survey of the programmes of work at some theatres, the target audience of young people gives a very specific intention to regular productions. Children's theatre is usually small-scale and rooted in story-telling: it is often improvisation-based and may well include dance, song and clowning. Its essential quality is that it relates to and engages an audience for whom 'live' entertainment may have become a rarity. Taking note of the attention-span of a young audience, the companies specializing in presenting plays for children invariably offer relatively brief but high-energy productions, combining humour, pathos and strong narrative with flexible and portable staging. The economics of a small cast, possibly working collaboratively, and a guaranteed audience make children's theatre an attractive option for young actors and particularly for those who have had some experience of working with young people. Some outstanding theatre companies for children have established permanent venues for their work and there have been notable improvements in the quality of scripts. However, the pattern of 'fringe'-style children's theatre is now threatened by the emergence of production companies presenting larger-scale productions of stage adaptations derived from well-known characters of current children's fiction. With the power of substantial commercial publishing and media companies behind them, such productions, designed to tour major theatres, rely more extensively on technology and familiar images to make their impact and may miss some of the intimacy of the fringe.

The broad characteristics of the fringe theatre are:

- small-scale venues generally in a city with large commercial theatres;
- emphasis on new writing;
- collective governance;
- tackling serious moral or political issues;
- situated in 'cultural districts';
- small casts and plays of variable length, most frequently short;
- experimental in approach;
- largely dominated by recently trained actors;
- self-financing.

Suggested activity

◆ Carry out your own survey of what 'fringe' theatre is available in London at any one time and compare this with your own situation.
◆ List the plays and their playwrights that are currently being presented on the fringe, noting the issues being addressed and, if possible, the size of the casts.
◆ List the cartoon and children's fictional characters who are now used as the basis for some children's theatre.

Total theatre or a new *Gesamtkunstwerk*

Consider this scenario. You have arrived at the Royal Court Theatre in Liverpool to see a production that is advertised as The Pool of Life presents *The Elements*. Although this large Victorian Theatre once had an auditorium filled with stalls and a proscenium stage and orchestra pit, you are now invited to purchase a drink in the bar and take it with you to drink at one of the many tables scattered around the empty auditorium from where you will watch the performance. The production is part of the celebrations of the fact that Liverpool has a large Chinese population and has been involved in cultural exchanges with China.

The first part of the performance consists of music played on traditional Chinese instruments: the *GuZheng* (a stringed instrument), the *Xiao/Di* (bamboo flute) and a Chinese version of the cimbalom. The musicians have all made soundtrack recordings for well-known films and are now accompanied by a piece of contemporary Chinese dance.

However, in the second part of the performance, the title *The Elements* becomes somewhat more explicit. Sections entitled Water: form-arrival; Wood: transformation-union; Fire: spirit-heart-red phoenix; Earth: people generations and Metal: soul lament all consist of an integration of music, dance, aerial ballet and Chinese calligraphy written on a huge screen. The music is now played by a section of the Royal Liverpool Philharmonic Orchestra but is composed and conducted by a leading Chinese musician famous for his film soundtracks. The choreography on aerial wires blends with the ground-based dances derived from martial arts and the text of the calligrapher creates vast visual and verbal symbols. The costumes are exotic and colourful. The audience is free to talk, drink, get up and walk about or read the extensive programme note with its mystical titles for the sections of the performance.

In your reaction to this description you might wonder what form of Theatre has been described. At this point, too, you might wish to look back at the Profile of Eugenio Barba in Chapter 1 and recall his ideas on **inter-culturalism**. Clearly, what was being attempted at Liverpool was some kind of artistic and cultural **fusion** in order to create a unique theatre form.

The concept of a stage work which combined and encompassed all known art forms was first articulated by the nineteenth-century German composer, Richard Wagner. Wagner is now primarily considered a composer of opera and it is easy to overlook the innovative nature of much opera in theatrical terms. It was, for example, the composer Gustav Mahler, working as a director of Wagner's operas, who first successfully employed a revolving stage; and it was the opera houses that led the way in the technological developments that transformed the theatre from the late nineteenth century onwards. Wagner, however, had a vision of 'the one total art form of the future', the *Gesamtkunstwerk*, that would achieve the integration of all theatrical elements. Wagner himself attempted to embody this aim; he composed the music, wrote the script, conceived and directed the *mise-en-scène*, arranged the lighting and décor and designed a new theatre in Bayreuth to contain his new form of stage-drama. The characteristics of his *Gesamtkunstwerk* were to be:

◆ the union of the arts in which their separate identity would be submerged in the total theatrical experience;

◆ music would be seen as the means of achieving this union and not as an end in itself;

◆ the use of myth dealing with archetypal characters;

◆ portrayal of the inner drama – what goes on inside a person; less concerned with externals such as 'plot' or what goes on between characters;

◆ through cathartic theatrical experience, society will be rejuvenated and reconnected with the profound experiences of life.

Although most critics would agree that Wagner never fully achieved his aims in his own stage works, he nevertheless initiated a debate that continues to this day and prompted some of the most stimulating experiments in modern theatre. Wagner's attempts and those of many who have continued his explorations constitute a search for **total theatre**.

This term was first used by the French actor, dramatist and theorist Antonin Artaud and was described in his seminal book *The Theatre and its Double* (1970). Artaud's concern was that Western mentality and its rationality were a block to a full understanding of the full metaphysical and emotional experience offered by such forms as those found in Oriental theatre. His theatre was an attempt to bypass the psychological tendencies of Western, script-based theatre through a host of non-verbal devices such as gestures, disassociated words, sounds, music or their combinations so that we could rediscover 'the idea of figures and archetypal symbols which act like sudden silences, fermata, heart stops, adrenalin calls, incendiary images surging into our abruptly woken minds' (1970, p. 94). Both performers and audience together should be 'victims burnt at the stake, signalling through the flames' (1970, p. 95). The implications of Artaud's **Theatre of Cruelty** as it became known, are both a challenge to the idea of detachment advocated by Brecht and an extension of the total, painful involvement of the audience that Wagner envisaged. Artaud was greatly influenced by his experience of watching Balinese dancers who seemed to have pared down the process of performance to its essentials.

Practitioner profile

Antonin Artaud (1896–1948)

Antonin Artaud worked with Lugne-Poe, Dullin and Jean Louis Barrault. For much of his life he suffered from mental illness and the effect of drugs. While his ideas were to have a profound influence on the theatre of the twentieth century, he was never able to achieve any great theatrical success himself.

◆ In 1926, he wrote:
The illusion we are seeking to create has no bearing on the greater or lesser degree of verisimilitude of the action. By this very act, each show becomes a sort of event. The audience must feel as if a scene in their lives is being acted out in front of them, a truly vital scene. In a word, we ask our audiences to join with us, inwardly, deeply ... Audiences must be thoroughly convinced we can make them cry out.

(1968, vol. 2, p. 18)

Artaud later elaborated on this ambition in terms of both practice and rationale, evolving the

concept of Theatre of Cruelty. The imagery he uses is both religious and revolutionary. Religion and revolution both relate to absolute principles and to fundamental and frequently holistic attitudes, and together they imply, at least in Artaud's terms, the discovery of new and purer socio-political and personal relationships.

Artaud wishes to reveal an 'occult equivalent' (1968, p. 22) of the moribund religion of his time. He aimed to extirpate 'our world's lies, aimlessness, meanness and two-facedness' (1968, p. 22).

He believed that a 'real stage play upsets our sensual tranquillity, releases our repressed sub-conscious, driving us to a kind of potential rebellion' (1968, p. 19).

Artaud sought a new sense of communion, a new sign system and a new priesthood in the theatre. The audience was to be 'encircled' so that direct contact could be made.

Another artistic movement that explored the idea of total theatre and has subsequently influenced theatre practice was the Bauhaus and it is Walter Gropius, the designer of a 'Totaltheater' in 1927 who is recognized as its leading figure (Figure 5.5).

Walter Gropius assumed the directorship of the Weimar School of Arts and Crafts in 1919 and reorganized it under the new name of Das Staatliche Bauhaus, Weimar. In 1926, the school moved to newly-built premises in Dessau and here, under such painters as Klee

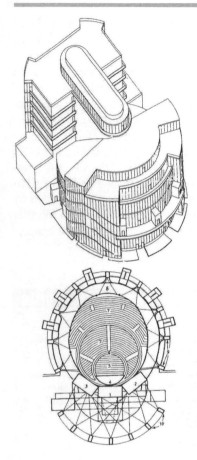

Figure 5.5 Walter Gropius's design for a 'total theatre'. Notes: 1, 2, 3 and 4 are the acting areas; 5 can be used as a revolve, with or without seating; the inner circle of seating at 7, together with 5 can be swung right around to create a theatre in the round; 8 shows the beam of light from one of the projectors housed in the pillars all round the theatre, e.g. at 9 and 10, making it possible for a director to surround his audience with an uninterrupted wall of images (using back-projection)

Source: (Barkhin, 'Architecture Teatra', Moscow 1947)

and Kandinsky, an ambitious programme of arts education was initiated. The Bauhaus evolved its own theatre/dance troupes as well as establishing links with directors such as Erwin Piscator and composers such as Hindemith and Schönberg. Revealing material on the search for new theatre forms is found in the diaries of Oskar Schlemmer, a painter who turned to dance in an attempt to create an integrated mode of performance. From 1916 until its final form in 1932, Schlemmer was working to develop his 'Triadic Ballet' that the Bauhaus troupe eventually performed in Paris and is now preserved on film. The triads were those of *elements*: form, colour and space; *dimension*: height, depth and breadth; *form*: ball, cube and pyramid; *colour*: red, blue and yellow; *constituent parts*: dance, music and costume. On a postcard to Otto Meyer in 1929, Schlemmer offered a 'recipe for Bauhaus theatre': 'One should be as free of preconceptions as possible; one should act as if the world had just been created; one should not analyse anything to death, but rather let it unfold gradually and without interference.'

And on 5 July 1926, Schlemmer wrote in his diary about his 'Triadic Ballet':

This speechless, theatrical dance, this non-committal muse who says nothing yet means everything, contains possibilities for expression and articulation which an opera or play could not offer in such purity; the theatrical dance, originally the form from which opera and the drama sprang, is free of constraints and thus predestined to furnish time and again the starting point for a theatrical renaissance.

(Schlemmer, 1972, p. 220)

The celebratory theatre

Muslims throughout the world acknowledge the festival of *Ashura* in various ways, but none more solemnly or dramatically than Shi'ite pilgrims on their way to Karbala. Pausing at a certain point they re-enact the martyrdom of Hussain, a grandson of the Prophet Muhammad at the Battle of Karbala in 680 AD. Using poetic text, song and ritual chest-beating, they recall this key moment in their faith in a public event that anyone can witness and experience.

Meanwhile, Christians of the Orthodox and Roman Catholic traditions have, since the Middle Ages, celebrated their belief in the death and resurrection of Jesus at the once pagan festival of new life, Easter. Solemn processions and re-enactments have taken and continue to take various forms, perhaps the most spectacular being on the Greek island of Corfu. Other highly sophisticated expressions of the events of 'holy week' are the magnificent **Mystery Plays** that have survived from the 'cycles' written for performance at the festival of Corpus Christi in a number of cathedral cities throughout Europe. In the case of Britain, these plays constitute some of the most important texts of early drama and their performance potential remains as remarkable as ever.

What we are labelling 'celebratory theatre' may take many forms, according to the community that is involved and the specific issues that are seen as a focus. One of the most interesting and significant examples of an entire community employing theatre as a means of a powerful collective statement and celebrations takes place every four years in the Swiss town of Altdorf. The tradition began in 1898 when the 'people's assembly' of the town decided that they were determined to stage the play *William Tell*, written in 1804 by the **neo-classical** dramatist Friedrich Schiller. The production of this play, recounting a key event in the history of the Swiss, was seen to be so important that it was decided to build a playhouse for the first performance in the following year. Now, ever since that time, the *Tellspielhaus* (Tell Playhouse) has seen a new production of the play every four years using local community performers and a professional director. Recent publicity for a new production of the play suggests that it has been, and continues to be, re-interpreted to respond to the 'spirit of the age' and to the differing expectations of audiences. The competition to play one of the major parts and the involvement of many members of the local population in aspects of the play make this a genuine piece of **community theatre**. A far better known example is that of the *Passion Play* presented every tenth year in the Bavarian town of Oberammergau since 1634 as a response to the population being spared from the plague. The event, as it now has become, is a major tourist attraction and has also resulted in the construction of a permanent theatre and the use of large numbers of amateur performers under professional direction.

The motivation of communities to explore aspects of their history through theatre was a notable development in Britain during the second half of the twentieth century.

The playwright, Ann Jellicoe, for example, spent time with local populations, listening to their stories, reading diaries, examining newspapers articles and minutes of meetings or looking at photographs and then moulding this material into performance using musicians, dancers and actors from the community. The projects have usually involved a small number of professional actors together with writers or composers who work with the local population. This kind of work has often been site-specific and frequently explored significant developments in a community's industrial, economic or agricultural past. Texts have sometimes used the actual words spoken at meetings or other event and this has come to be known as **verbatim theatre**. Most frequently, productions have been characterized by the direct simplicity of the performance style and by the fact that many of the performers have rarely, if ever, participated in an event of theatre.

Processions, pageants, parades, some ceremonies and rituals, demonstrations, fairs, street celebrations, South Asian *Melas* and even protest marches are aspects of what we may term **carnival**. One of the major contributions to the debate concerning carnival was made by the Russian literary critic, Mikhail Bakhtin (1885–1975) who developed his theories in a book concerned with early Renaissance literature *Rabelais and His World*. Bakhtin argued that the term *carnival* could embrace the event, its environment and the behaviour of the participants. He pointed out that medieval feasts and festivals were often characterized by bawdy humour, colloquial language and generally unconventional conduct. We might recall one of the Shepherds in the *Wakefield Second Shepherds' Play* who tells a rogue character to 'take out that Southern tooth and set it in a turd' as an example of the rough mixture of vulgarity and piety that coexisted in that form of celebration! Bakhtin's thinking on the nature of carnival centred on its social function and he considered this to be ambivalent. On the one hand, carnival was irreverent, challenging to authority, organized outside the immediate influence of the predominant secular or ecclesiastical authorities; on the other hand, carnival was permitted through licensing and the declaration of 'holy days' and thus was never a dangerous challenge to the status quo. Bakhtin's ideas were developed from his study into the strange blend of foolishness, grossness and anarchy that accompanied celebrations of profoundly held religious beliefs and his key observations were:

- carnival images closely resemble the artistic form we term 'spectacle' because of their sensuous nature and strong element of play;
- carnival belongs to the border between art and life;
- in reality, it is life itself but shaped according to a certain pattern of play;
- carnival acknowledges no distinction between actors and spectator;
- while carnival lasts, there is no life outside it;
- carnival is not a spectacle seen by people, they live in it;
- carnival celebrates temporary liberation from the established order;
- there is no rank or hierarchy during carnival;
- a special kind of communication is possible during carnival because of the suspension of rank;

◆ carnival laughter is the laughter of all the people;

◆ a major feature of carnival is grotesque realism.

(See Counsell and Wolf, 2001, pp. 216–20)

If you study the list above carefully, you will observe that some of the features represent an in-between state of existence, a borderland between two states of being. This is what is termed a **liminal** state and has become one of the most interesting aspects of enquiry in Theatre Studies. Theatre frequently inhabits a territory between the 'real' and the 'unreal', the 'off-stage' and 'on-stage'. We shall encounter **liminality** again in a future chapter.

The influential Brazilian theatre director and teacher, Augusto Boal (b. 1931) has argued strongly against Bakhtin's view of carnival. For Boal, all such events are an instrument and device of oppression conceived by the status quo to ensure that the public remains passive. Carnival, he argues, may act as a 'safety valve' for the release of tension but does not empower in the way that he believes the theatre can and should. Boal's own particular approach to empowering communities through theatre has been his development of a technique he calls **forum theatre**. In this approach, Boal takes a group of professional actors into a community where a local issue is causing great concern and where the population feel impotent in the face of perceived oppression. A play is devised using the information supplied by the local people and presented to them. Spectators are invited to interrupt the performance to propose alternative strategies in order to bring about change or resist bureaucracy. The play or incident is then acted out again to see if a more satisfactory outcome might be achieved.

Boal's approach may seem to belong to a different world from yours, but you might like to consider if a population fed a constant diet of sport, celebrity or royalty is not equally impotent when it comes to changing the attitudes or policies of the governing elite.

We would also wish to make a distinction between **ritual**, a frequently repeated set of actions that has deep significance for all participants and **ceremony**, a symbolic event involving both doers and spectators.

■ Conclusion

In this chapter we have suggested that, in order to study Theatre effectively, you must be aware of the multiplicity of theatrical activities going on around you. In order to consider the many differing forms that these activities may take ,we have provided extensive examples and suggested the following headings: the *predictable* theatre, the *unpredictable* theatre, the theatre of *images*, the *popular* theatre, the *fringe* (including *children's*) theatre, *total* theatre and *celebratory* theatre. None of these categories is an entirely comprehensive definition and plays or performances may fit into more than one. However, we offer these labels as a basis for your personal exploration of and thinking about Theatre.

We have argued that many approaches to the study of Theatre have traditionally been too narrow and that it is important to be open to all forms. The chapter has included details of some practitioners and playwrights who have experimented with new forms, challenged the expectations of audiences and debated the nature of Theatre itself. We have also considered the possibility of artistic and cultural fusion or integration through the medium of performance.

Topics for discussion and reflection

◆ In your survey of your local theatre, how many plays by well-known English dramatists were performed?

◆ Were many plays for children scheduled for performance at school holiday times?

◆ How much 'new writing' was evident in this season?

◆ What kinds of audience do you think this programme might attract?

◆ Is it possible to achieve a fusion of the arts in order to create a piece of Theatre?

◆ Study Gropius's design for a 'total theatre' very carefully and consider its practicality.

◆ Why do Oriental forms of theatre seem to have inspired many of the modern innovators in performance?

◆ Why do so many recent performances appear to have abandoned the written text as a starting-point?

◆ What do you understand by the concept 'total theatre'? Have you ever experienced it?

◆ Discuss a local event in the light of your understanding of carnival and of the distinctions between ritual and ceremony. Decide whether you follow Bakhtin's point of view or Boal's.

■ Further reading

Artaud, A. (1968) *Collected Works*, 2 vols, trans. V. Corti, London: Calder and Boyas. Artaud is often misunderstood because students rely on his reputation rather than reading what he actually said and believed.

Baugh, C. (2005) *Theatre Performance and Technology*, Basingstoke: Palgrave Macmillan. A very accessible and informative volume by a leading scholar and theatre designer.

Berghaus, G. (2005)*Avant-garde Performance*, Basingstoke: Palgrave Macmillan. A comprehensive consideration of recent work.

Boal, A. (1979) *Theatre of the Oppressed*, trans. L. McBride, London: Pluto Press. Written with passion, this book sets out the basis for some of the most remarkable work in the modern theatre.

Pavis, P. (ed.) (1996) *The Intercultural Performance Reader*, London: Routledge. Provides a broad and fascinating perspective for the investigation of performance.

Striff, E. (ed.) (2003) *Performance Studies*, Basingstoke: Palgrave Macmillan. An excellent resource for reflection and discussion.

■ Website

For an example of ritual, carnival and celebration, see our website: www.palgrave.com/foundations/pickering

Theatre in Context and Understanding the *Zeitgeist*

6

In this chapter we shall be discussing the concepts and approaches needed for what has become known as 'Contextual Studies' in relation to Theatre. We shall consider how the original physical, social and philosophical conditions of creation and writing/devising of a piece affected how it was written and how those factors and current attitudes impinge on its **afterlife** in performance now.

Learning outcomes

By the conclusion of this chapter, you should be able to:

▶ understand the concept of contextual studies as applied to theatre;

▶ identify the skills and knowledge necessary for a full appreciation of a play text;

▶ use the concept of the *Zeitgeist* in a meaningful way;

▶ use various sources to reinforce your understanding of a play;

▶ draw examples from several periods of theatre history including the Restoration and the nineteenth century;

▶ employ knowledge and understanding of an historical period to enhance your study of a play;

▶ appreciate changes in performance style and theatre buildings;

▶ read a play with greater perception and understanding;

▶ identify areas of knowledge that will be appropriate to a fuller understanding of theatre;

▶ discuss some of the factors that will contribute to the 'afterlife' of a play.

The *Zeitgeist*

Many aspects of the theatre of the past have survived into our modern world but the principal legacy of any theatrical period consists of the plays that have been preserved in written form. In order to understand these we need to have some concept of the spirit of the times in which they were written: in short, we must appreciate what the German philosopher Hegel called the **Zeitgeist** (spirit of the times). You may recall that, when discussing the *William Tell* play performed in Alstadt, the organizers explained that new productions of the play reflected 'the spirit of the age'. The original German text of the publicity used the expression *Zeitgeist* at that point.

There are many examples of using the *Zeitgeist* of the contemporary world to give new significance to an ancient play. One of the most striking was a recent London fringe production of *The Provoked Wife* by the seventeenth-century dramatist Sir John Vanbrugh. With virtually no changes to the text this was presented as if it were an episode of the TV series *Footballers' Wives*. The success of this remarkable production was that it was clearly based on a profound understanding of the *Zeitgeist* of the time when the play was written, particularly the attitudes to wealth, celebrity and marriage as well as of the contemporary world.

The production of plays from an earlier period is not archaeology, it is the process of recreating a living art form. We have taken the expression 'afterlife' of a play from the British director Jonathan Miller (1986) to indicate the idea that the theatre must be a place where works are given new life every time they are presented and that our understanding of the original conditions of their creation is an essential element in that activity.

If you think about the relevance of your current studies to a possible situation you might encounter in the future, you could find the following scenario. You are an actor who has just completed a course of Theatre Studies and you have been cast in Sheridan's play *The Rivals*. You discover that this play was first performed at Covent Garden and is set in the playwright's contemporary world. Your production will be in the Olivier Auditorium at the National Theatre in London. Making use of the textual homework that you have acquired in a Module of study that may have been entitled 'The Performer and Text' you know how the first scene (in which you appear) would have been staged when the play was new. You understand that the text exploits the relationship between the performers and the audience which theatre at that time offered and will understand such devices as the 'aside'. Sensibly, when passing through Richmond in Yorkshire, you went to look at the Georgian Theatre still in use there. As the Olivier stage is completely different you wonder how the first scene will be staged.

When it comes to the technical rehearsals, you admire the huge black and white **backcloth** of a view of Bath, like some enormous eighteenth-century print, and you enjoy making your entrance through the auditorium and sitting on the front of the stage. This does, indeed, seem like an equivalent of the original staging, as the Director had suggested. You wonder if you might feel **upstaged** by the huge view of Bath behind you and by the attendants bringing on the furniture for the second scene: but you remember your performance discipline of focus.

In performance you get very little audience reaction and ask the Company Manager to suggest to the House Manager that latecomers are kept out until the end of scenes. Being so near the front row of the audience you were very aware that people were looking at their programmes and obviously watching the furniture shifters behind you. Friends who attend confirm that there was a tendency to watch the activities going on upstage and that those who did not know the play did pick up the plot eventually because the playwright repeats a good deal of the information!

The student parties you had rather dreaded turn out to be well-behaved and responsive, possibly because they had been provided with excellent information packs in advance from which the students quoted when asking questions in the 'post-show' discussions. In fact, you really prefer them to the tiresome 'look at me' kind of audience members who leap to their feet clapping even after a poor performance.

Now you wonder if playing the same play at Richmond would have been the same experience and if you really needed to see the entire audience, as you had when you attempted Stand-Up comedy some time previously.

If you are puzzled by the relevance of this imaginary account you need to realize that performance does not take place in a vacuum. It is affected by the buildings or found spaces it takes place in, by the culture of the day, which may differ widely from the culture of the day in which the play was first performed, or even from the culture of the region in which it was first seen. It is equally affected by the working methods and preconceptions of those involved in performance. However, if you are involved in Theatre in any capacity, a thorough reading and understanding of a play's text will be an absolute requirement.

■ Models for plays in context

One of the most impressive publications in the field of Theatre in context is James Shapiro's *1599: A Year in the Life of William Shakespeare* (2005) and we would strongly recommend that you obtain and use this book as a model of such scholarship. Professor Shapiro points out that, because Shakespeare is often thought of as a 'playwright for all time' we often make the mistake of overlooking the fact that he was very much a writer of *his* time. A number of different aspects of context combine to give us a fuller understanding of the plays attributed to William Shakespeare:

◆ *Theatrical context*: in 1599, Shakespeare's company of actors moved a building known simply as The Theatre timber by timber across the frozen Thames from the north bank to a new site on the south bank and reconstructed it as The Globe. A modern reconstruction stands on the same site today. At the time in question, London was a centre of theatrical activity and, in spite of the fact that it was then a relatively small city, there were literally hundreds of new plays being written and performed there. The construction of the Globe is well documented in terms of dimensions and costs and we can be fairly certain that, in many respects, it resembled the Swan (Figure 2.8).

◆ *Political context*: in 1599, an English army was sent to crush a revolt in Ireland and the nation lived under the threat of another Spanish Armada. The question of succession to the throne was becoming ever more urgent as the childless Queen Elizabeth grew older. The East India Company, which was to provide a major source of wealth and power to the nation, was in its formative years.

◆ *Social context*: in the absence of the media as we know them, we learn from contemporary comment that 'the English pass their time, learning at the play what is happening abroad'. Interest in political and personal scandals, power-struggles, discovery, rumour and gossip was as keen then as it is now, but it was largely the theatre that provided the arena for such issues.

Bringing together these three strands, Shapiro demonstrates the activities of one remarkable year in the life of William Shakespeare. During 1599 the playwright completed the plays *Henry V, Julius Caesar* (both of which explored political situations which would have resonated with the audiences of the day), *As You like It*, and a draft for *Hamlet*. If you have ever tried writing a play, particularly without the use of word-processing, you will appreciate the scale of this achievement. *As You Like It* contained several coded references to the death of the playwright Christopher Marlowe, together with some topical jokes that remain virtually impenetrable to a modern audience. We can surmise that the astonishing creativity of 1599 was partly a result of the new theatre in which Shakespeare's plays could be performed, away from the puritanical presence of the city (situated on the north bank) and exploiting developments in playhouse construction that were favourable to a more imaginative and dynamic form of writing. The plays attributed to Shakespeare from this period carry clear indications of the **context** in which they were written. They are a response to the events and the *Zeitgeist* of 1599 but they do not constitute a documentation of actual happenings. The risks in portraying actual events were too great. Shakespeare had already seen several of his playwright contemporaries imprisoned and tortured but intelligent audiences probably had little difficulty in making connections with living people and situations.

Suggested activity

◆ Conduct your own research into a year in the life of Shakespeare or any other dramatist. Consider the significant national events and/or inventions of that year and the organization of the theatre. List the plays written, the kind of theatre in which they were performed and any events in the life of the playwright that might have contributed to the nature of the plays.

◆ Discover as much as possible about the style and conditions of performance. For example, we know that Shakespeare's plays all used boys to play the parts of women; what implications did that have?

Establishing the context: a working example, *The Country Gentleman*

Discoveries concerning the circumstances and attitudes surrounding the **Restoration** play, *The Country Gentleman* (1669), written by Sir Robert Howard and the Duke of Buckingham, provide an intriguing example of the kind of investigation that is sometimes necessary to establish the context of a stage work. The play is one of a number of unpublished stage works dating from the years of the reign of Charles II in England that were subsequently thought to have been 'lost'. Fortunately for posterity, the play and its unexpected effect are mentioned several times by the diarist Samuel Pepys and in a number of other contemporary documents which form important **primary sources** for our enquiry. From these we learn that the play caused a national scandal and very nearly the death of government officials. It was banned from performance during its initial rehearsal period and it was only the remarkable discovery by two scholars in 1975 of a manuscript copy in the Folger Library in Washington that has enabled us to piece together the rest of the picture. We can now consider what we can deduce about this play from some of the evidence we have available.

The text itself

If we examine the list of characters we can begin to sense what type of play this is. The characters, together with their editorial glosses, now appear as:

Roger Trim – a scheming barber, formerly a servant to Sir Richard Plainbred; determined to arrange a profitable marriage for his daughters.

Mistress Finical Fart – a scheming landlady, a middle-aged pretender to gentility who affects French words and phrases.

Jack Vapor and Tom Slander – two lying fops, scheming cowards who hope to marry Isabella and Philadelphia for their money.

Sir Cautious Trouble-all and Sir Gravity Empty – two grave 'men of business', caballing fools; also courting Isabella and Philadelphia for their money.

Worthy and Lovetruth – two country gentlemen of wit and sense; in love with Isabella and Philadelphia.

Sir Richard Plainbred – an exemplary country gentleman, wise and witty, who detests city fashions and believes in old-fashioned country virtues.

Isabella and Philadelphia – Sir Richard's witty daughters; heiresses; in love with Worthy and Lovetruth.

Kate and Lucy – Trim's daughters.

Ned and Will – boys in Sir Richard's household.

From this cast list alone, you may be able to deduce the following:

◆ a complex story involving intrigue, scheming and lying;
◆ characters obsessed by fashion and affectation;
◆ characters whose names suggest their personal qualities;
◆ comedy and satire;
◆ a reversal of the usual Restoration preference for the town over the country.

If you have studied the Restoration theatre previously you will also know that actresses appeared on the English stage for the first time during this period and that many of the plays concerned sexual intrigue and aspects of marriage. The list of characters here indicates that these factors exist in this play. But the text of the play itself, though witty and fast moving, does not entirely explain the play's particular history. For this we might consider the playwrights themselves.

The playwrights

Richard Villiers, the second Duke of Buckingham, was the son of James I's assassinated favourite. He was a notorious womanizer and party-goer with a ruthless sense of ambition, who had managed to remain on the right side whenever there was political danger. In 1667, he was part of a conspiracy to oust the Lord Chancellor and, in 1668, he also set out to destroy Sir William Coventry, an honourable Commissioner to the Treasury. He aimed to achieve this by persuading his friend, the playwright Sir Robert Howard, to insert a scene into a new play that would insult, lampoon and infuriate Coventry and his associate Sir John Duncomb.

Sir Robert Howard is probably best remembered today as the brother-in-law of the much more famous poet and playwright, John Dryden, but in his time he and three brothers were considered important dramatists. It is, perhaps, rather surprising that Buckingham and Howard became friends as the former had led a disgraceful brawl to interrupt the performance of a play by one of the latter's brothers. However, Buckingham clearly impressed Howard by his political cunning and obviously shared his contempt for Coventry, who was somewhat proud and ponderous.

Other primary sources

Pepys' diaries and some contemporary letters, tell us that, as a result of the insults which Coventry had got wind of during the rehearsals of the play, he challenged Buckingham to a duel and threatened a major political crisis. The King, hearing of this, asked to read the play and ordered that the rehearsals be stopped. He sent the unfortunate Coventry to the Tower of London and during his imprisonment there, Pepys was a frequent visitor.

We can learn from Pepys that the offending scene was in fact Act III. Sc.1 and that the character of Sir Cautious Trouble-all was a thinly disguised portrait of Coventry and Sir Gravity Empty of Duncomb. Both men are shown as dull, without humour or imagination. In the inserted scene, Trouble-all is seen sitting on a swivel stool at a huge table surrounded by papers in exactly the same fashion in which Coventry was known to operate. Tediously he labours through his affairs and demonstrates a complete lack of self-awareness.

From all the information we have now accumulated, it would be possible to decide if this play had the potential of an afterlife and whether, indeed, you would wish to bring that into realization in the theatre.

■ Studying a play

The study of Theatre involves a careful consideration of plays as potential pieces of live performance and we can only gain a comprehensive and balanced view of the meaning and nature of a play when we think about it in relation to its staging. It follows, therefore, that, although their ultimate goals may be different, the kind of 'study' in which an actor, director or student might engage is largely the same, for the idea of performance must always be present.

Many college and university courses employ a different method, concentrating entirely upon literary analysis of the text and students are never forced to test their ideas in the laboratory of real or possible performance. Such an approach may lead to one level of understanding but it fails to take into account many of the aspects of a play which only emerge in the theatre.

In Theatre Studies we have also to realize just how many issues can and do affect the performance of a play: factors which may include the nature of its staging, the style of acting, the attitude of the audience and the piece's topicality. From a large number of such factors, it is possible to discern *two* major strands.

First, there are those qualities indigenous to the play itself: the author's **intentions** discernible from the text with its characters and plot and in **stage directions** (where these exist) and an author's preface. Scholars are divided as to whether the notion of 'intention' has any validity, but we prefer to take the view of the playwright David Hare (2005, p. 2) when he says: 'Please reject absolutely the crazy Jonathan Miller suggestion that playwrights don't have intentions. Or that there is no need for directors to seek to discover them. They do. And there is.'

Second, there are those qualities that the players, playhouse and audience bring to the performance of a play. Clearly, when writing a play, the playwright may be influenced by the knowledge of who is to perform it and in what conditions, but if the play is not contemporary, we, who wish to perform the play again, are left to explore the links between the two sets of qualities we have mentioned. To make these links, a play must be examined in the context of the theatre conditions that were current when it was first written. However, before we can consider the importance of players and playhouses, we need to look at plays in the context of the social conditions and attitudes and the movements within the arts which existed at the time of their creation.

Does this mean that a student of Theatre must also be a student of social and political history, the history of moral or religious beliefs and of the arts? To the extent that Theatre both reflects, and is capable of dealing seriously with, some of these issues, the answer must be 'Yes.'

Theatre, the most public of all the arts, always involves people; either the imaginary characters of a play or the real people who give them substance and the real people who watch. Therefore, any aspect of the human condition may become the business of the dramatist, the performer or the student of Theatre. This does not mean that we should begin our study of a play with comprehensive research into the history of the period in which it was written. This mistake has adversely affected theatre and drama studies in the past when, for example, students of Shakespeare have been asked to acquire an 'Elizabethan World View'. Obviously some knowledge of contemporary customs, fashions and attitudes is helpful because the dramatist peoples a play with characters who move, speak and think like his or her contemporaries and an appreciation and understanding of the *Zeitgeist* is vital.

Approaching the study of plays

In establishing an appropriate method for gaining contextual information, the first principle must be that the play itself will reveal what is relevant. Instead of asking, 'What information about the author and his times is necessary for a full understanding of this play?', we should initially ask two questions:

1. What can we learn about the author and the social conditions, attitudes and *Zeitgeist from* this play?
2. What are the relevant issues on which we require further information?

Both these questions will help us to recreate imaginatively the conditions in which the play was first written and performed: a vital process if we hope to examine its afterlife. This will not provide the complete picture, because we are setting aside for a moment the history of the theatre itself, but we often fool ourselves into thinking that a play is really about one set of issues because we are bringing our current beliefs and attitudes to bear upon it when, if we examine the play in its original context, it turns out to be about something quite different.

We can illustrate our method of enquiry and the possibility of detecting social attitudes from a play text by considering views on marriage expressed in *The Man of Mode* by the Restoration dramatist George Etherege. During the course of the play various characters make statements about marriage; here are some of them:

(a) *Shoemaker.* 'Zbud, there's never a man i' the town lives more like a gentleman with his wife than I do. I never mind her motions, she never inquires into mine, we speak to one another civilly, hate one another heartily, and because 'tis vulgar to lie and soak together, we have each of us our several settle beds.

(Act I Sc. 1)

(b) *Dorimant.* She's a discreet maid, and I believe nothing can corrupt her but a husband.
Medley. A husband?
Dorimant. Yes, a husband. I have known many women make a difficulty of losing a maidenhead who have afterwards made none of a cuckold.

(Act 1 Sc. 1)

(c) *Old Bellair.* You need not look so grum sir; a wife is no curse when she brings the blessing of a good estate with her; but an idle town flirt with a painted face, a rotten reputation and a crazy fortune … is the devil and all.

(Act II Sc. 1)

(d) *Harriet.* I think I might be brought to endure him, and that is all a reasonable woman should expect of a husband.

(Act III Sc. 1)

This is only a small sample of the many references to marriage in the play, but from these, two things are apparent:

◆ the expectations of marriage, of what it will bring and its chances of success, are extremely low;

◆ a very different scale of values from those now current in society is reflected here for, although there are now many broken marriages and marital chaos is a favourite subject for 'soaps' and stand-up comics, these words would be unlikely to appear in a contemporary play, at a time when expectations of marriage are extremely high.

It is a reasonable supposition that the characters of Etherege's play are intended to be believable seventeenth-century people: they may have exaggerated traits but in the main the dramatist appears to be showing us a representative group of upper-class people talking, intriguing, falling in love, going to the theatre, and so on. Therefore we can assume that the hard-headed things they have to say about marriage represent attitudes that were quite common in such circles. But was Etherege commenting on a particular social attitude?

Further evidence from other plays of the period will help in answering the question. In his play *The Beaux Stratagem*, from the same period, George Farquhar has included a scene in which Mrs. Sullen meets her sister-in-law and describes in vivid detail the shortcomings of her husband.

Suggested activity

Read this aloud, if possible, with a partner:

Dorinda. Morrow, my dear sister; are you for church this morning?

Mrs. Sullen. Anywhere to pray; for Heaven alone can help me. But I think, Dorinda, there's no form of prayer in the liturgy against bad husbands.

Dorinda. But there's a form of law in Doctors-Commons; and I swear, sister Sullen, rather than see you thus continually discontented, I would advise you to apply to that: for besides the part that I bear in your vexatious broils, as being sister to the husband, and friend to the wife, your example gives me such an impression of matrimony, that I shall be apt to condemn my person to a long vacation all its life. But supposing, madam, that you brought it to a case of separation, what can you urge against your husband? My brother is, first, the most constant man alive.

Mrs. Sullen. The most constant husband, I grant ye.

Dorinda. He allows you a maintenance suitable to your quality.

Mrs. Sullen. A maintenance! Do you take me, madam, for an hospital child, that I must sit down, and bless my benefactors for meat, drink, and clothes? As I take it, madam, I brought your brother ten thousand pounds, out of which I might expect some pretty things, called pleasures.

Dorinda. You share in all the pleasures that the country affords.

Mrs. Sullen. Country pleasures! Racks and torments! Dost think, child, that my limbs were made for leaping of ditches, and clambering over stiles? Or that my parents, wisely foreseeing my future happiness in country pleasures, had early instructed me in rural accomplishments of drinking fat ale, playing at whisk, and smoking tobacco with my husband? Or of spreading of plasters, brewing of diet-drinks, and stilling rosemary-water, with the good old gentlewoman my mother-in-law?

Dorinda. I'm sorry, madam, that it is not more in our power to divert you; I could wish, indeed, that our entertainments were a little more polite or your taste a little less refined. But, pray, madam, how came the poets and philosophers, that laboured so much in hunting after pleasure, to place it at last in a country life?

Mrs. Sullen. Because they wanted money, child, to find out the pleasures of the town. Did you ever see a poet or philosopher worth ten thousand pounds? If you can show me such a man, I'll lay you fifty pounds you'll find him somewhere within the weekly bills. Not that I disapprove rural pleasures, as the poets have painted them; in their landscape, every Phillis has her Corydon, every murmuring stream, and every flowery mead, gives fresh alarms to love. Besides, you'll find, that their couples were never married: – but yonder I see my Corydon, and a sweet swain it is, Heaven knows! Come, Dorinda, don't be angry, he's my husband, and your brother; and, between both, is he not a sad brute?

Dorinda. I have nothing to say to your part of him, you're the best judge.

Mrs. Sullen. O sister, sister! If ever you marry, beware of a sullen, silent sot, one that's always musing, but never thinks. There's some diversion in a talking blockhead; and since a woman must wear chains, I would have the pleasure of hearing 'em rattle a little. Now you shall see, but take this by the way. He came home this morning at his usual hour of four, wakened me out of a sweet dream of something else, by tumbling over the tea-table, which he broke all to pieces; after his man and he had rolled about the room, like sick passengers in a storm, he comes flounce into bed, dead as a salmon into fishmonger's basket; his feet cold as ice, his breath hot as a furnace, and his hands and his face as greasy as his flannel nightcap. O matrimony! He tosses up the clothes with a barbarous swing over his shoulders, disorders the whole economy of my bed, leaves me half naked, and my whole night's comfort is the tuneable serenade of that wakeful nightingale, his nose! Oh, the pleasure of counting the melancholy clock by a snoring husband! But now, sister, you shall see how handsomely, being a well-bred man, he will beg my pardon.

(Act II Sc. 1)

Contextual issues

Mrs Sullen's observations in the above extract seem to confirm the views on matrimony expressed by the characters in *The Man of Mode*, and a study of other plays from the period provides an understanding of the attitudes to marriage among fashionable classes of the late seventeenth century. To modern eyes their marriages seem more like business transactions or essays in diplomacy and the titles of many of the plays of the period show a concern for, and interest in, marriages of convenience, marriages of old men to young women, infidelity and other sources of tension. Such plays as *The Country Wife* (Wycherley), *The Provoked Wife* (Vanbrugh), *The Provoked Husband* (Vanbrugh and Cibber), *The Tender Husband* (Steele), *A Bold Stroke for a Wife* (Centlivre), *The Careless Husband* (Cibber) all reveal a fascination, almost an obsession with the nature of marriage among Restoration dramatists.

Other features of the context in which seventeenth- and early eighteenth-century dramatists were writing may be discovered by a consideration of the **action** and **activities** of the main characters in any one of the plays mentioned. The most striking feature is that few of them ever appear to work in the modern sense; they enjoy infinite leisure, considerable fortunes and complete mastery of their time and are able to devote most of their energy to love affairs, fashion, entertainment and gossip. They revel in scandal and move only in titled and court circles; they despise the country and glory in the elegance of the town; they travel in sedan chairs and inhabit gracious and spacious houses. We can see why *The Country Gentleman* both complemented yet contradicted the playwriting fashion of the times.

Such matters written about on so wide a scale indicate the nature of the audience for whom the plays were intended: a comparatively small, aristocratic circle revolving around the court, which gave its patronage to the theatre in the form of royal patents. Many of the plays carry dedicatory prefaces or speeches addressed to a particular member of the royal family or aristocracy and, as we have seen in an earlier chapter, many of the theatres established at the time still bear the name Theatre Royal.

A further working example

Before extending our discussion into methods of deriving information about such important factors influencing initial conception as audiences, playhouses or other theatre spaces it will be useful to apply our method of enquiry to a play from a contrasting period. *A Doll's House* by the Norwegian playwright Ibsen was written in 1879 and once again contains a large number of statements concerning the nature of marriage. The play deals with the relationship between a husband, Torvald Helmer, and his wife Nora. Torvald has recently been promoted to the position of bank manager when his attractive wife is visited by an old friend, Mrs Christine Linde, who is now a widow. In studying the following short pieces of dialogue it should be possible to build up a picture of the play's underlying attitudes and assumptions. Consider each carefully:

(a) *Nora.* Oh, yes, Torvald, we can be a little extravagant now. Can't we? Just a tiny bit? You've got a big salary now and you're going to make lots and lots of money.

   Helmer. Next year, yes. But my new salary doesn't start till April.

(b) *Nora.* ... Tell me, is it really true you didn't love your husband? Why did you marry him then?

(c) *Mrs Linde.* Well, a wife can't borrow money without her husband's consent.

   Nora (tosses her head). Ah, but when a wife has a little business sense and knows how to be clever ...

(d) *Mrs Linde.* And you've never told your husband about this?

   Nora. For heaven's sake, no! What an idea! He's frightfully strict about such matters. And besides he's so proud of being a man – it'd be so painful and humiliating for him to know that he owed anything to me. It'd completely wreck our relationship. This life we have built together would no longer exist.

   (extracts (a)–(d) from Act I)

(e) *Nora.* ... You see, Torvald's so hopelessly in love with me that he wants to have me all to himself – those were his very words. When we were first married he got quite jealous if I as much as mentioned any of my old friends back home.

(f) *Nora.* Don't look at me like that, Torvald!

   Helmer. What, not look at my most treasured possession? At all this wonderful beauty that's mine, mine alone, all mine?

(g) *Nora.* It is true. I loved you more than anything else in the world.

(h) *Helmer.* You have loved me as a wife should love her husband. It was simply that in your inexperience you chose the wrong means. But do you think I love you any the less because you don't know how to act on your own initiative? No, no. Just lean on me. I shall counsel you. I shall guide you. I would not be a true man if your feminine helplessness did not make you doubly attractive in my eyes ... There is something indescribably wonderful for a husband in knowing he has forgiven his wife.

(i) *Nora.* We've been married for eight years. Does it occur to you that this is the first time we two, you and I, man and wife, have ever had a serious talk together? ...you're not the man to educate me into being the right wife for you.

(j) *Helmer.* But to leave your home, your husband, your children! Have you ever thought what people will say?

(k) *Nora.* What do you call my most sacred duties?

   Helmer. Do I have to tell you? Your duties towards your husband and your children.

   Nora. I have another duty which is equally sacred.

Helmer. You have not. What on earth could that be?

Nora. My duty towards myself.

Helmer. First and foremost you are a wife and a mother.

(extracts (e)–(k) from Act III)

The whole tone of these fragments of dialogue suggests that we are on much more familiar territory than in *The Man of Mode*: this is the stuff of modern marriage guidance, of a great deal of our fiction and television drama. The questions raised here are within our experience, although some of the opinions expressed are clearly quite unacceptable today. It is not necessary to be familiar with the whole play to detect that we are witnessing the breakdown of a marriage and that Nora painfully makes the transition from submission to a particular concept of a wife's role to independent self-assertion. Unlike the characters of the Restoration plays, these people appear to have very high expectations of what marriage should be and achieve and consequently the failure of a marriage to attain such high ideals is a subject of tragedy rather than humour.

From your careful reading you will see that each of these extracts reveals something of the context of social attitudes and conditions in which Ibsen was writing.

In (a), the husband and wife are discussing their changed financial circumstances in a way that suggests that they have both been aware of the need for economies and have, to that extent, shared a problem in a way that no characters from Restoration drama would have done. The wife, as in the Restoration plays, is shown as the more extravagant of the two and this traditional source of tension reveals not only a difference in temperament but a slightly uneven partnership. The view that women are really inferior managers and slightly irresponsible lies behind this exchange.

In (b), the incredulity of Nora that anyone should consider marriage for reasons other than love shows the basis on which she thought she was building her own relationship. Love as the only socially acceptable foundation for marriage is, in fact, the irony against which the action is played; but a major source of conflict is the social ideal of love, suggesting a sharing, equal partnership and the reality which assigns unequal roles to husband and wife.

This reality is reinforced by the law as shown in statement (c), and requires a rebellious and even devious woman if it is to be circumvented.

A very clear statement of the complex pressures and prejudices that lay behind the marriages of many nineteenth-century women is made in extract (d). Compare the almost sacred and reverential approach of Nora with the cavalier Mrs Sullen. Nora is reiterating the late nineteenth-century Protestant view of the sanctity of marriage: a relationship that had to be worked at, based on the father as head of the household and breadwinner, the wife as mother, homemaker and comforter and the home as the foundation of society.

It is only against this background that we can understand the impact of the dialogue in (k), and appreciate why the audiences who first saw this play found it so indescribably shocking.

Both (g) and (h) show the sharing but male-dominated partnership; the husband's behaviour is governed by a common conception of how a husband ought to behave but to us he may have acquired a Jehovah-like self-image. Infinitely more frightening is the extension of male dominance that sees the wife as the sexual possession of the husband, for it was by no means an uncommon nineteenth-century view that it was a wife's duty to provide sexual gratification regardless of her own feelings.

That Helmer somehow manages to incorporate this belief into his supposedly caring concern for Nora is shown in his outburst in (f). In contrast with the possessiveness and concern for appearances, which appears to be the real root of Helmer's marriage, Nora has aimed at the ideal of love and is to pay a bitter price for it.

If you have not been able to make these deductions from the text, you must develop this skill by constant, close attention to published plays.

Other plays from the period as sources

The need to cover up the cracks in marriages that failed to achieve the unity which society deemed desirable, the deeply painful experiences of the partners and the whole question of sexual taboo concerned a number of nineteenth-century dramatists. Ibsen's contemporary, Strindberg showed in his play *The Father* (1886) how a marriage can become a living Hell, producing precisely the opposite effect to the desired state of bliss. Both Ibsen's and Strindberg's wife characters make a telling contrast to the self-effacing and eternally faithful wives we can find if we turn to Tom Taylor's *The Ticket of Leave Man* (1863) or T.W. Robertson's *Caste* (1867), although both these plays are credited with having contained elements of social comment. We can build up a detailed picture of the problems of marriage in the second half of the nineteenth century if we compare all these plays with Sir Arthur Wing Pinero's *The Second Mrs. Tanqueray* (1893) which exposes many of the pressures and prejudices.

If you study these plays carefully you may also detect a growing debate on the wider issues of women in society; consider, for instance, the questions raised by such an apparently simple statement as the following from Strindberg's *The Father*:

> But I don't want to play the pimp and educate her just simply for marriage – if I do that and she stays single, she'll become one of these embittered spinsters. On the other hand, I don't want to train her for some masculine vocation that'll need years of study and be completely wasted if she does get married.

(Act I .Sc. 3)

However unacceptable we find these views now, they form a vital part of the original context of the plays of this period. Dramatists were writing seriously about marriage for a very different kind of audience from the Restoration playwrights and again we can deduce something of the nature of that audience by an examination of the characters in plays by Ibsen, Chekhov, Strindberg or Wedekind.

In striking contrast to the leisured and titled characters of the seventeenth-century the nineteenth-century plays are peopled by those who have worked to achieve their position, frequently in some profession such as banking, teaching, medicine, architecture or the armed forces. Many now enjoy comfortable middle-class affluence but, because they may have climbed from humbler origins, their inferiors in the social scale will play an important role in the drama. A random selection of stage settings from the period reflects a deliberate lack of ostentation, emphasizing the virtues of simplicity and sobriety: 'Dr. Stockmann's living room – humbly but neatly furnished', 'A large kitchen', 'Room in Grant's Cottage', 'The room occupied by Mary Edwards in Miss Willoughby's house – humbly but neatly furnished', and so on. When large houses are occupied, as in Chekhov's *The Cherry Orchard*, they are shown as a financial burden to their owners or as the symbol of achievement through business acumen.

The inhabitants of such settings are often concerned by change; change of status, loyalty, belief or relationships. They are interested in the inner self, the effect of powerful personal drives and the analysis of human conduct. At the same time, they are troubled by the need for outward respectability and for success as the middle-class world sees it. They seek happiness through the conscious working out of philosophical ideas and, above all, they subscribe to the Protestant work ethic: the view that unflagging self-help and industry bring their rewards in this life as well as in the life to come, and that a life of dissipation is rewarded by a Hell on earth.

Obviously such a range of topics would only interest a cross-section of the public familiar with the situations and problems under discussion. This was in fact the case, for the serious-minded audience for whom Ibsen and his contemporaries were writing consisted largely of those for whom the Industrial Revolution and the advance of science had brought increased affluence and education.

▇ Interpretation and the afterlife of plays

So far we have been concentrating on how much the playtext alone can tell us about the *Zeitgeist*, social conditions and attitudes. We have seen that, in the characters of Etherege and Ibsen, behaviour is governed by a particular set of social assumptions. These are clearly embedded in the text of any given play and vary greatly from one period to another. Directors and performers will often use the production of a play from an earlier period to make statements about current issues. At times they delude themselves that the play was saying in *its* time what they want to say in *their* time but, as we have noticed with the *William Tell* play, it is perhaps inevitable that, in a new production, a play will take on some quality of the age in which it is performed if it is to continue to exist as a living work of art.

Frequently the manipulation of a production to highlight a social or ideological point can be a fruitful and stimulating exercise, as in the performance of the *Provoked Wife* we have already described (see p. 102) or when Edward Bond translated Frank Wedekind's play *Spring Awakening* (1891) for its first English production at the National Theatre in 1974. Bond obviously felt a considerable affinity with the play and in his lengthy introduction to the published version wrote passionately of the failure of modern industrial society; suggesting that *Spring Awakening*, though written over 90 years ago, had become even more relevant. 'The play isn't out of date. It becomes more relevant as our armies get stronger, our schools, prisons and bombs bigger, our means of imposing discipline more disciplined and veiled, and our self-knowledge not much greater.'

Statements and ideas of this kind of attitude often give rise to accusations of betrayal and critics will argue that, in a case like this, Bond has used Wedekind's play to serve his own purposes rather than respecting those of the original work. Every new production involves a reordering of the play's priorities and it is virtually impossible to draw a line between the 'faithful' and the 'unfaithful' revival. Every performance is a primary source for understanding aspects of the age in which it takes place; we can, for example, learn a great deal about artistic trends in the nineteenth century from records of Victorian productions of Shakespeare, but we may learn very little about Shakespeare from the same source. We need to examine carefully the question of trying to reproduce the physical conditions of original performance in order to achieve a true, authentic interpretation of a playwright's intention. But for the moment we must deal with other means of discovering factors that influenced the creation of a play.

■ Sources from outside the play

Useful information for the student, director or actor in helping them to establish the nature of the original play may be found by exploring:

1. publications likely to have been influential and available to the playwright and his potential audience;
2. private correspondence of the playwright;
3. journals or newspapers of the time;
4. play reviews;
5. programme notes or any introductory material that a playwright might have written for his own work.

We can demonstrate the value of such sources if we continue, briefly, our consideration of Ibsen's *A Doll's House* and its effects on Strindberg. Ibsen returned to Norway in 1874, after an absence of ten years, to find the issue of women's rights a fierce debating point. John Stuart Mill's *On the Subjection of Women* had been translated into Norwegian in 1869 and provoked a mass of publications on the subject. Ibsen's play, therefore, gained enormous impact from its topicality and it is hardly surprising that, as Michael Meyer (Ibsen, 1980, Introduction) puts it, 'by the end of the century there was scarcely a civilized country in which it had not been performed'.

Ibsen's private correspondence reveals that the genesis of the play was, in part, dictated by the climate of opinion on women's rights and the inviolability of marriage and partly by his own personal experience. The critic Georg Brandes had suggested to Ibsen that a character from an earlier play, *The League of Youth*, who accuses her husband of having dressed her up like a doll and played with her, might form the basis of a future play. At a slightly later date Ibsen became involved with a woman whose predicament resembled that which the playwright created for Nora, and in 1878 we find him writing in some notes:

> There are two kinds of moral laws, two kinds of conscience, one for men and one, quite different, for women. They don't understand each other; but in practical life, woman is judged by masculine law, as though she weren't a woman but a man ... A woman cannot be herself in modern society. It is an exclusively male society with laws made by men and with prosecutors and judges who assess female conduct from such a standpoint.

> (Ibsen, 1980, p. 12)

We have now pieced together from some of the sources suggested a useful body of information that throws light on Ibsen's major concerns and by the use of further evidence from such sources many editors and historians have given a vivid picture of the reception accorded the play. This has been done most economically and stylishly by Michael Meyer in his *Ibsen, Plays 1–4* (1980).

What of the effect on Strindberg? The published version of *A Doll's House* together with the ferment it had created were both available to Strindberg when, in 1886, he read a magazine article by Paul Lafargue propounding a theory that the human family was originally a matriarchy. Strindberg's own deeply unhappy marriage, coupled with his contempt for Ibsen, whom he termed the 'Norwegian Bluestocking', combined with a suspicion of women that was fuelled by the Lafargue article made him determined to write plays that would redress the injustice and damage which he felt had been done to men by *A Doll's House*.

Accordingly, he wrote *The Father* in 1887, followed by *Miss Julie* in 1888, to which he provided a very revealing introduction. It is obvious that Strindberg was considerably affected by the intellectual climate of his times: his gloomy view of the relationship between the sexes as a struggle for dominance and survival clearly owed something to the ideas of Darwin and to the emerging science of psychology with its concern for man's primitive, innate drives. By a careful check of dates we can see that Darwin's *Origin of Species* (1859), *The Descent of Man* (1871) and *The Expression of Emotion in Man and Animals* (1872) were all available in translation in Sweden by the time Strindberg was writing; furthermore, only two years before he wrote *The Father* Freud arrived as a student at the Salpêtrière clinic in Paris where he was to achieve a revolution in psychological investigation. In 1882, Tuke and Bucknill's *Textbook of Psychological Medicine* showed that even before Freud there was extensive interest and research into the workings of the subconscious mind.

We have devoted considerable attention to the example of that period in the nineteenth century that produced a number of plays that are still frequently performed today. We could have extended our investigations further into the music, poetry, architecture, technology or religious attitudes of the times but we may have done sufficient to detect the *Zeitgeist*. The continuing popularity of these plays indicates that they have qualities that may transcend their time or appear to have a particular relevance to our own *Zeitgeist*.

■ Performance in theory and practice

It will be obvious from our discussion in this section that we are neither providing nor advocating a conventional 'history of theatre'. At one time, courses in Theatre or Drama Studies involved an historical progression from 'The Ancient Greeks to the Present Day', but this is no longer the case. Sometimes such approaches have merely been replaced by an historical survey of great and influential directors, but this has the same limitation of not demanding a practical response.

Clearly, there are some benefits in studying key texts from selected periods and traditions in order to acquire an overview of the development of theatre and such an approach will rely on the great plays which have survived in performance or simply in print. But this creates a number of problems. The canon of so-called 'great plays' may have been deemed worthy of study because of their literary rather than their theatrical merit, for we must remember that prejudice against the study of Theatre or even Drama as a performing art as opposed to a branch of literature has been, and to some extent remains, strong.

Plays selected and considered in the quiet of the study provide, at best, an incomplete picture and by looking at other sources we can see that some of the most interesting and creative periods in the history of theatre were those from which few plays have survived. The fact that a play has not survived is not necessarily a guide to its merits either. The whole business of staging a play is so complex and costly that thousands of good plays, and perhaps some great ones, have simply been lost or remained on the page. A musician wishing to revive some music from a past age gathers together a group of instrumentalists or singers, provides them with copies, has a couple of rehearsals, gives one performance, and the public is satisfied; but the revival of a play will involve the learning of many lines, the blocking of moves and enough performances to repay the time and effort (or the management) involved.

In recent years there has been a growing appreciation of the fact that playwrights have gained much of their impetus from the advances in performance style, technology and public taste which took place in what have frequently been considered 'bleak periods' in drama and that many of the playwrights working in these periods (such as the early to mid-nineteenth century in Britain) were craftsmen of considerable skill. One of the most striking facts to emerge from studies of the careers of performers and the history of playhouses is the vast repertoire of once popular and now forgotten plays which engaged the energies of actors and actresses and the interest of audiences. If we add to this the fact of the rapidly changing tastes of the public, we can see how unreliable a guide to quality is survival. Some kinds of play are more durable than others; in **situation comedy** and **melodrama**, the essence of the drama lies in the action and not in the words, so such plays appear to have little merit on paper. Moreover, even enthusiastic critical acclaim cannot guarantee the continued, long-term success of a playwright.

Critics invariably reveal something of the context of the writing and original production of plays. Such contextual issues, with which this section has been concerned, can help to explain why certain plays are popular at certain times, and what world events might bring about changes in taste.

▌ Conclusion

In this chapter we have explored the idea that all plays and performances are, to some extent, the product of their times and that, in order to understand them, we need to appreciate both their theatrical and their historical context. We have worked through a number of examples in some detail in order to demonstrate the importance of recognizing the *Zeitgeist* and theatrical conditions which have shaped dramatic texts and influenced the style of their original performance. We have emphasized the importance of developing a willingness to undertake considerable research as a means of placing any stage work in its context.

As we have considered the attitudes, events and theatrical conditions that have shaped plays and their performances in the past, we have moved towards an understanding of how a stage work may be given an afterlife in performance now. Furthermore, we have demonstrated that any performance today will be as influenced by the current *Zeitgeist* as was the original text.

We have taken our examples from three key periods of theatre history, all of which had a largely predominant form of theatre building that both shaped and was shaped by the plays written. However, examples of the interaction of theatre buildings, current attitudes or national events and the plays and performances of the time may be taken from any period of history, including our own.

Topics for discussion and reflection

◆ Do you consider from the information you now have that *The Country Gentleman* could have an afterlife?

◆ How many plays from the Restoration period contain the word 'wife' or 'husband' in their title? Compare these with the titles of plays by the French dramatist Molière. Why might there be a connection?

◆ What technological inventions and social attitudes contributed to the *Zeitgeist* at the time when Ibsen, Strindberg or Chekhov were writing?

◆ David Hare's recent plays *The Permanent Way* (on Britain's railways) and *Stuff Happens* (on the war in Iraq) explore recent events, issues and attitudes using verbatim theatre and the impersonation of recognizable political figures. How does the current *Zeitgeist* enable such plays to be staged?

◆ How is the current *Zeitgeist* reflected in some of the production and performance modes outlined in Chapter 5?

■ Further reading

Holland, P. and Orgel, S. (eds) (2004) *From Script to Stage in Early Modern England*, Basingstoke: Palgrave Macmillan. The two books edited by Holland and Orgel recommended here contain excellent examples of the scholarship involved in understanding performances in their historical context.

Holland, P. and Orgel, S. (eds) (2005) *Performance to Print in Shakespeare's England*, Basingstoke: Palgrave Macmillan.

Kermode, L. and Scott-Warren, J. (eds) (2005) *Tudor Drama Before Shakespeare, 1485–1590*, Basingstoke: Palgrave Macmillan. Provides a fascinating insight into the pre-Shakespearean theatre.

Luckhurst, M. and Moody, J. (eds) (2005) *Theatre and Celebrity in Britain, 1660–2000*, Basingstoke: Palgrave Macmillan. An ever more relevant topic explored with perceptive scholarship.

Shapiro, J. (2005) *1599: A Year in the Life of William Shakespeare*, London: Faber and Faber. A model of living history.

Worthen, W. B. and Holland, P. (eds) (2003) *Theorizing Practice: Redefining Theatre History*, Basingstoke: Palgrave Macmillan. Offers new ways of thinking about what has often been seen as 'difficult and irrelevant' to current practice.

■ Website

For playwright profiles and further activities, see our website: www.palgrave.com/foundations/pickering

Devising and Writing for the Theatre

This chapter aims to equip you with the necessary skills for the creation of an original work for the stage. We are assuming that your course of study may include a module that either requires the devising and presentation of a performance or the writing of a play. We discuss the various options available to you as a potential creator of stage works and offer practical suggestions, while emphasizing the necessity of drawing upon your complementary skills in performance and critical thinking.

Learning outcomes

By the conclusion of this chapter, you should be able to:

▶ build on the experience of previous chapters to assist in your writing and devising;

▶ participate meaningfully in creating a thematic programme for performance;

▶ devise a short theatre piece;

▶ make a stage adaptation of a novel;

▶ write stage dialogue;

▶ plan and write a short play;

▶ understand the principles of effective writing for the stage;

▶ discuss the various processes involved in writing and devising with understanding.

◼ Creating a new work

Every year, thousands of works are created for the live theatre in addition to the large number intended for the screen or radio. Of these, the majority will be scripted plays and of those a small proportion will be performed. An even smaller proportion (approximately one in every seven hundred submitted to publishers) may be published and achieve some measure of 'afterlife'. Other works may be devised for particular events or spaces and their text may never be finally fixed in written form. Some 'devised' pieces, such as those by the playwright and film- maker Mike Leigh, will finally achieve a 'fixed' state as a script after a long period of experimental work whereas others may be intended for a single performance which could not be repeated.

The process of creating and presenting a play or other stage work is highly complex and opportunities for the performance of stage works are relatively rare. Theatre companies, directors and producers are constantly inundated by unsolicited scripts from 'new' playwrights and the instances of such initiatives resulting in a production are very few. If you are participating in a module or course in writing and devising, it is important for you to grasp this opportunity to 'try out' your work and see it performed.

Successful writing or devising for the theatre is very difficult: David Hare, one of Britain's most celebrated dramatists, emphasizes the degree of difficulty in his stimulating collection of lectures *Obedience, Struggle and Revolt* (2005a) and admits that his favourite playwriting story is of the great Bertolt Brecht who failed to convince anyone in Hollywood that his idea for a movie based on 'boy meets girl, so what?' had any future.

Richard Hoggart, whose book, *The Uses of Literacy* (1996), inspired generations of teachers and thinkers in the field of culture, describes his own complete failure as a playwright in his autobiographical musings:

> The drama? Years ago, a BBC producer urged me to write a play. So I began; and gave up after Act 1, Scene 1. The reasons were very clear and simple. My poor characters, insofar as they existed at all, were endless talkers, of monologues, though now and again they let others have a go. Worse, they did not move. I could not see them in three-dimensional space in which they came and went, had their exits and entrances. They talked all the time, quietly or heatedly, and stayed tied to the one spot. No one came in to introduce a new element. No one left, if only to answer a call of nature. Not even a loo-chain was pulled off stage, to suggest other humans outside. All the characters stayed talking perhaps but also mutely begging for release, to be taken out of the selfish world of the single authorial voice, and to be granted an instance of dramatic surprise.
>
> (2000, p. 115)

Although we have begun by emphasizing the difficulties and sheer effort involved in creating a stage work, you should not allow this to discourage you. The English playwrights Shelagh Delaney and Andrea Dunbar, the Scottish playwright Paula McGee and the American Trish Harnetiaux all wrote very successful plays as students, or as very young women, and although you may encounter many gloomy predictions that the play is 'dead' as an art form or that only **site-specific** plays have any future, if you have an ambition to write and create new works, you should respond to that ambition in the knowledge that humanity constantly seeks re-enactments of its concerns and beliefs in some tangible form.

You are not being asked to begin without a foundation. These have been established in previous chapters and you should aim specifically to build upon:

◆ your work on monologues
◆ your understanding of the effect of place on the nature of performance

◆ skills and experience in story-telling

◆ your investigations into a wide range of performance modes and styles.

▇ Advice from playwrights

Hare's lessons

You may wish to consider some practical lessons which David Hare claims to have learned throughout his long career as a 'political' playwright:

1. The playwright is not going to control an audience's reaction to anything s/he writes. Therefore the playwright should not give the audience 'easy handles with which they can pigeonhole you'.
2. The first lesson of theatre is that there is no such thing as an unimportant performance.
3. In this business your enemies will follow you to the ends of the earth. (Hare described how one famous theatre critic has voiced the view that he wished the playwright would 'just go away!')
4. You can will a theatre into existence. You cannot will a play.
6. The creation of a great political play will demand exactly the same measure of genius, torture and art as the creation of any other.
7. No play exists in its description, in the ambition of what you would wish it to be. It exists only as it is, the thing, not the design.

(2005a, pp. 8–22)

These statements may have considerable significance for your intended work in writing and devising and you may wish to compare them with some statements by the American playwright, Richard Foreman (b 1937). At first reading these may seem almost impenetrable but they reward carefly consideration. Eventually, you should aim to be able to construct your own **paradigm**.

Foreman's paradigms

Foreman presents the following contrast between the theatre of the past and his own:

> *Old Paradigm*: Universe consists of forces that solidify into units (Gestalts, objects, events) to which we *respond*.
>
> *New Paradigm*: Universe consists of forces that leave traces which are not fully identifiable consciously, of which we see only residual evidence – and if we respond it is 'error' of responding to what we *project* into those traces.
>
> If you follow the old paradigm your art tries to make something visible, and the life copied by that art is a responding-to-input from the 'world'.
>
> If you follow the new paradigm, your (my) art tries to erase things (because they are obstacles) and the life copied by that art is a 'something else' that tries to resonate to inner output.

(quoted in Cohn, 1991, p. 152)

The qualities required for successful devising/playwriting

In order to achieve any success as a creator or works for the stage, you will need to be:

◆ *observant*: notice the way in which human beings behave, move and deal with other people in public and private situations. Do they manipulate, intimidate, support or oppose? How do they reveal their attitudes, beliefs and value systems?

◆ *listening*: be an avid listener to the way in which language is used in every conceivable situation. Take time to listen to conversations in pubs, cafés, public places; listen to speakers and those being interviewed in the media. Notice the patterns of voices and speech and how dialogue is constructed.

◆ *open*: be open to the possibilities of all theatrical forms; listen to advice and suggestions.

◆ *hungry*: for experience in the theatre. Attend every possible performance you can, even if the performance is 'bad', you will learn something from the process. Notice how plays and performances are constructed, the conventions they employ. Read plays extensively and note the ways in which the playwright has provided a blueprint for performance, how dialogue and stage directions are set out on the page and how ideas are explored.

◆ *perceptive*: to the use of space in relation to performance. Notice how a performance and a text are, to some extent, shaped by the space. Gain wide experience of differing styles of production and different theatre spaces.

◆ *passionate*: about topics that would inspire you to write/devise a piece. If you are not totally committed to your topic and its expression in the theatre, nobody else will be.

◆ *patient*: you may not achieve what you want to achieve at the first attempt. Be open to the possibility of making changes as a result of readings and rehearsal.

■ Three initial decisions

It is highly likely that you are studying this chapter because the creation of an original piece of theatre is a requirement of your course. You may be the sole creator or you may take part in a collaborative act of creation; you may be required to perform in or direct the piece or provide technical and artistic support. Whatever your precise role you will inevitably have to confront three initial areas of choice:

1. What is the topic or theme of the piece?
2. Where is it to be staged?
3. What **genre** will be employed?

As we have seen from previous chapters, these three areas are interrelated and must all form part of the total concept. Let us consider each of them separately before seeking to make connections.

Topic or theme

It is important to concentrate on an issue that engages your individual or collective energy for the duration of a project. This will almost certainly mean that the topic will arise from some deep concern or area of interest. Students often make the mistake of imagining that they have to find some new, witty or obscure area that they think might be amusing to work with rather than creating something that is about life as it now is and impacts on them. Fantasy and science fiction are areas best avoided for the inexperienced theatre practitioner unless they serve to illuminate some aspect of life as is appears to the creator. If you consider the range of topics covered by a week's viewing of 'soaps', you will see that Brecht's famous 'boy meets girl: so what?' is subject to an almost infinite number of possibilities alone. But it may well be that, like David Hare, you will wish to research and present material related to current political and social matters. Hare has ranged over the state of Britain's railways, the conflict in Israel/Palestine, the war in Iraq, the Church of England, the judiciary, the Labour Party and other aspects of life in modern Britain while steadfastly refusing to write 'to order' about any topic. What interests you, what disturbs you, what infuriates you, either in terms of topical themes or in terms of performance, should lie beneath the initial decision to focus energy and attention for a considerable period of time.

Space

From the outset, you must be thinking of the kind of theatrical experience you want for your audience and how this might be shaped by the performance space. Similarly, that space may well define the genre you select as a means of expressing your ideas and will certainly help to shape the nature of the performance of the work itself. Writing or devising a play or creating some other form of performance text and *then* wondering where to perform it is the *wrong* process. From the outset, your piece must be conceived in spatial terms and may either determine, or be determined by, the space that is available to you. One common mistake is to create a play or performance piece 'on paper' and then, at some stage, hope that it will 'work' in a space allocated. It is this interrelatedness that has largely brought about the popularity of the concept of the **found space**: far too many pieces with good potential have been strangled almost at birth by the restrictions of a particular theatre or stage whereas a successful work will virtually grow out of the nature of the space. The potential of certain spaces may well provide the initial inspiration for your creation and you should take time to explore widely what might be available to you.

Genre

In Shakespeare's play *Hamlet*, a troupe of actors visits the castle at Elsinore. The rather tedious Lord Chamberlain, Polonius, introduces them as:

> The best actors in the world, either for tragedy, comedy, history, pastoral, pastoral-comical, historical-pastoral, tragical-historical, tragical-comical-historical-pastoral, scene individable, or poem unlimited.

(Act II Sc ii)

UNIVERSITY OF WINCHESTER
LIBRARY

Although this is a satire on the scholars' classification of different types of drama, it shows that the concept of multiple possibilities for types of performance is by no means new. Even if you decide that you wish to write a relatively straightforward one-act play with two or three characters, the nature of that play will still involve a great deal of choice. But if you consider the wide variety of performances we have already encountered, you will now understand that the process of selecting your genre is both complex and vital. It is possible that aspects of that selection will be dictated by the forces and talents available to you. For example, you may be restricted to a certain number of performers of specified gender or you may be given a precise time limit. You should not look on such apparent restrictions as inhibiting: it is quite common for writers to be commissioned to create a performance text for a specified number of performers or for a particular company or venue. Such a commission may well include indications of time and the agreement for rewrites during the course of rehearsal. If you have the requisite skills for writing and devising, you should eventually be able to respond to opportunities of this kind.

If you are on a course there will inevitably be restrictions on what you might attempt: it is, for example, unlikely that you will have access to aerial performers of the calibre described in two of the productions mentioned in Chapter 5, but you may well have fellow students with skills in singing, dance or physical theatre or actors anxious to use the approaches of Stanislavsky or Meisner who will welcome the opportunity to work on a new text. Think carefully about all the resources available to you before you plan your piece.

■ Four options for creating a new piece

When creating a new piece for the theatre in the context of a course of study, there would appear to be four main options:

1. making a **compilation** or 'thematic programme' using already existing sources;
2. making an **adaptation** from another literary form such as a novel or poem;
3. **devising** a new work from a variety of sources and working collaboratively with a group of performers;
4. *writing* a new text and bringing it to life during rehearsal.

We shall examine each of these options in turn and provide substantial examples of ways of working in each case.

■ Devising a thematic programme

At the beginning of April 2008, London's West End theatres between them were staging 25 musicals, a fact that caused some critics considerable concern. (You may also like to consider if that is a good 'use' of fair-sized proscenium arch theatres in a capital city.) Four of these musicals were 'compilation/anthology shows', still further upsetting the critics, on the grounds that these productions weren't even 'proper' musicals, just an opportunity to trawl through the 'back catalogue' of such performers as Abba, Queen, Buddy Holly and The Four Seasons.

In fact, such productions employed a number of devices for linking the musical 'numbers' as did some of their predecessors. For example, earlier shows based on the musical output of Cole Porter, Noel Coward and Stephen Sondheim relied on a linking narration, though *Cowardy Custard* also utilized scripted scenes from Coward's work.

Whatever views may be held on such productions, they do suggest interesting possibilities for Theatre Studies situations. A theme may be selected embracing play extracts, material from books and newspapers, poems, singing, appropriate dance and, depending on the ambitions of the design aspects of the course, film, video or specially created 'effects', utilizing various electronic means.

Ideas for creating a compilation may be obtained by a study of the historical framework of the staging of Alan Bennett's *Forty Years On* (reflected in the published Stage Directions) or the structure of *Oh, What A Lovely War!*, devised by Charles Chiltern and Joan Littlewood.

There are obvious possibilities for research and contextual studies and the outcomes may be reflected not just in the final staged work but in programme notes and foyer displays. Enthusiasts will almost certainly discover rarities and a few surprises and in all probability, given a good theme, too much material will result. A wealth of good material will lead to interesting work in shaping the production's structure with due regard to the comparative weight of items, variety, balance and thematic clarity or the logistics of potential 'doubling' by performers.

A working example

A theme which would certainly provide too much material might be entitled 'Tea and Terror', viewing the period from 1890 to the present through the contrasts between the horrific conflicts of the period and, in part, plays which (unfairly) may be thought of as merely 'cup and saucer/anyone for tennis?' work related to staging with a box set.

In the interests of the theme you may well achieve some surprises. Who, for example, do you imagine wrote this impassioned outburst from a young officer in a company headquarters in a quiet section of the Front Line in the spring of 1917?

> It isn't poor old England; it's poor old Human Nature. There isn't a hope for it anywhere, all this proves it ... watching kids like Armitage torn to pieces, screaming in bloody pain ... Imagine his mother's face when she opens the telegram. He's an only son, I believe. He had his twenty-first birthday last week when we were out of the line – we had a grand evening you remember, you were there ... Aren't you touched by it any more? Not now, I don't mean now when everything's comparatively quiet, but when we're in the thick of it floundering through mud in an attack, treading on men's faces, some of them not dead, with the bloody din of the barrage in our ears, and thin human screams cutting through it quite clearly, like penny whistles in a thunderstorm ... and when it's over and we fall back sometimes, back over that idiotic ground, having to go quickly, not hearing people groaning or crying for water-when we flop down in a dug-out, safe, for the moment, time to think then, isn't there-can you help thinking then? ... And the civilian public doesn't have the remotest suspicion of what really happens. They'll never know, whichever way it goes, victory or defeat ... They'll smarm it all over with memorials and Rolls of Honour and Angels of Mons and it'll look so noble and glorious in retrospect that they'll start itching for another war, egged on by dear old gentlemen in clubs who wish they were twenty years younger, and newspaper owners and oily financiers, and the splendid women of England happy and proud to give their sons and husbands and lovers ... They'll never know, never, never, never, never!

At first glance, this might appear to be from the best-known of all plays dealing with the First World War, R.C. Sherriff's *Journey's End* but, in fact, it is from Noel Coward's anti-war rarity *Post-Mortem*. Or is it? If you look carefully at the play's first scene in Volume 2 of Coward's collected plays you will see that this is an amalgam of several speeches that have been 'cobbled together' for the purpose of a particular thematic performance where a single voice was required. Your observation will therefore introduce you to the concept of **cobbling**.

Another Coward rarity, *Peace in Our Time*, could also be an interesting addition to the programme because it is written as if the Germans had won the 1939–45 War.

Once you become involved in a thematic exercise like this, there are endless possibilities. Shaw's *Arms and the Man* connects cavalry and guns, his *Major Barbara* links – through Lady Britomart and her children – the world of Lady Bracknell to the morality of the arms trade. Though Somerset Maugham's *For Services Rendered* would seem an obvious source, some of the thoughtless prattle of his young characters in *The Breadwinner* piquantly links 'tea' and 'terror'.

You may go on to compile your own lists but, without even naming any recent plays which touch on Western involvements in Iraq and Afghanistan, you might consider Peter Whelan's *The Accrington Pals*, Stephen Lowe's *Touched*, C.P. Taylor's *And a Nightingale Sang*, Willis Hall's *The Long and the Short and the Tall*, John Osborne's *The Entertainer* (for the Suez Crisis of 1956), the final speech of Act 1 of Alan Bennett's *Forty Years On*, Terence Rattigan's *Flare Path*, and – for the Blitz and concentration camps – another rare source, Rodney Ackland's *Absolute Hell*.

Commercial theatre pieces could well add to the mixture – explore *Seagulls over Sorrento*, *Reluctant Heroes* and *See How They Run*. And to mention Peter Nichols's *Privates on Parade* is to move towards the potential musical side of such a thematic programme.

That telling points may be made by the juxtaposition of material was definitively proved by *Oh, What a Lovely War!*, in itself a reminder of the many available 'war songs' from Ivor Novello's 'Keep the Home Fires Burning' to numbers associated with the Second World War's 'Forces' Sweetheart', Vera Lynn. *Cabaret* is a rich source and the wreckage of Lionel Bart's *Blitz* might be searched. The various 'dance crazes' of the (lengthy) period to be covered would provide excellent material for the 'linking' sections of such a production, for 'continuity' in thematic entertainments always needs careful thought.

If any recorded classical music is to be used, there is a good deal to be explored from Elgar, Butterworth, Vaughan Williams and Holst to Britten and Karl Jenkins's *The Armed Man* and beyond. Poetry related to both World Wars is abundant and accessibly anthologized and it may be through research into poetry that the more recent horrors of armed 'terror' might find a place in the performance.

Clearly this particular theme would produce far too much potential material and editing, shaping and rigorous adherence to a 'through line' would be necessary. But this type of themed work can arouse enthusiasm among participants and, incidentally, often offer a greater range of roles and activities than a 'conventional' play. Thus we can see its value in study and training situations but also its potential in providing stimulating, even challenging, fare for audiences.

Perhaps two cautionary notes should be sounded:

1. *Performing rights.* Within a study situation and to an invited audience, the use of extracts may be in order but any more elaborate, public, let alone 'commercial', performance

should probably be preceded by enquiries to relevant agents as to implications regarding the use of extracts.

2. *Cobbling*. If you have investigated how the speech from Coward's *Post-Mortem* was 'written', you will have realized what cobbling means and how it may be used in a themed production. Additionally, cobbling done responsibly may produce Audition Speeches which – refreshingly – are not in the published collections of Audition Speeches. But be careful if applying to a Drama School to note if the regulations forbid 'cobbling'.

■ Adapting for the stage

Interchange between various literary forms, the stage and the screen has become an important aspect of recent writing. We can see this in the work of the playwrights Harold Pinter and Christopher Hampton who both have produced successful screen-plays from famous novels. In the live theatre there have been remarkable works ranging from the stage adaptation of the world's oldest written story, *The Epic of Gilgamesh* by the Caravan of Dreams Theatre, the dramatization of Chaucer's poem *Troilus and Criseyde* and the medieval poem *Sir Gawain and the Green Knight* by Michael B. Herzog to the epic stage versions of Dickens's *Nicholas Nickleby* by David Edgar and of Tolstoy's *War and Peace* by Helen Edmunson. Adaptation is part of the craft of playmaking and students may well find that, initially, the dramatization of a small fragment of a novel is a highly productive exercise.

In order that you might follow this suggestion, we include below some advice from one of the most prolific and skilled of recent adaptors, the playwright and theatre director, Philip Dart. Many of his adaptations were made for Chalkfoot Theatre Company for their tours of rural communities and small-scale Arts Centres in response to local demand for dramatized versions of well known works of literature.

Over the past twenty years or so stage adaptations have become increasingly popular with producers.

Audiences like adaptations: even if they do not know the book, they will have almost certainly heard of the title, and that is why these productions normally do well at the box office.

As the Director of a small-scale theatre company, I have adapted over ten novels for the stage. I really enjoy the creative process involved and adaptations give the company a chance to produce new and exciting work that is calculated to appeal to a large audience base.

There are no hard and fast rules about adaptation, but here are a few questions you should ask before you begin, together with some suggestions and advice that might help you when you start writing.

What about copyright?

Copyright in a literary work lasts until 70 years after the death of the author. This means that there are many works you might wish to adapt that will require permission to do so from either a living author (or the author's agent) or a deceased author's Estate.

This is not always an easy process. You might have just read the most brilliant new best seller, but as an unknown writer you are unlikely to be granted the performance rights you will need to adapt it for stage.

If, however, you are lucky enough to obtain permission, you will normally be expected to pay 'up front' for the rights of the novel: bear in mind that a proportion of box office royalties will also be payable to the book's author.

For a beginner, adapting a book outside the copyright law is, of course, a much easier option. There is a wealth of suitable and stimulating titles available and choosing an older work does not mean that your approach cannot be innovative.

However, you should remember to work from the date of the death of the writer, *not* the date of publication. For example, H.G. Wells wrote '*The Invisible Man*' in 1897 but did not die until 1946 (so the rights will not be available until 2016).

Is this the right book for me?

Naturally, your choice of book is crucial to the process. It should be a novel that you have loved reading and you feel passionate about.

Adaptation is a creative process and it is important to be on the same wavelength as the writer. It helps if you are familiar with the work of your chosen author and have an appreciation of its style.

An affinity with and a knowledge of the book's subject matter together with an appreciation of the historical period in which it is set are also an advantage.

Is the book suitable for adaptation?

Once you have an idea of the novel you want to adapt, it is important to take a realistic and dispassionate look at your choice before you begin.

Can you really transform this book into a stage play? You need to ask whether the novel is too long or the plot too complicated to transfer to the stage in just two hours' playing (modern plays tend to run no longer than this and you should beware of making your audiences restless).

You also need to consider whether the essential components of the novel can withstand the process of adaptation, e.g. how would you represent the supernatural element in Henry James's *The Turn of the Screw*? (Imaginative solutions to these problems are normally possible but it is best to consider these questions early on in the process.)

Are there too many characters? If so, is it possible to reduce them? Unless the play is intended for a large cast, there may be limits on the number of actors available.

Of course, doubling or trebling is possible, and may even be preferred, but that can cause additional complications. In my own company professional actors often take multiple roles, but you need experienced performers to make this work.

What approach should I take?

Adaptation means you must identify the best parts of the story – including dialogue – and craft them into text which will work in performance.

You are creating a new artistic work out of an existing one and for a different medium – the theatre. It is important to ask yourself what you want to achieve, and what the audience will get from watching your play.

How will it be staged?

You will also need to envisage how your adaptation will work in performance. Although it will be the Director's job to 'stage' your adaptation, it is important to offer your own views on how this might be achieved.

Most novels are very episodic and take place in many different locations. You will need to think about how you are going to set the scene and inform the audience of any movements in time. Consider innovative ways of creating the atmosphere of the novel you are adapting: much can be conveyed with effective lighting and a basic set. Music or sound effects can be added to suggest time and place, and narration is useful, provided it is imaginatively introduced and not overused.

When I adapted Jane Austen's *Emma* for the four actors I decided on a simple set – just a floor cloth and drapes, with very minimal changes to costume. The actors mimed everything and the action moved swiftly along as the storytelling was unfettered by props or complicated costume changes.

Here are some steps that might help once you begin your work on the adaptation:

1. Read and re-read the novel – make sure you are very familiar with it.
2. Write a brief synopsis of the book – you will naturally find yourself editing the story and tightening the structure.
3. Go back to basics – remind yourself why you wanted to adapt the book – what inspired you. This will help you make the right decisions when you are writing.
4. Decide on the approach. Do you have a vision on how the play will work? A strong concept here is very helpful. Although it is frequently done, you could opt for the 'play within a play' convention. e.g. in the West End hit *The Woman in Black* two characters 'enact' the supernatural experience of one of the characters.
5. Could you set the play in a different period in time? This is often done in film, e.g. the 1995 film *Clueless* was a contemporary re-working of Jane Austen's *Emma*.
6. What is your concept for the narration? Are you going to use direct address to the audience? Are you using a single character as narrator or proposing narration by a number of characters? Narration is a useful device if you want to make the action really clear and keep the story moving. However, avoid making your narration too wordy – remember it's a play, not a book.
7. List the main characters – which are the most interesting and essential to the plot?
8. Write a scene breakdown. Make a list of scene locations and note what characters are involved. (This can change as you work on the piece, but it is good to have something to work from.)
9. Attempt a first draft – remember to be radical and bold. Be brave – cut whole sections if you have to (your first draft is likely to be too long anyway).
10. Leave it at least a week and then re-read your first draft and ask the following questions: Are the story lines clear to someone who hasn't read the book and who is

watching this for the first time? Are the characters well developed and believable? Is the dialogue realistic and are you using the right language? It is acceptable, and often desirable, to take dialogue from the book, but be careful! Dialogue on the page is not always actable and can be rather verbose – particularly in the case of nineteenth-century novelists. You must ensure that the style of the dialogue you have added yourself matches the style of the writer. Will a Director be able to stage this successfully? Are there too many cumbersome scene changes or character changes for the actors?

11. Write a second draft and then get friends and colleagues to read your script. Is the story clear to them and are the relationships believable? If the play is too long, use a red pen and cut what is not essential, however much it hurts!

12. Write a third draft and stage a reading. There is nothing better than listening to your own play being read in order to gauge how it is working. Listen to the way it sounds and take on board the performers' comments, particularly if they find any of the dialogue difficult to read or understand.

After further revision, your play should be ready for rehearsal, but the process is not finished. Try not to be too protective about your work and if the director and actors ask to change dialogue or alter scenes and can justify their requests, listen to them. Of course, if you really feel strongly defend what you believe is right and stand your ground!

To summarize:

Choose carefully when selecting a book to adapt.

Make sure it is one that you will really enjoy working on (adaptation is a lengthy process and you will be working with this material for many months).

Come up with a strong concept.

Visualize your adaptation in theatrical terms and be imaginative and bold in your approach.

Thoroughly research your book's subject matter and the period in which it is set.

Do not be afraid to write many drafts and to listen to, and take note of the comments of others.

Go for simplicity and remember that, above all, you are a story-teller.

(© Philip Dart, 2008. Philip Dart is the Artistic Director of Chalkfoot Theatre Arts (www.chalkfoot.org.uk))

■ Devising

The dramaturgy of the actor

What is the **dramaturgy of the actor**? We have taken this term from Eugenio Barba (see Chapter 1) to define the actor-generated texts which have become an essential part of the modern theatre. The creation of a text by a company of actors is not a new phenomenon: we know that the scenes presented by **Commedia dell' Arte** troupes during the Renaissance were devised by the performers, following certain **conventions**. This form of theatre, that was at its height in Europe during the early seventeenth century, involved a process whereby the actors were provided with a *soggetto*, which was an outline plot with brief descriptions of the scenes. The actors then improvised all the dialogue, action and business. They were provided with **stock characters** and, during the course of their work, would develop a repertoire of memorized speeches, known as *concetti*, that could be inserted into a performance. Knock-about comic business (*lazzi*) was handed down to new generations of commedia actors and, although the troupes were eventually to disappear, their influence on subsequent theatre practice was considerable. Shakespeare, who might well have seen a commedia performance, makes reference to improvised dialogue from comic characters in a speech in *Hamlet* where the protagonist is giving some advice to a visiting company of actors. Improvisation and actor-generated texts were probably a feature of Elizabethan Theatre: a recent programme note to a production of *The Massacre at Paris* by Shakespeare's contemporary, Christopher Marlowe, outlined the director's belief that the relatively short printed version from which he and his cast had been working was probably the product of a company of actors who took the play on tour after its London premiere. Needing to use a smaller cast and without, possibly, the one 'book of the play', they relied on their recollection of the original and interspersed the text with fragments from other plays when their memories failed them. If that conjecture is accurate, the traditional skills of the Commedia dell' Arte had clearly survived.

However, it was in the second half of the twentieth century that devising as we now understand the term, came into prominence with the growth of companies committed to more experimental work and more open systems of governance. We see examples in the work of Jean-Claude van Itallie in the USA, Mike Leigh in Britain, Robert Lepage in Canada, Joan Littlewood at the Theatre Royal in Stratford East London, and the Market Theatre in Johannesburg.

Jean-Claude van Itallie

The Belgian-born van Itallie is most often associated with the actors' workshops at the Open Theatre in New York. Using the personal discoveries made by the actors themselves, he embarked on a series of devised plays that were little more than sketches in their early form. *War and Four Other Plays* explores the generational conflict between two actors whereas *The Hunter and the Bird* demands role reversal. The 'playwright' explores the notion of time in such pieces as *Almost Like Being* and *I'm Really Here* that ironically take their titles from songs made famous by the film star, Doris Day. Many of van Itallie's plays depend on the exercises undertaken by actors. In *Interview*, there is an on-stage chorus that takes part in a series of enactments involving a 'transformation technique' in which each actor is required to 'transform' into a new character type. Juxtapositions of priest-confessor, psychiatrist-patient, acrobatic opponents, subway riders, square dancers and rhetorical politician-silent public culminate in a moment when the actors line up 'like marching dolls' one behind the other, having responded without sensitivity to their social roles. Perhaps the most famous of Jean-Claude van Itallie's plays to emerge from the exercises at the Open Theatre was *America Hurrah*, the first play to transfer from Off-Off Broadway to Off-Broadway. It was conceived as a trilogy but devised to respond to the situations that existed in the theatre 'off Broadway'. In the major part of the trilogy, a motel manager talks about her work while grotesque figures scribble graffiti and eventually dismember her.

Mike Leigh

Few recent practitioners have divided the opinions of actors and critics more sharply than Mike Leigh, the British playwright/director who is probably best known for his play *Abigail's Party*, a series of memorable television plays and his more recent films such as *Secrets and Lies*, *Career Girls*, *Topsy Turvy* and *Happy-go-Lucky*. All these works, which exploit the poison that seems to lurk beneath the surface of much 'family life', are particularly interesting for the reappearance of a relatively small group of actors who have embraced working in Leigh's idiosyncratic way, a method deeply rooted in intense improvisation. Actors either warm to working with Leigh's approach or are repelled and disturbed by it: even those who return to his methods find the experience demanding and, at times, frightening.

Leigh's initial meeting with his potential cast takes place without the existence of a text. Some kind of governing idea and theme or topic is introduced, together with the most important of Leigh's ingredients: the idea of character. From this point onwards the actors are required to discuss the characters that might appear in the drama and, after initial agreement as to their identity, to embark on a period of intense personal research into their roles. The lengthy preparatory period may extend for several weeks. Only after its completion are the actors brought back together so that their characters can interact with the others in a series of situations. These may either be contrived by the director or created in response to what might arise in the course of improvisation.

The experience of confronting 'in role' another actor who is also 'in role' can be alarming when there has been no relaxed reading of a script or any other means of preparation for the unexpected. However, the results may well be profound. Leigh tends to lead his characters to breaking points and to dwell on the damage that humans seem to inflict upon each other in relationships but he insists that his actors base their work on careful observation of physical and psychological characteristics

Only after extensive improvisation of dialogue and scenes is the play or film scripted in any permanent form and debate continues to rage as to where, precisely, the credit for 'writing' it lies. However, like Joan Littlewood before him, Leigh's ability as a facilitator has led to his methods being employed by students and tutors to enrich the sense of characterization and to produce texts of disturbing and accurate detail.

Robert Lepage

Lepage is one of the most fascinating directors of our time with a strong commitment to devising theatre. In this process he has embraced the **RSVP Cycles** method of collaborative creation developed in San Francisco during the late 1960s. Standing for Resource, Score, Valuation and Performance, this approach uses objects, places, fragments of music or memory as its resources and stimuli for performance. The *score* consists of the material that arises from the research, discussion and improvisations undertaken by the actors and from characters, settings and events. The phase of *valuation* entails selecting, evaluating and shaping the collected material through discussion and practical engagement resulting in a performance draft. Performance, though obviously the moment when the material is shown and shared in performance is part of an ongoing process as implied by the term *cycles*. Ideas are constantly revisited, revised and reshaped in response to audience and performer feedback.

Lepage's work is usually open to many influences: his collaborative methods have led to multi- lingual pieces and a profound sensitivity to objects, spaces, metaphors and technical aspects of theatre. His pieces are frequently episodic and evolve over many years. Through the use of lighting and multi-media innovation he has created a powerfully visual theatre that has also extended into some remarkable productions of classical texts such as Strindberg's *A Dream Play* and Shakespeare's *A Midsummer Night's Dream*

Joan Littlewood

A great deal has been written about Joan Littlewood and her influence on the British theatre of the 1950s and 1960s but it is her contribution to the devising process that concerns us here. Working in the faded grandeur of a theatre in what was then one of the poorest areas of London, Joan Littlewood established her 'Theatre Workshop' as a company without 'star' performers dedicated to new plays, popular theatre techniques, improvisation and a sense of 'freshness' that she often achieved by moving the various objects on stage a few moments before the beginning of a performance. Responsible for bringing the playwrights Brendan Behan and Shelagh Delaney to the attention of London audiences through a careful reshaping of their material and the use of music hall techniques, Joan Littlewood's most successful 'devised' piece was *Oh, What a Lovely War!* for which Charles Chilton, best known for his radio drama *Journey into Space*, was eventually credited with the text. Using documentary evidence from diaries and casualty statistics that were flashed across the stage in lights, the play juxtaposed the horrific slaughter of the First World War with the pomposity and foolishness of British officer-class attitudes. Presented as a performance by a troupe of Pierrots, the play included song, comic routines, satirical sketches and 'realistic' moments of action. Taking some of her ideas from Brecht's *Mother Courage*, Joan Littlewood created a powerful piece of theatre that, almost uniquely among devised works, continues to have regular performances today.

The Market Theatre, Johannesburg

During the 1980s the Market Theatre in Johannesburg established itself not only as South Africa's most famous theatre but also as one of the major centres of artistic opposition to the apartheid regime. The playwright Zakes Mda (Kruger, 1999) made a distinction between **protest theatre**, epitomized by the plays of Athol Fugard and supported by the Market, and **theatre for resistance** that emanated from the black townships. The former, he argued, was intended to disturb relatively privileged audiences by its exposure of injustice whereas the latter represented a means for oppressed people to empower their own resistance. However, during the years that led to the eventual demolition of apartheid, the devised plays and workshop texts that were presented at the Market employed many techniques and performance styles, such as physical and verbal comedy, multiple roles and direct address to the audience to challenge the status quo in what Loren Kruger (1999) terms a theatre of testimony. Successfully integrating black and white actors, directors and writers, the theatre drew upon the real-life experiences of those who suffered under the oppressive regime and through constant workshop experimentation produced a body of work that explored every aspect of political life in South Africa.

One of the leading figures in developing the Market Theatre's unique impact was Barney Simon who had worked backstage at the Theatre Royal, Stratford East, and had seen Joan Littlewood in action, transforming texts and ideas into 'a democratic theatre event' with her workshop techniques. Collaborating with the black actors Mbongeni Ngema and Percy Mtwa, Simon created what was to become, perhaps, the Market's most powerful play, *Woza Albert* (Albert Arise, 1981). Using a vaudeville approach and a series of comic sketches linked to the idea of the Second Coming of Christ to South Africa, the devised piece showed the influences of Grotowski and Peter Brook and yet employed clowning and the sadness of the underdog to make a specific attack on the intolerable situation that might remind us of Boal's *theatre of the oppressed*.

The devising process: strategies and possibilities

In surveying a number of key practitioners in the field of devising, we have touched upon a considerable number of approaches for you to employ in devising your own piece. Many devised pieces are *autobiographical* because it is only through a level of introspection that a drama concerning the self can be created and this can often be best realized by the eventual creation of a work involving significant objects and places. In such cases the piece may involve only a single performer, but may also benefit from the use of technical additions such as voice-over, music, moving or still images or items of costume.

A great deal of devised work will have a specific audience in mind and be **site-specific**, largely because both of these factors profoundly influence the nature and shape of the material devised. Once the basic decisions concerning audience and place have been made, and the number of performers agreed, the process of devising may involve the following activities:

◆ *research*, either individual or collective, is an essential prerequisite to any devising project. This may include interviews, visits, listening to music, looking at documents, exploring performance techniques, reading or watching news items and discovering statistics. As we have seen, research will also include intensive work on establishing or creating character.

◆ *brain-storming* will enable a project to begin with a sense of energy and commitment. Ideas from all participants produced in a limited and focused period of time will ensure that the quality of the work has richness and variety. Finding ways to pool ideas is vital: one technique is literally to throw ideas (written on paper) into a circle and then survey what has come up.

◆ *improvisation* of any potential meetings, encounters, confrontations, scenes, situations or events can provide the basis of a text and enable a shape to develop. Drawing on exercises mentioned in the chapters on acting will enable participants to establish a good working atmosphere.

◆ *tableaux* can help establish key moments in a drama. 'Still' pictures of groups and individuals in a variety of situations can simulate a 'family album' of events and characters. The activity may be accompanied by 'OK' questions from the watching members of the group, i.e. questions that contain no adverse criticism but are aimed at elucidating factual answers. The tableaux can be brought to life and linked to form the foundation of a longer scene.

◆ *role-play* may be an extension of improvisation in which single performers may play multiple roles. Experiment with devices such as changes of hats or shoes to indicate changes of role. Recall the descriptions of Jean-Claude van Itallie's work.

◆ *liminality* is a concept which permeates theatre and can be explored within devised pieces. The term means 'neither here nor there' or 'in between states' and has obvious applications to acting or staging. Is the space you have 'found' a stage or is it a place for the audience? Where precisely is 'off stage' or is it that fluid imprecision that gives a space its power? Is an actor him or her self or is s/he somebody else? Is the piece to be devised durational, or does it have a precise start or finish, or is there another possibility? When does the performance begin and how does that relate to the arrival of an audience?

■ Playwriting

As a student of Theatre, you have a considerable advantage over anyone else who might wish to write a play. You have investigated many aspects of the life of the theatre and can bring skills, knowledge and understanding from your experience to the playwriting process. It is difficult to name a single successful playwright who has not been deeply involved in the theatre: we might think of Shakespeare and his company physically moving their own theatre, Sheridan who managed a major London theatre, Strindberg and Ibsen who worked in all aspects of the theatres they helped to establish, Chekhov who was so fascinated by actors that he wrote two plays about them and was constantly in the company of directors, Harold Pinter and David Hare who have acted in their own plays and David Mamet, whose play, *A Life in the Theatre* demonstrates his profound knowledge of the medium.

The craft of playwriting is not simply another branch of English Literature at which you can 'try your hand' without any concept of how performance issues impact upon the writing; it demands insights into such matters as acting, environments, staging, design and theatre technology.

However, this is not a manual of playwriting: there are many of these and accessible to those who simply wish to attempt to write plays. As a student of Theatre, you are required to reflect upon and analyse the processes in which you are involved in order that you are able to articulate your understanding. For this reason we are providing some indications of the areas in which you need to make decisions and the issues that might affect those decisions rather than provide a step-by-step guide to writing a play.

You will find that much of the advice offered in Philip Dart's article on adaptation is applicable to playwriting.

Understanding the dramatic concept

A play may take many forms but it will have been created as a *concept* in the mind and imagination of the writer. In order to make a play (and we must remind you that the term 'playwright' implies a 'maker' of plays), the creator must have a concept that enables various devices to be employed. These would include:

◆ *themes*: in the broadest sense, a play is 'about' something and although there are many examples of playwrights who are, or have been, reluctant to elaborate on their themes in interviews or writings, there needs to be some sense that the theme or themes can be identified. No audience, director or actors are likely to be engaged by a play with no discernible theme, even if that theme may be the potential for chaos or the impossibility of making sense of the Universe.

◆ *genre*: throughout this book we have stressed the multiplicity of works for the theatre but eventually you, as the playwright, must make a decision as to which genre you will employ. The most accessible genre for a novice playwright will be a short play with few characters but it may be a comedy or a tragedy even in that short space. You should refer back to our earlier section on genre on p. 123.

◆ *character*: a play in which the characters are of no interest to the audience is unlikely to be a success. The characters may be named and have fully explained situations, they may simply be known as 'I' or 'M', as in the plays of Maria Irene Fornes, or A, B and C as in some plays by David Campton, or they may be robotic figures or clowns but their words and/or actions must engage the spectator and there must be a sense in which we care about their destiny.

plot: a summary of the intended story line of a play is considered essential by potential producers. The plot should, ideally, be simple so that the dilemmas of the protagonists are clear and powerful. Unexpected 'twists' to the plot may well add a feeling of suspense and dynamic movement.

emblems: consider using images and objects that represent something other than themselves.

symbols: use objects or acts to suggest deeper meanings or unconscious or repressed conflict in the characters.

text: employ monologue, dialogue or narrative or any combination of these. Verse, prose, ritual utterance or song are all possibilities. Remember that characters rarely speak in complete sentences; they frequently pause and often pick up the cues of words spoken by the previous speaker. Other characters do not listen but all have a distinctive pattern of speech, shaped by regional, ethnic and class pressures or by personal, psychological states.

Styles of writing

The style you decide to adopt will be influenced by the subject matter and intended mode of performance. You should consider:

linear structure: in which the events follow sequentially and, probably, closely upon each other. Locations will remain largely within a small radius.

episodic structure: in which events are presented in brief episodes, including the possibility of 'flashback' or incidents that occur simultaneously or many weeks, months or even years apart. Locations may change with ease.

narrative structure: in which an actor or actors relate the events directly to an audience or intersperse acted events with monologues. Story-telling of any kind may be employed

documentary structure: in which 'real' events are both described and acted out with the use of narrative, original text from documents or from recorded media.

Constructs and conventions

The play that has been constructed in the mind of the playwright is an image or series of images that must be realized on stage. In order for this to happen, the playwright must invoke some of the **constructs** and conventions of Theatre. These may include:

a tacit agreement with the audience that they do not enter the performance space;

a tacit agreement with the audience that the boundary of the performance space may represent a wall, a window or any desired unseen object;

performers behaving as if they were not being watched or admitting that they are being observed, possibly addressing the audience directly;

◆ the passage of time indicated by a notice or some other device;

◆ the audience using their imaginations to recognize a shift of location or time;

◆ actors playing several parts;

◆ a smooth transition from dialogue into song or dance;

◆ symbolic actions or realistic events created by people known to be actors;

◆ the deliberate flouting of any of the above for dramatic effect.

It is usual, in preparing a play, to make a plot summary, a list of characters and a sample scene before submitting a draft of the entire play. This procedure from the theatre might well be followed by students and tutors with advantage so that problems can be addressed at an early stage.

■ Conclusion

In this chapter we have explored four options for the creation of a new stage work: compilation, adaptation, devising and playwriting, and have provided practical guidance for each possibility. We have emphasized the qualities that students must bring to these tasks and underlined the fact that the successful genesis of an original piece for the theatre depends on extensive knowledge and understanding of the processes of Theatre. Considerable emphasis has also been placed on the research and careful planning that must precede any writing or devising of a text for performance.

In order to demonstrate the many ways in which a performance text might evolve, we have considered the work of, and studied statements from, a wide range of successful practitioners. It is entirely possible to adopt and adapt the working methods of others but we hope that you will find your own, distinctive approach. You should have observed that our chapter presupposes that any work you may create should have the possibility of performance and that you should take advantage of the unique situation of being a student of Theatre Studies in order to experience work being shaped by practice. We have emphasized the fact that writing for the theatre is not the same as creating other literary forms and must often involve bold experiment involving the contributions of actors and other theatre practitioners.

Topics for discussion and reflection

◆ After reading Richard Hoggart's experience of playwriting on p. 120, what do you understand by the 'selfish world of the single authorial voice' and how might you work differently?

◆ List all the obvious faults in Richard Hoggart's playwriting attempt and discuss which of them you have encountered.

◆ How might you use actors' exercises as a stimulus for devising?

◆ Which aspects of Mike Leigh's work on character might you employ?

◆ What would happen if you adopted the RSVP Cycles method?

◆ How might you achieve the multi-faceted nature of Joan Littlewood's work?

◆ Would you consider using clowning or music hall techniques for a serious work?

Further reading

Ayckbourn, A. (2002) *The Crafty Art of Playmaking*, London: Faber and Faber. A practical man of the Theatre explores many aspects of 'playmaking', drawing on his highly successful plays as examples.

Brown, L. and Gawthorpe, A. (2007) *Teach Yourself: Writing a Play*, London: Hodder Education. A step-by-step guide offering sound advice.

Emmet Long, R. (ed.) (2008) *Writing: Working in the Theatre*, New York: Continuum. A rich source of ideas and opinions.

Fountain, T. (2008) *So You Want to be a Playwright*, London: Nick Hern. This and the following book, offer clear, realistic and helpful assistance to an inexperienced playwright.

Greig, N. (2005) *Playwriting: A Practical Guide*, London: Routledge.

Landes, W. (2008) *How to Get Your Play Published*, Studio City: Players Press. Although relatively few plays are published, this book provides essential information and help for writers with that ambition.

Website

For a case study on adaptation, see our website: www.palgrave.com/foundations/pickering

Undertaking a Research Project

The prospect of writing a research project can be quite daunting, partly because it will represent a very considerable commitment in time and energy and also because it may well be the most substantial piece of sustained writing you have ever undertaken. This chapter will guide you through the process but it is essential that you check with your university or college the precise requirements for word-count, format and referencing. These may differ slightly from one institution to another and no book can cover all such possible variations.

Learning outcomes

By the conclusion of this chapter, you should be able to:

▶ plan a research project;

▶ write a research paper/dissertation;

▶ understand various methods of information-gathering;

▶ use sources efficiently and correctly;

▶ plan interviews and questionnaires;

▶ conduct a **desk-based**, or field-based, project;

▶ understand the range of topics available for research;

▶ pace your work to comply with deadlines.

▇ Research in the Performing Arts

Until fairly recently, the idea of 'research' in the Performing Arts or any other subject was largely confined to post-graduate courses or to what would be termed 'graduate school' in the USA. The kind of research envisaged in such situations was largely 'desk-based' and mainly involved the use of books and documentary sources. Now, however, it is common for Theatre Studies courses and programmes to demand a final research paper or dissertation and students are frequently ill-equipped to deal with them.

There are a number of important reasons for the movement towards research in Theatre Studies. First, the subject has moved away from the shadow of English Literature and with this new-found confidence has recognized that the artefacts which provide much of the basis for research into theatre are uniquely valuable. Second, ever since practitioners such as Peter Brook established centres for 'theatre research' during the last century, there has been an emerging emphasis on 'practice as research' in theatre and those involved, including students like yourself, are expected to have a far wider perception of what constitutes the act of 'research' than hitherto.

What is research?

Richard Courtney, one of the great pioneers of in the arts in education, wrote the following helpful statement about research into the arts as long ago as 1986:

> It is often said that artists conduct research while they create and, in a popular sense, this is true. Artists discover new ways of knowing, use innovative methods to explore meaning, and are on the 'cutting edge' of the future. They focus on the mental processes of imagining, seeing possibilities and then expressing them in action in an artistic medium. That is, artists engage in experiential enquiry: they find new ways to explore knowledge as they create. This is similar to how we operate in everyday life. It is also like such techniques as 'experiential workshops' and human activity in general. What makes artists different is the medium in which their exploration takes place: their art.

(1987, p. 1)

This is as good a definition of the new concept of practice as research as you are likely to find, but there are, of course, other forms of research and those who engage in this activity as an academic profession tend to take a more limited view of what is involved. In the context of your studies, you may wish to adopt the more conventional approach in which you wish to study the creators, teachers, events or practitioners of theatre and discover if they were or are effective. In this case you will need to distance yourself from the subject and attempt to be objective and dispassionate about it. Indeed, you may see yourself more like an analytical scientist than an artist. Remember, however, that the artist and the scientist both have their own methods of discovering meaning and knowledge and no one way is more valuable than any other.

What are likely topics for research in theatre?

As we have seen in this book, the area of Theatre Studies is vast and seems to be growing in scope. Possible areas of research might be:

- theatre history: including the history of specific actors, companies or buildings;
- playwrights and their work in the theatre: to include living playwrights;
- the work of specific practitioners or theatre companies;
- styles of performance;
- performances of a particular genre;
- texts for the theatre and the media;
- particular projects undertaken by the researcher or some group or individual well known to him/her;

◇ approaches to design or technical aspects of theatre;

◇ the use of different performance spaces;

◇ costume or make-up in theatre;

◇ attitudes towards aspects of theatre;

◇ multimedia performance or the use of music or images in performance;

◇ aspects of the *mise-en-scène* in a particular context.

These are only a few of the areas you might wish to consider but there are two absolute rules to observe when making your selection: (1) be certain that you have access to the sources of information; and (2) be certain that your topic reflects your interest and is a natural extension of your work and objectives.

For example, if you decide that you wish to research the work of a living practitioner, ensure that you have access to substantial quantities of information that is not simply downloaded from the internet and, if necessary, the opportunity of seeing work at first hand or talking to key people, preferably including the subject of your study. Similarly, the study of this practitioner's work must have some relevance to your own. Will you, for instance, adopt this practitioner's methods into your work in some form?

What forms of research are open to you?

◇ *Desk-based* **research**: this is the traditional method that still has great validity and potential. It focuses on a survey of all the relevant literature available in books, journals and on the internet. Above all, this type of research demands detailed and accurate notetaking and rigorous documenting of all references. The initial stage of this form of research is always the **literature review**.

◇ *Field-based* **research**, which may include practice as research, might involve the use of various means of a gathering data. These will include **experiential** activities, surveys and questionnaires, interviews and case-studies. The results must be carefully documented and may well be presented in a way that includes recorded material. Some universities have encouraged the presentation of entire research projects on DVD.

◇ *Qualitative* **research**: this term embraces all forms of research which depend on discovering and exploring qualities, attitudes and ideas rather than on the exploration of facts that can be accurately measured. It is the most likely form for you to adopt in Theatre Studies. It could be either desk- or field-based.

◇ *Quantitative* **research**: research that depends on the accurate measurement of facts and results.

◼ Sources and data

The success of any research project will depend on two factors: (1) the nature of the sources used; and (2) the method with which data is gathered and analysed.

There are two basic kinds of source material:

1. **Primary sources**: These will be the actual products of the 'subject' of your study. They might include books, or other texts written or produced by the object of study,

records, documents or diaries by individuals or organizations, performances witnessed by the researcher, speeches given by the individual being studied. For example, if you decide to research the career of a living actor, an interview a book or a live performance of theirs will be a primary source.

2. **Secondary sources**: This is material that offers some commentary on, or critique of, the primary source. So, for example, if you were researching the work of a living actor, a book written *about* them would be a secondary source. The term is also sometimes used to describe a source to which you refer but cannot quote from directly.

3. **Supporting material**: This material will be included as an Appendix to the main study and will consist of anything you wish to supply as supporting evidence to what you have said in the text. This might include a sample of a questionnaire you have administered or the complete recording of an interview you arranged.

Methods of gathering data

Professional researchers, particularly in the Social Sciences, distinguish between two main methods of gathering the data that forms the basis of any research project. There is that data that is there waiting for you to find and that is termed **capta**. On the other hand, there is data that will only emerge if you structure a means of discovering it, and is termed **generata**.

Shulamit Reinhaz (1992) suggests 24 methods of data capture in her book *Feminist Methods in Social Research* and these include the analysis of talk and behaviour. You will notice that we have introduced the term **discourse** to embrace all forms of talk and words relating to a topic. Casual talk, structured discussion and argument, writing or passionate verbal exchange, e-mails, text messages or phone conversations are all forms of discourse. You must become adept at using all forms of discourse as a basis for research. It was, in fact, the use of Mass Observation techniques by the British government during the Second World War which led social scientists to recognize that listening to casual talk (capta) was frequently as informative and useful as gaining information from structured interviews (generata). What we are suggesting, therefore, is that some informal information gathering may be a valuable part of your research. For example, you may discover a great deal about the way in which a particular theatre company works by sitting in a theatre bar listening to the actors talking after a production or during rehearsal. This is all the more reason to maintain a notebook/journal of all your discoveries.

It is a useful exercise as you prepare your research strategy to draw up a table similar to the example shown in Table 8.1.

Table 8.1   Some types of data (evidence)

Data found or made?	Words (discourse)	Visual (images)	Interview	Observation	Documents	Other
Capta?						
Generata?						

What is discourse analysis?

In introducing the concept of discourse we are suggesting the use of what has become known as **discourse analysis** as one of the methods you will possibly need to employ. Discourse analysis, in its broadest sense, refers to an interpretative examination of how language, discourse, or discourses achieve particular effects in specific contexts. It will include a consideration of institutionalized language and what we might think of as 'jargon'. However, few discourse analysts agree on precise conceptual or operational definitions of what they are doing, how and why! There are some tensions between two 'styles' of discourse analysis in all research – discourse-as-interaction and discourse-as-practice. These styles are rooted in different philosophical traditions; they focus on different kinds of 'data' (e.g. conversations and interviews versus media texts and documents) and analyse discourse in order to answer different kinds of research questions. You may feel somewhat apprehensive about using discourse analysis but it will be well worthwhile to become ware of its possibilities.

Using the Internet

The information revolution created by the world-wide web has radically changed the face of scholarship and research. It is now possible to obtain vast areas of information and opinion by a mechanical process and, used responsibly, this is of great benefit to students of Theatre Studies. However, the fact that something appears on the internet does not necessarily mean that it is reliable or 'true'. It is as important to check the authorship of something you read on a website as it is for a book or journal. Unfortunately, authorship of internet articles is often difficult to determine and any expression of opinion should be regarded with some scepticism unless it is clearly acknowledged or attributed. The fact that it is possible to download complete articles on almost any topic has led to two major problems:

1. Students stop thinking for themselves. Remind yourself at all times that the internet is not a substitute for thought. It is an excellent means of gathering information but the use and analysis of that information remains the responsibility of the student.
2. A great temptation to commit plagiarism. College tutors and university examination boards waste hundreds of hours each year in dealing with this problem. Remember that if you attempt to pass off an internet article as your own writing the change of 'voice' will immediately be recognized and, more importantly, you will have learned and achieved nothing. Always provide the full details of any website you have used for your research.

■ Planning and presenting your research: a stage-by-stage guide

Stage 1: Establish two preliminary ways of working

◆ Note the final submission date and establish a clear set of goals and routines in order to complete your work with time to spare.

Keep a notebook/card index with you at all times and note the full details of ANY material that may be useful. If this is a book, website or article, ensure that full publication details are kept.

Stage 2: Decide on your subject in broad terms and begin to survey sources

Ensure that the topic excites you and that you can 'live with it' for several months.

Acquaint yourself with the learning resources available to you and how they operate.

Stage 3: Ensure that you have ascertained the style of presentation required

How is the research to be submitted?

What referencing system is to be used? It is now likely to be the Harvard System so ensure that you have a 'style sheet' giving full details of this or any other system used at your college.

Stage 4: Define your central research question (CRQ)

Think carefully, and read extensively, about your topic and decide what it is that you wish to discover.

Review the supporting material likely to be available to you and decide if it is adequate.

Develop your literature search.

Stage 5: Find simple, clear ways of expressing what you intend

Submit your ideas in the form of a proposal to your tutor.

Work to refine your intentions: do you aim to inform, persuade, explain, influence or make suggestions as a result of following your CRQ?

Stage 6: Define your research strategy/method

Will your work be desk-based or field-based?

Is this 'practice as research'?

What methods will you employ to gather information/data?

Stage 7: Begin your detailed research

Maintain careful notes of all your critical reading and field-based work.

Ensure that any quotations you wish to use are fully referenced and accurately copied.

◇ Carefully record the details of any websites used.

◇ Decide if the information you have begun to gather has affected your view of your CRQ. Modify it if necessary!

Stage 8: Create an outline for your research paper/dissertation

◇ An Introduction and Conclusion, together with a Bibliography, are essential.

◇ What other chapters will you need?

◇ Consider the logical structure of your research paper so that the eventual reader will be led through your discovery and thinking process easily.

Stage 9: Complete your information gathering

◇ Reading, note taking and such field-work as interviews and questionnaires must now be completed.

◇ Organize the material ready for analysis.

◇ Take time to reflect on what you have gathered/experienced and allow it to assume some shape in your mind.

Stage 10: Make a final decision on the outline of your writing

◇ Plan the contents of each chapter.

◇ Ensure that your tutor is satisfied with the CRQ and its supporting material.

◇ Prepare for the process of 'writing up' your findings by detailed timetabling of your writing schedule.

Stage 11: Analyse the results of all field-work

◇ Reflect upon what is revealed by your questions, observations, capta and generata.

◇ Begin writing those sections deriving from any field-based or practice-based research.

Stage 12: Write draft versions of each of the main chapters in turn and seek feedback

◇ Do not yet write an Introduction. You have nothing solid to introduce as yet!

◇ Give each chapter to your tutor for initial comment and remember that rewriting is an essential aspect of academic writing.

Stage 13: Compile your Bibliography and list of other sources

◆ Ensure that you list Primary sources first and Secondary sources second. List in alphabetical order and follow the precise instructions for giving details.

◆ Study examples of Bibliographies and dissertations to assist you in determining the appropriate sections.

Stage 14: Complete at least two more draft versions of your work and write the Introduction

Allow time to return to a chapter after (at least) several days' break. You will be surprised by the results.

If possible, read each chapter aloud to yourself and note where the expression seems clumsy.

Now write your Introduction!

Stage 15: Write, edit and format the final version of the entire research paper

If you are doing the final version yourself, ensure that you have complied with all the requirements. If you are using someone else to word-process and format the work, ensure that they are fully acquainted with the requirements.

Stage 16: Final Stage: Proof-read your work meticulously and then submit it

Allow time for this process.

Do not wait until the final deadline to submit your work.

Be *absolutely sure* that there are no instances of plagiarism in your project. Plagiarism is a very serious offence and will lead to the rejection of your work.

Notes on the use of this suggested set of stages

Use this to plan your work over the entire period from the moment that the project is initiated until the moment you complete it. Allocate dates for the completion of each section in conjunction with any timetable of tutorials/supervisions issued by your tutors.

Our constant emphasis on ensuring correct referencing may seem tiresome but you should remember that, as a student whose course is validated by a university, you are expected to use generally valid methods of recording information. This ensures the free flow of information and learning across the entire world.

■ Undertaking field-based research

Some guidance for interviews and questionnaires

Students frequently decide that they wish to engage with people as part of their research projects and this is to be encouraged. However, the decision to gather information and opinions through interviews and questionnaires often raises issues of protocol and research design that must be addressed. If you have decided that one of these methods of data-collection is appropriate for your research, you should keep the following questions in mind from the outset:

◆ Are the 'subjects' of any interview likely to take part willingly? We recently heard of a student who approached a famous director for an interview and, although this was granted, the first part of the resulting interview was taken up by the director reprimanding the student for disturbing him and communicating by e-mail.

◆ What is the best and most gracious way in which to approach a 'targeted' subject or group of subjects? Almost certainly this should involve a formal and polite letter.

◆ Is the request for an interview likely to cause resentment? Although many theatre practitioners welcome the interest of students and are anxious to help, there are others who regard such approaches as a tiresome intrusion or a form of exploitation.

◆ How can I plan an interview to ensure that my needs are met?

◆ Is a large enough sample, or an appropriate sample, available for a questionnaire? A few fellow students do not make up a satisfactory sample.

◆ What proportion of those approached will be likely to take part? Be prepared for many questionnaires not to be returned even though you have secured initial agreement.

■ Stages of research

Step 1: Identify Central Research Question (CRQ), Theory-Based Questions (TQs), and Interview Questions (IQs)

We have suggested that every piece of research has a **Central Research Question (CRQ)**. This is often a general question, such as 'How does a small theatre company promote ideas of social justice?' Or it can be rather practical: 'How does the director of Chalkfoot Theatre set about adapting a novel for a tour of village halls?' In either case, the CRQ identifies what you want to know.

Of course, any researcher should have read a great deal of literature on a chosen research topic. This literature typically identifies possible answers to the CRQ – and often identifies several of them. For example, if we read widely in the field of Political Theatre, we might come to the conclusion that promoting the idea of social justice through Theatre may depend on gaining access to various strands of society and that we must question those levels of organization in society that deal with such issues. Or we might want to investigate the process of adaptation for the stage but find that this seems to be linked with audience-demand. This will lead us to wish to discover how such information is obtained.

Wengraf (2001) calls such questions **Theory-Based Questions (TQs)**. After identifying one's CRQ, one needs to identify several TQs that, taken together, allow one to answer the CRQ.

The TQs that we may construct are, however, likely to be still too general. One needs to 'operationalize' them – break them down into smaller parts that real people can understand and answer. For example, it would *not* be a good idea to ask a sample of people who attend the performances by Chalkfoot Theatre in their village hall if they are influenced by 'postmodernist approaches to the found space'. Few informants speak such academic jargon, and only some of those who don't will have the courage to say, 'Huh? What's that supposed to mean?' Most will say something that sounds like an answer, but they won't really tell us much. People need to understand clearly what they are being asked, if they are to provide details.

The researcher thus needs to create a series of Interview Questions (IQ) from each Theory-Based Question (TQ). Informants' answers to these IQs should, collectively, answer the TQ. The answers to the TQs, taken collectively, should answer the CRQ.

Step 2: Turn these *Interview Questions (IQs)* into a usable interview protocol

In a development from Wengraf, Spickard (2007) suggests a further stage. Interviews need not only to be logical and clear; they also need to engage our informants. Asking a long string of rather specific questions seldom does so. It does not encourage informants to give us more than we asked for – the rich detail that enlivens their accounts and deepens our understanding of them.

Fortunately, this is relatively simple to correct. One takes the list of IQs generated, and rearranges them so that they both engage informants and flow cleanly. One may, for example, ask our potential audiences about times when they were truly inspired by the visit of a theatre company. Depending on how the story unfolds, we might then probe about the expectations that they had developed. We would certainly want to know if such stories were typical of our informants' experiences – and we can ask this directly. The point is, one can call on our informants' imaginative creativity, as well as on their logic, to get a fuller picture of their experiences.

We must ensure that our protocol includes questions, stories, or reflections that elicit answers to all of our IQs and that everything will have been covered.

One way to do this is to construct a table. Put your TQs, IQs, etc. across the top, and your interview protocol down the left side. Go through the rows, putting check marks beneath the IQs that each interview question answers. Make sure that every column has at least one check mark in it; if it does not, you need to revise your protocol so that the IQ in question gets answered.

Step 3: Interpreting the results

As you can imagine, this method keeps things clear. It reminds you why you are asking each question. And it should guarantee that you ask the right questions in the right order to get the response you need.

It has the further advantage of helping you to interpret your data. Remember that answering the IQs lets you answer the TQs, which (collectively) answer your Central Research Question. To answer any IQ, just read down the proper column, pulling together all of the answers in the rows that you have checked. Then, reading through them, you know what your informants had to say about the matter. Do that for each column, combine the IQ answers to answer the applicable TQs, and you are well on the way to having answered the question with which your project started.

By the way, it makes no difference whether you sort your interview transcripts into actual piles on the living room floor, as one did in the old days, or with the help of qualitative analysis software, The sorting logic is the same.

■ Open and closed questions

A semi-structured form of interviewing is characterized by an emphasis on relatively open questions. An **open question** invites an extensive, and possibly rambling, response. You might, for example, ask 'How do you see the value of touring theatre?' However, you may wish also to put certain **closed questions**, such as: 'What was the last touring production you saw?' Consequently, what is crucial is the capacity first to recognize the difference between open and closed questions and, second, to be able to generate the one or the other rapidly in an interview situation. It is always surprising to discover how difficult this is, not so much in theory, but rather in practice under pressure. Here, as elsewhere, preparation and planning beforehand are invaluable.

As always, the important thing is to know that some TQs require precise information that may entail closed questions, and that other TQs will require open questions. And some TQs require both. Hence, the crucial need to develop clear TQs, so that the IQs (open, closed, or a mixture of both) serve their purpose clearly.

What we have said here concerning interviews ought also to provide you with sufficient guidance as to the construction, framing and interpretation of questions on a questionnaire.

■ Approaches and methods to writing up a project

Researching and 'writing up' a project should be one of the most satisfying and enriching aspects of Theatre Studies but it does require a considerable degree of commitment and personal organization. Before we leave the subject of research we suggest that you study the following advice provided by the distinguished Theatre Historian, Paul Ranger. Although this relates to a project in Theatre History, his description of his meticulous approach to research into the theatres of Winchester would serve you well as a guide and inspiration for your own work, whatever your topic.

> Research implies an orderliness in keeping one's materials. Although the following points seem pedantic, experience has shown me the need to be systematic in collecting materials. Each theatre that I work on has its own loose-leaf binder. I can then enter into that file information relating to the building and to the companies that performed in it. With each book that I consult it has become habitual to record: the full name of the author, the full title of the book, the place

of publication and the date of publication. I also keep a marginal note of the page numbering alongside the information. It is necessary to be able to distinguish one's own summary of the information from direct quotation and here an indentation for all quotations is a useful ploy. A sturdy pocket inside the cover of each file is useful for keeping photographs safely. In addition to the theatre files, I have found a series of biography files and files relating to plays useful in my research. These are arranged in alphabetical order. As the material grows a simple cross-referencing system is necessary: an index built up on small record cards is one answer.

When I began my forays into theatre history I concentrated on one theatre in Winchester, The Market House Theatre of 1620, and eventually wrote up my researches in the *Hampshire County Magazine* (February 1974). This then expanded into a study of later Winchester theatres until the last of the managers, ruined by debts, packed the show in. An edition of the *Proceedings of the Hampshire Field Club* (1976) has been devoted to this further development. Students should consider the possibility of having off-prints made, as I have done, to form a limited edition to be sold commercially in bookshops and museums. An exhibition of playbills in the City Museum and an accompanying slide lecture helped to announce the publication. Modest trumpeting is no bad thing. Additionally I wrote, in a more popular style, articles for the local newspapers.

Expanding to work on other theatres, I discovered that, occasionally, a modern theatre manager would welcome a brief article for one of his programmes: the Theatre Royal at Windsor, for example has an attractive magazine programme, *Curtain Up*, which formed a suitable outlet for a description of Henry Thornton's management of the Windsor Theatre in the eighteenth century. Similarly the pamphlets issued by local history associations are a further means of promulgating one's researches.

Ambitious research projects are well within the range of any student with a spirit of curiosity and enquiry. It has been known for students to see their work published in limited form and for them to progress to producing substantial booklets, books and DVD features, often supporting the ambitions of local museums, theatre groups and companies. Research is an integral part of the study of the phenomenon we call Theatre and we often need to employ methods from the historian, the anthropologist, the social scientist or the literary scholar to assist in our explorations.

(This article originally appeared in the journal *Speech and Drama* and is used by kind permission of the Editor.)

Conclusion

However careful and regular their supervision, students can feel very isolated and insecure when they are finally required to undertake an individual research project: for the first time in their course of study they may have total control over the subject matter and method of study. If you are in this situation we hope that this chapter will have provided the help and reassurance you need and we would draw your attention to extensive suggestions for further reading as additional sources of help. We have outlined the various potential areas of study for a student of Theatre Studies and have considered a number of research strategies, giving particular attention to notoriously difficult areas.

In providing a suggested plan for the writing of a research paper or dissertation we are very aware that there will be differences in time-scales and expectations. However, we have sought to establish the principle that 'to fail to plan is to plan to fail' and have underlined the fact that it is entirely your responsibility to adhere to required deadlines and formats, to discover the expected method of referencing and to avoid plagiarism.

Topics for discussion and reflection

◆ What constitutes a realistic CRQ (Central Research Question) for the culmination of a Theatre Studies course or programme?

◆ How do mechanical means of recording contribute to our ability to 'study' Theatre?

◆ What are the problems involved in administering questionnaires?

◆ Compare experiences in conducting interviews as a means of research.

◆ What resources are available to you for the conduct of 'desk-based' research?

◆ What are the advantages and shortcomings of the system of referencing used at your university or college?

■ Further reading

Bell, J. (1999) *Doing Your Research Project*, Milton Keynes: Open University Press. This, and the two following books, will provide a systematic guide to any research project relating to aspects of Theatre.

May, T. (2001) *Social Research: Issues, Methods and Process*, 3rd edn, Buckingham: Open University Press.

Neuman, W. (2006) *Social Research Methods*, Boston: Pearson International.

Seale, C., Gobo, G., Gubrium, I. and Silverman, D. (2004) *Qualitative Research Practice*, London: Sage. A particularly clear treatment of what is often a vague area of research.

Spickard, J. (2006) *How to Construct an Interview Protocol*, London: University of East London. A most helpful approach to one of the most frequently misused aspects of research.

Taylor, G. (1989) *The Students' Writing Guide for the Arts and Social Sciences*, Cambridge: Cambridge University Press. Provides stimulating and practical support for any student lacking confidence in writing.

■ Website

For the full details of Dr. Ranger's Theatre History project, see our website: www.palgrave.com/foundations/pickering

CHAPTER

9 # Audiences and Spectators

In his lecture entitled 'The Play Is in the Air', the dramatist David Hare said: 'A play is not actors, a play is not a text; a play is what happens between the stage and the audience.' Much of this chapter will be an exploration of the validity of this statement and will demand considerable critical thinking on your part. We have seen from the outset that the audience is so vital an element of Theatre that it cannot be said to exist without it. It is remarkable, therefore, that Theatre Studies has traditionally taken so little active interest in the nature and function of audiences and many students embark upon the devising or rehearsal of performance pieces with little or no thought for the audience-experience that their work will lead to. We shall be illustrating our points with examples that you should consider with care.

Learning outcomes

By the conclusion of this chapter, you should be able to:

◆ develop a discourse on the subject of audiences;

◆ cite historic examples of differing actor/audience relationships;

◆ explain the growing emphasis on manipulation of the audience;

◆ discuss how audiences 'read' a play, using insights from communication studies and critical theory;

◆ recognize, and respond to, the importance of the audience in your own practical work;

◆ account for a progression from audience to spectator;

◆ discuss examples of plays that seem to indicate particular attitudes and intentions towards audiences;

◆ explore the relationship between performance spaces and audiences.

■ The importance of the audience

Why should a highly successful modern playwright like David Hare wish to draw our attention to the chemistry between stage and audience as if it were the life-blood of a play and why do so many contemporary productions take audiences to unexpected places both literally and metaphorically? There are two possible explanations:

1. The development of the 'laboratory' and 'research' approach to theatre in the hands of such practitioners as Joan Littlewood and Grotowski has progressively stripped theatre bare of many of its traditional 'overlays' such as scenery, lighting or other aspects of 'production', leaving only the actor and the audience as all that it needed for theatre to take place. In this context, many theatre practitioners have increasingly seen the audience as integral to a performance, rather than as a group of passive observers.

2. The recorded media – film, television, DVD, and, to some extent, radio – have usurped many of the areas that traditionally belonged to the theatre. Spectacular effects, close-ups, lavish costumes, transformations of all kinds are easily achieved by technological devices but the one thing the media cannot achieve is the live interaction between performer and audience. Even when a studio audience is imported, its function is strictly regulated and the constant awareness of the camera profoundly affects the ways in which audiences react.

It would appear, then, that only the live theatre retains the performer and the audience as unique features and a growing awareness of this fact has led to many new experiments in the creation of theatrical events. In order to illustrate and explore this development let us consider two examples of productions attended by the authors of this book 50 years apart. The first took place in 1956 and may now read like the description of an event from a world that has almost entirely disappeared: a 'tea matinée' in the weekly schedule of a repertory theatre. What was known as 'weekly rep' provided a training ground for many successful actors and the rhythm of daytime rehearsals of one play, and evening performances of another, together with matinees on certain afternoons, was an established tradition. The paying audiences relied on local publicity and word of mouth to discover the name of the next play.

Read the following detailed account of a performance event carefully:

It is 3 p.m. at a seaside resort on the coast of Britain and an audience of two hundred or so people (mainly fairly elderly) has gathered in a theatre built just behind the promenade on the seafront. They know that they have come to see the matinee performance of a new 'thriller' and, in the comfortable stalls of plush red they wait with some expectancy for the curtain to rise to reveal the opening 'picture' on the proscenium stage.

Many of the audience are frequent supporters of this theatre; there is a new production of a play each week and they are so familiar with the actors who appear regularly in the various plays that they almost feel they know them.

Some of the audience sit in an upper gallery that runs around three sides of the theatre. This necessitates sitting in what are virtually padded 'dining room chairs' and, for those at the sides, having to look sideways towards the stage, of which they may only obtain a partial view. This discomfort, however, is cheerfully accepted as part of the experience of attending a performance in the longest-running repertory theatre in the country.

Recorded music is played as the audience gathers, some of whom place orders at the box office for later refreshments. As the music fades and the house lights dim, a hush replaces the animated chatter of the audience. As the curtain rises to reveal an interior setting of a room (constructed with painted wood and canvas) with the view of a garden outside the 'french windows' the audience applauds the scenery as a maid and a butler move around the interior of the room. Only when the applause has died down does the dialogue between the two characters begin. At this point some of the stage 'business' involves the maid coming downstage and apparently lighting a fire in an unseen fireplace that clearly exists in the '**fourth wall**' of the room through which the audience watches the action. There is some amused but discreet laughter when some members of the audience notice a puff of white powder rising from the head of the butler as he moves. This is a young cast member who has 'greyed' his hair and the audience recognize him as the same actor who played the gardener and the detective in the previous production.

In as many aspects as possible the play performance is 'realistic': real cups and saucers, real telephones, real lamps on tables, real furniture; all of which evoke a genteel image of an England that might have recently passed, but that 'reality' is temporarily shattered when the 'leading man' enters. Most people in the audience know that he is the manager of the theatre company that presents the season of plays and that he invariably plays the main part. Very often his wife plays the female lead. His appearance is greeted with yet another round of applause that he acknowledges with a slight

nod of the head. He then engrosses himself in the plot, only demonstrating an awareness of the presence of the audience by never turning his back on them and projecting his voice so that every line of his dialogue is heard. Even when he forgets one of his lines and asks for a prompt and thanks the prompter before continuing, the audience applauds him.

As the action of this 'murder mystery' progresses, the audience responds with laughter, gasps and very quiet whispers to neighbours and the excitement and tension engages them so entirely that the interval arrives almost without their being aware of the passage of time. The safety curtain is lowered and the audience begins to discuss what they have seen.

However, for those sitting in several of the Stalls seats, the interval brings yet another part of the entire event. The usherettes employed by the theatre bring trays of sandwiches, cake and tea and the audience members who have ordered this luxury now fix their trays to the rear of the seat in front of them and begin to consume their 'afternoon tea'.

Those members of the audience continue to eat sandwiches and cake or pour tea long after the curtain has risen for the second half of the play and there is a quiet background sound of their activity throughout the rest of the play.

When the play finally comes to an end with a resolution of the mystery, the audience have seen action take place in several locations because the 'flats' on which the scenery is painted can be reversed or moved to reveal another setting. As the applause is in full flow, the leading actor steps forward to quieten the audience. He thanks them for attending and tells them about the next play that opens on the following Tuesday (Monday is always reserved for final dress and technical rehearsals). The audience then leaves the theatre without any further interaction with the actors.

Now compare the experience, expectations and probable attitudes of the audience at the 'tea matinee' with those of the audience described in the following performance that was offered as part of higher degree studies by an experienced practitioner who had devised the entire concept and performance. The audience consisted of an invited group of friends and scholars in the field of Theatre Studies. The event took place in 2006.

A group of about 12 people has gathered outside a small hotel because they have been invited to attend a performance of a new play. There appears to be no means by which this small 'audience' can enter the hotel because the main entrance is closed. However, at the precise time when the performance is due to begin a well-dressed woman appears at the door and invites the waiting people to follow her into an inner courtyard where a drinks reception involving six people is already taking place. Some of the 'audience' accept the offer of a glass of wine.

The six 'actors' (because that is what they turn out to be) are engrossed in fairly animated conversation as they stand around with their drinks and the audience moves as comfortably close as possible in a confined space. After a while, however, two of the 'characters' appear to be involved in a violent argument and storm off into the building and they are heard climbing the stairs. Others follow and the audience is made to follow too. Still aware of shouting and argument in the distance, the audience is led into a bedroom on the second floor and asked (or subtly enticed) to sit on a large double bed that occupies much of the room. As they sit there,

they become aware of some of the people they have seen earlier rushing into the room, gathering items of clothing and disappearing again. The two who had started such a fierce argument make spasmodic, separate appearances but then those sitting on the bed become aware of a mounting climax of verbal exchange between them in some distant room and there is a constant sound of loud footsteps and movement.

After what seems like a very long time the 'audience' sitting on the bed notices that a television screen mounted in the corner of the room has come to life and they can see what is going on in one of the bedrooms.

Some of the snippets of overheard conversation have combined to suggest that the event is actually a pre-nuptial party and that the two engaged in argument are the prospective bride and groom. The audience now witnesses a strange sexual ritual in which the woman asks to be tied to a bed while the man makes love to her in slow motion. However, the image fades from the screen and the onlookers are led by one of the original party-goers down to a larger room where they are all given a drink and invited to take part in a discussion of the performance.

Suggested activity

Now that you have studied both descriptions critically, consider and/or discuss the audience experience of both events using the following headings:

◆ the relative 'value' of the theatrical experiences;
◆ socio-economic factors determining the make-up of the audience;
◆ the probable reactions of the two audiences;
◆ the causes of the differences in approach by the actors to the two audiences;
◆ why the events, 50 years apart, appear so different;
◆ all the factors that may have brought about the changes;
◆ how you would react to an 'after-show' discussion in either production?;

◆ in each case, who largely determined the nature of the audiences' experience?;
◆ the relationship between the nature of the performance spaces and the audience experience;
◆ the theatrical conventions present or absent in the two descriptions;
◆ which style of production and attitude toward the audience is likely to most nearly reflect the work with which you are familiar?;
◆ the relationship between the performers and the audience;
◆ the point at which the performers considered the audience as a factor during their preparation for the performance;
◆ why **weekly rep** appealed to many people and why it hardly exists today.

The complex issues to which you have applied some critical thinking are typical of the many considerations that permeate discourse about the theatre and we can trace their gradual changes through study of plays themselves.

The intellectual climate, or *Zeitgeist*, that affects a playwright may also be expected to shape the opinions of an audience. It follows, then, that the assumptions and composition of such audiences comprise an essential element in establishing a contextual understanding of a play. We are now used to the idea that the approach to the audience is determined by the director or theatre company but we must not overlook the way in which audiences influence the texts of the plays themselves. The act of writing a play involves commitment to communication with a public: every playwright craves a public hearing for his or her work. However much playwrights may shun publicity, disregard reviews or hate watching their work performed, their aim is invariably to provoke a response from their live audience. Playwrights may despise their public, or wish to shock them; more commonly they will aim to please them; but, whatever their attitude, their awareness of their audience will shape the way in which they write.

Students of Theatre and those who are considering the production of a play need to be able to determine something of a playwright's attitude to his or her audience, together with the ideological assumptions, social and economic conditions under which that audience may live.

As an example, we can take some of Strindberg's remarks about his audience from a letter to Adolph Paul in 1907: '*Miss Julie* (without an intermission) has gone through its ordeal by fire and shown itself to be the kind of drama demanded by the impatient men of today: thorough but brief' (Strindberg, 1976b, p. 3). Strindberg's sense of 'impatient men' composing his audience was very different from George Etherege's ideas of the people for whom he wrote *The Man of Mode* that we considered in Chapter 6. These were members of fashionable society who brought a far more casual attitude towards sexual behaviour to the theatre. Etherege's audience were in no hurry; they could afford to listen with mild amusement to a lengthy prologue written by Sir Car Scroope, Baronet. This included an appeal to the audience not to be too severe in their judgement, asked for sympathy for 'poor poets' (playwrights) and made reference to imported tastes in French fashion and dancing.

The study of audiences, and of playwrights' attitudes towards them, is thus an important step in recreating any 'period' play for a performance in a modern theatre. This fact emerges very clearly when we come to Shakespeare, although many would argue that his plays transcend the considerations of their original performance conditions.

▮ Shakespeare's audience

In our chapter on theatre spaces we have already considered some of the implications of performance in the permanent theatre building current at the time of Shakespeare. Scholars continue to dispute the authorship of the plays that appear under the name of William Shakespeare but, whoever he was, we can ascertain from his plays that he was steeped in the life of the theatre. In addition to demonstrating an awareness of and a facility for exploiting the physical nature of the theatres and audiences of his day he also reveals experience of performance in more private venues such as great halls and, possibly, palaces and other found spaces. For, as Yvonne Adams (2008) has pointed out:

> Elizabethan stage performances inevitably bring to mind the wooden 0 as exemplified by the Globe, the Rose, and the Swan on London's south bank. But these purpose-built theatres were by no means the only venues where audiences gathered to participate in the ever popular activity of play going. Amongst buildings used or adapted for occasional stage performances were inns, town halls, guildhalls, churches and chapels, Oxford and Cambridge college halls, Inns of Court, private houses and royal palaces – in fact any building which had room to accommodate actors and their accompanying stage properties and provide space for an audience. Outdoor venues included the market place, village greens, college courts, churchyards, tilt-yards, and even streets. All these sites, of course, predate the purpose-built theatre by many years, some of them even by centuries.
>
> (Marlowe Society *Newsletter*, p. 6)

Shakespeare's plays are permeated by references to plays, players and playhouses: he often refers to actors as 'shadows' and uses the theatre as a metaphor for life itself. However, he was keenly aware of his audiences. In *Henry V* for example, his **Chorus** figure addresses members of the theatre audience directly and asks them to employ their imaginations within 'this wooden O'. Both *The Tempest* and *A Midsummer Night's Dream* conclude with an appeal for applause and include scenes where a play is presented to an 'on-stage audience'. But it is in *Hamlet* and *A Midsummer Night's Dream* that we find the most extensive references to the audiences for plays and it is in these two plays that groups of actors visit a court to give their performances.

In Shakespeare's *Hamlet*, the young prince of that name is given to believe that the current King, his uncle, has murdered his father, the former King, and married his mother. Hamlet, a university student with a passion for theatre, is delighted when he hears that a troupe of actors is about to visit the castle and the prospect of their coming lifts his state of depression to some extent. Much of the fascination of the play lies in a study of Hamlet's inability to act upon the knowledge of his uncle's deed and he constantly procrastinates and seeks reassurance and confirmation. One way in which he hopes to prove his uncle's guilt is to arrange for a performance of a play to which the court will be invited and to insert into the action a speech that will challenge the conscience of the king (Act II Sc. 2). Incidentally, the title that Hamlet gives this play, *The Mousetrap*, has become part of modern theatre history because of its association with one of the longest-running plays ever in London's West End.

On his second meeting with the players (Act III Sc. 2), Hamlet delivers a speech of advice to the actors and this speech has been much quoted and examined as containing Shakespeare's opinions on acting and the nature of drama itself. You should certainly familiarize yourself with it for these reasons alone, but it also contains significant references to audiences. At one point in the speech where Hamlet is urging a more restrained acting style, he suggests that some actors: 'split the ears of the groundlings, who, for the most part, are capable of nothing but inexplicable dumb-shows and noise'.

The groundlings were the poorer theatre-goers who stood on the ground in the open courtyard of the theatre, where there was no flooring or seating. Hamlet is assuming that they constitute the least cultivated part of the audience and are usually only able to appreciate the action of the **'dumb-show'**, a mimed version of a story.

At a later point in the speech Hamlet, who has continued to recommend an acting style that is not 'overdone' says:

> Now this, overdone, or come tardy off, though it make the unskilful laugh, cannot but make the judicious grieve; the censure of which one must, in your allowance, o'er weigh a whole theatre of others.

(ll. 23–7)

Here, we see Shakespeare's (Hamlet's) awareness of the views of of a more discerning type of playgoer and Hamlet continues in this vein when he suggests that the clowns in the play should refrain from improvised dialogue because these antics will 'set on some quantity of barren spectators' to laugh too; though, in the meantime, some necessary question of the play was then to be considered.

Interestingly, Shakespeare uses the term 'spectators', that is 'watchers', to refer to the least attentive part of the audience and the speech implies the desirability of intellectual engagement with the language and substance of the play. The idea of careful listening was obviously at odds with the potential for rowdiness in the audience. Modern audiences attending performances at 'recreated' Shakespearean theatres, such as the Globe, often have difficulty in knowing how to behave as groundlings and modern actors might well find themselves discomfited if a high level of authenticity were to be reproduced in this regard.

When the play is finally performed at the court (Act III Sc. 2. l. 85 onwards), it has the desired effect and the king flees noisily from the room. This is a small audience and an intimate performance of the kind that Shakespeare's own company must have experienced. The spoken text of the play is preceded by a dumb-show revealing the manner of the murder of the previous king by the pouring of poison in his ear while he was asleep in the orchard. Although scholars can find little evidence that it was current theatre practice to duplicate the plot through both dumb-show and text, in *Hamlet* it is clearly designed to create mounting pressure on the one member of the audience at whom it is principally aimed.

Suggested activity

As an exercise in practice as research answer the following questions by considering Act III Sc.2 of *Hamlet* from line 49 onwards:

◆ Where is the **play-within-a-play** staged?
◆ Who attends?
◆ Where do they sit/stand in relation to the action?
◆ How might this affect the 'real' audience watching *Hamlet*?
◆ How does Hamlet ask his friend Horatio to behave?
◆ How does he react to this?
◆ Do the actors appear to have taken the advice offered by Hamlet earlier in the play?
◆ What is your reaction to Hamlet's behaviour towards the Queen and Ophelia?
◆ At what point does the dumb-show or play disturb the king?
◆ How and when is this shown?
◆ How effective is theatre as a means of disturbing the conscience of the audience?

■ The on-stage audience: an extended activity

By far the most extensive treatment of the subject of theatre audiences in Shakespeare occurs in his play *A Midsummer Night's Dream* and this repays some in-depth consideration. Like *Hamlet*, the play is set in a court at which a group of actors present a play: in the case of *Hamlet*, they are a professional troupe, whereas in the *Dream*, they are a group of enthusiastic amateurs.

This group of craftsmen or 'mechanicals', as they are called, have met in a wood outside Athens to rehearse a play which they hope will be presented at court as part of the celebrations of the marriage of Duke Theseus. The play they are rehearsing is a version of the story of the doomed lovers Pyramus and Thisbe and in the early scenes of their involvement they struggle with some of the conventions of theatre. How, for example, will they construct or represent a wall? How will Pyramus and Thisbe whisper through this wall? How will they convey the idea of moonshine? What effect will a lion have on the female members of the audience and how can this be offset? You can explore the proposed answers to these issues and the group's preparation of the performance in Act I Sc. 2 and Act III Sc. 1.

The actors are constantly concerned with their effect on their audience: Bottom, who takes the tragic role, intends to move them to tears; Quince, who is the 'teller' (the organizer of the play with the only complete text) is anxious not to terrify them; Bottom realizes that his death by his own sword may upset the ladies; Snout proposes that a prologue must explain that the actor playing the lion is not a lion but a man; Bottom, however, suggests that the lion could have a gap in his costume through which he can explain that he is not, actually, a lion. Obviously their inexperience leads them to doubt the power of conventions with which the sophisticated audience to whom they will perform will be familiar. It is this clash of cultural expectations that lies at the heart of the comic elements of these scenes.

In Act V Sc. 1, we see Shakespeare dwelling equally on the performance and the on-stage audience and for this reason we suggest that you should begin by reading rapidly the two scenes we have briefly described and then embark on a detailed scrutiny of the text.

The context of the scene

After a series of misunderstandings and adventures in the woods, four lovers, Lysander and Hermia, Demetrius and Helena, have come to the court where their nuptials will be celebrated at the same time as that of Duke Theseus and Hippolyta, the Amazon Queen. The entire court is seeking entertainment and the group of amateur players led by Peter Quince have offered their play as part of this process.

On a first reading consider the following questions:

◆ How many characters are on stage at the start of this scene?

◆ What are their roles?

◆ Where are they?

◆ What is the difference in attitude between Theseus and Philostrate?

What can be learned about Elizabethan plays and theatre from the text and any notes in any edition you may be using?

What examples of direct address to the audience are encountered?

Why does Theseus say that he will 'hear' the play? What would you say in a similar situation today?

What examples of interaction with the audience are given? Which are intended and which unexpected?

What is your first impression of the constant comments by the audience?

At this point you should aim to 'workshop' the scene, deciding the precise physical positions of the on-stage audience and the actors in the play-within-the-play. Try to experience and understand the nature of the audience's interjections and the effect these have on the actors. Notice the verbosity and complexity of the 'wit' of the onlookers and decide on your reaction to their behaviour. Enjoy the slapstick humour of the scene and use your physical and vocal resources and skills to create a committed performance by the 'mechanicals'. Total engagement with, and focus on, the task will result in your appreciating more profoundly the effect of the presence of the on-stage audience but you will also need to consider the off-stage audience for whom the performance is intended. Was Shakespeare making some telling points about the behaviour of audiences he had encountered by this scene? After your research, answer the following questions:

What is the effect of acting when there is no darkened auditorium and the audience pass frequent comment in full view and hearing of the performers?

Is this on-stage audience trying to impress by its verbal wit?

How does this audience compare to that described in the 'hotel' performance in the early part of this chapter?

What are the essential differences between private and public performances?

What is the importance of the discourse concerning acting, shadows and imagination between Theseus and Hippolyta?

What impression of Theseus as a theatre-goer or patron of the arts do you form? How does his attitude compare with that of the other characters as a member of an audience?

Compare the first meeting of the 'mechanicals' for rehearsal with the scene of their eventual performance. There are considerable developments; what do you imagine took place in the rehearsals we are not shown?

Why do we no longer go to 'hear' a play?

The expression to 'hear' a play was common in Shakespeare's day and, in fact, it persisted well into the seventeenth century when the diarist Samuel Pepys recorded that he would go to 'hear a play'. The prologues and epilogues of plays from the same period suggest that the thrust of theatre was largely achieved through language and dialogue, although there was no shortage of physical action. This was an important factor in ensuring that one of the considerations in the design and construction of new theatres was their acoustics. The fact that both Restoration plays cited in our brief consideration of prologues and epilogues referred to playwrights as 'poets' also emphasized the literary nature of theatre which continued well into the eighteenth century.

Some scholars would maintain that it was the gradual development of theatre technology in the eighteenth and nineteenth centuries that led to our current practice of saying that we will 'see a show', rather than 'hear a play'. Early experiments in stage lighting during the time of the great actor-manager David Garrick resulted in the idea of darkening the auditorium and lighting the stage. Before that time actors and audience had usually shared a commonly lit space. The lighting of the stage and the growing complexity of scenic construction and stage machinery made possible a range of effects and images that had been unthinkable in Shakespeare's day or in the Restoration theatre and, by the nineteenth century, plays were able to depend on both visual and verbal elements equally. In the popular theatre this resulted in shows that were almost exclusively visual and even Shakespeare was cut and reduced savagely in order to accommodate spectacular scene changes or the use of real horses and rabbits Towards the end of the nineteenth century the introduction of more comfortable (and expensive) seats changed the audience's behaviour to the relatively quiet and attentive state most familiar today. In this atmosphere, and with the wide use of lighting, playwrights such as Ibsen were able to exploit subtle and frequent light 'states', varied scenic backings, interior settings of great detail and audiences prepared to follow the arguments of their plays.

■ Theatre audiences

Imagine, for example, the audience brought together for the production of Chekhov's *The Seagull* in 1898. Drawn from the Moscow intelligentsia, this group shared an interest in a new theatre that had only been open for a few months and that claimed by its name to be offering a new repertoire of high artistic standards for a broad audience – the People's Art Theatre, as the future Moscow Art Theatre was then known. They did not share the common religious beliefs of a medieval audience watching a Mystery Play. Indeed, some of them would have been atheists or agnostics and some believers. The multitude of new attitudes to religious belief in late nineteenth-century Russia is made abundantly clear in Dostoyevsky's novel *Crime and Punishment* (1865).

But Chekhov's audience did share the belief that the latest developments in artistic style were important enough to merit serious, even reverential consideration. When Stanislavsky came to describe the opening night he spoke of 'a roar in the auditorium' and a production that had 'held the audience mute for a time before it began to roar and thunder in mad ovation' (2008b, p. 356).

The reaction described clearly suggests a collective state of mind in which a group of people, lost in rapt attention to what they are witnessing, wake, as it were from a dream at the end of the performance, It is almost as if they are the same audience that Puck has in mind when he says in the final speech of Shakespeare's *A Midsummer Night's Dream*:

> Think but this, and all is mended –
> That you have but slumbered here
> While these visions did appear.

> (Act V Sc. 1)

They then take some time to recover their critical faculties which eventually find expression in applause. This was an audience that did not expect to participate in a sense of communal celebration of belief, as a medieval audience might have done, nor engage in the soliciting and other activities familiar from Pepys' Diaries in the Restoration era. Instead, it came for the pleasure of losing itself in a fiction presented with maximum realism through the use of acting-styles and technology. As we have seen, in order to achieve this sensation, the auditorium lighting was not left on, as mainly it was until the nineteenth century; thus the audience felt itself to be observing a 'slice of (real) life' which seemed to take place as if they were not there and whose participants never realized that they knew they were being watched.

This audience/performer relationship became the model for many 'art' theatres all over the world in subsequent years and is chiefly defined by the audience's concept of what constitutes dramatic art. The pleasure its members expect to derive from a visit to the theatre will not necessarily be related to the play which absorbs them. It will also depend on a sense of belonging to an elite group that is aware of, and interested in, the latest developments in theatre. However, this social function is firmly subordinated to the belief in the value of the work of art. Such an audience, whatever Strindberg's view, is prepared for a play that demands a lengthy and intense period of attention. From experience, it was accustomed to witnessing a single dramatic episode involving the same small group of people inhabiting a single location, usually a drawing room or apartment similar to the one they have left behind in their own homes. The visit to the play, therefore, flatters their belief that important events do indeed occur within their social stratum and in the special space which they have created for themselves.

Alternative models

In his now classic book, *A Good Night Out* ([1981] 1996), the late John McGrath, former director of 7:84 Theatre Company, evokes a working-class audience which contrasts very sharply with the middle-class audiences we have met for Chekhov or the 'tea matinée'. With great humour and without condescension, the writer stresses the vitality and participation of a working-class audience in a club or bar but also shows its unwillingness to pay attention unless it is totally convinced that what is being presented actually concerns it.

Brecht was particularly critical of the self-importance of the established middle-class audience and, working in the German theatre during the 1920s, he sought to draw upon the qualities of popular working-class entertainment. He complained of:

> All those establishments with their excellent heating systems, their pretty lighting, their appetite for large sums of money, their imposing exteriors together with the entire business that goes on inside them, all this doesn't contain five pennyworth of fun.

('Emphasis on Sport', in Willet, 1964, p. 7)

Brecht's ideal audience was like the public at a boxing or soccer match: passionately involved in the action, yet able to stand back and take a dispassionate view of the skills of the participants. In his Preface to the play, *In the Jungle of Cities*, (1923), he outlined his ideas: 'Don't worry your heads about the motives for the fight, concentrate on the stakes. Judge impartially the technique of the contenders and keep your eyes fixed on the finish.'

Just as a boxer or a musician tries to show off his or her technique, so Brecht wanted theatrical techniques and means to be clearly visible to his audience. From this desire emanated all those familiar aspects of his production style: the curtain only half-lowered that did not hide the preparations, the use of very bright lighting from visible sources and an acting style that aimed to 'demonstrate' rather than 'incarnate'.

Brecht's concept of the relationship between actors and audience was developed and refined during the 1920s and early 1930s during which he was becoming convinced that he must take sides in the political struggle dividing Germany. In such circumstances, it seemed vital to prevent his audiences from identifying themselves with rapt and dream-like attention to the events being portrayed. Thus, his model became the club, café or bar audience that McGrath later discussed. Such an audience retained its detachment and independence of mind and was prepared to intervene if it disagreed with, or objected to, what was being presented on stage. Accordingly, Brecht wrote a number of plays specifically designed for production in schools, halls or workers' clubs with the intention that they would provoke political discussion. In Brecht's view, far from making theatre performance boring, this type of approach could re-introduce some of the fun that he had found missing in middle-class theatre. He anticipated that his audience would experience a particular pleasure in discussing, learning and confronting new ideas:

> The theatre of the scientific age is able to make dialectics pleasurable. The surprises of development as it proceeds logically or by leaps and bounds, the instability of all states, the humour of contradictions, etc., these are enjoyments of the vitality of men, things and processes, and they heighten the art of living.
>
> ('Appendix to *Short Organum*', in Cole, *Playwrights on Playwriting*: 84)

The idea that theatre is a means for the communication of Marxist philosophies has since been adopted by a number of British writers, but for David Hare this aspect of Brecht's influence has been a negative factor because, he maintains, 'the questions have been answered before the play has begun'. The Marxist playwright, he argues:

> thinks that because the play itself is part of the class struggle, he must first say which side he is on and make that clear, before he proceeds to lay out the idea of the play as fairly as he may. To me this approach, is rubbish; it insults the audience's intelligence; more important, it insults their experience; most important, it is also a fundamental misunderstanding of what a play is ... a play is a performance. So, if a play is to be a weapon in the class struggle, then that weapon is not going to be the things you are saying; it is the interaction of what you are saying and what the audience is thinking.
>
> ('The Play is in the Air', 2005a, p. 118)

■ The audience and its conscience

After his first meeting with the players who arrive at the castle of Elsinore, Hamlet finally resolves on a plan to trap the King's conscience:

> I have heard
> That guilty creatures sitting at a play
> Have, by the very cunning of the scene,

> Been struck so to the soul that presently
> They have proclaimed their malefactions;

(Act II Sc. 2)

As he describes how he will insert a speech into the play and observe the King's reaction, he concludes:

> The play's the thing
> Wherein I'll catch the conscience of the king.

(Act II Sc. 2)

The effect of this rhyming couplet as an exit line in memorable and it highlights the use of theatre as means of stirring the conscience. We have already seen how the Market Theatre in Johannesburg employed what Zakes Moda termed '**protest theatre**' to disturb the consciences of white audiences in the era of apartheid. Perhaps an even more remarkable example of a protest against racial discrimination was the kind of audience envisaged by the playwright Jean Genet when he wrote his play *The Blacks* in 1959. This is a rare example of a play that goes so far as to specify that it has been designed for performance to a particular audience:

> This play, written, I repeat, by a white man, is intended for a white audience, but if – which is unlikely – it is ever performed before a black audience, then a white person, male or female, should be invited every evening. The organizer of the show should welcome him formally, dress him in ceremonial costume and lead him to his seat, preferably in the front row of the stalls. The actors will play for him. A spotlight should be focussed upon this symbolic white throughout the performance.

(Preface to the published edition, trans. Frechtman, 1960)

The Preface demonstrates an exceptionally sensitive attention by the playwright to the function of the audience in constructing a meaning for his play. The reason for the insistence on the presence of a white audience is that his play is not a story but a ritual: it does not describe events, it attacks attitudes. The theatre event produced by the play is a ceremony for exorcising the often shameful European, or white, view of black or African people. The ceremony is directed at the traditional white-skinned view that black skins represent the primitive, the obscure and the threatening. The ceremony aims to realize as fully as possible these figments of the white imagination in order, ultimately, to destroy them. Since it does not represent the reality of black people, but only the image imposed upon them by white people, it is essential to have a white audience for this act of protest.

Genet, in fact, requires a quality in his audience that is very much akin to the quality of belief in a medieval audience. The images presented on stage only acquire force as a result of the beliefs of the white audience. If we were to ask what kind of pleasure the audience might expect to derive from attending a performance of *The Blacks*, the answer must also be couched in almost religious terms. It is certainly not the pleasure of flattery that we noted in Chekhov's audience, or the sense of self-indulgence. In this play and many subsequent plays that challenge the conscience, it can only be described as the pleasure of seeing an indefensible myth undermined and exploded from within and the sense of release that may come from recognizing the evils embedded in one's own culture.

Audiences may well have experienced something similar when seeing David Hare's play *The Permanent Way* which exposed the scandalous neglect of Britain's railways to which so many of the population have directly or indirectly contributed, or when leaving the production of the play *Baby Killer*, by the American playwright Steve Wilmer. This play explores the corrupt fashion in which a global corporation persuades mothers in developing countries to use their powdered milk product. When it was first presented, the audience, no doubt aware of their tacit support for this company through their purchase of coffees and chocolate, left in total silence.

The Theatre of Cruelty

We have already encountered Artaud's concept in Chapter 5 but his ideas have particular relevance to our discussion of audiences. He wished the audience to be 'encircled' so that direct contact could be made. Seated in the centre of the action in swivel chairs, the audience would change their focus according to the movement of the drama around the hall which he hoped would be architecturally similar to a 'holy place'. There was to be no vacuum in the audience's 'mind of sensitivity' (Artaud, 1968, p. 84): their attention was to be persistent and persistently committed. 'Intensities of colour, light or sound . . . vibrations and tremors, tonality of light . . . tremoring gestures' were to fuse, to create discords and to envelop the whole space and people so that the experience was immediate and primal, 'as exactly localised as the circulation of the blood through our veins' (1968, p. 70).

Artaud sought 'true magic' and the 'hypnotically suggestive mood where the mind is affected by direct sensual pressure' (1968, p. 84). However, the performance was not aimed at involving only the minds or the senses of the audience but their 'entire existence', plumbing and revealing 'the most secret recesses of the heart'. Artaud likens the experience he aimed to create to that of a snake being charmed: 'I intend to do to the audience what snake-charmers do and to make them reach even the subtlest notions through their organism.' He had argued that is was not just the music that affects a snake but the vibrations in the ground with which the creature comes into contact through its long body.

It is this profound and complete audience experience which characterized what Artaud called his Theatre of Cruelty, a theatre in which the 'unconscious' was to be liberated and the individual's inner driving force revealed and recognized: a state that many seek to achieve through therapy. It was to be 'cruel' because it denied the audience a passive observer's perspective and forced it into a 'tangible laceration', a full and 'whole' commitment to the event. Expressing his belief in the theatre as a place where life-forces were discovered and released, he wrote:

> The theatre
> is the state
> the place
> the point
> Where we can get hold of man's anatomy and
> through it heal and dominate life.

> ('Aliéner l'acteur', 12 May 1947,
> quoted in Esslin, 1976, p. 76)

Audience experiences and choices

In the work and ideas of Brecht and Artaud, we discern a considerable change from a situation where the audience's tastes and demands determined the nature of the action on stage to a point where manipulation and utilization of the audience become common. A student of Theatre Studies today can draw on multiple examples of the ways in which playwrights, directors and companies have engaged and involved their audiences in a manner that was virtually unthinkable during the early years of the twentieth century. Even today, some of these approaches are regarded as daring when set alongside what we have termed the '**predictable theatre**' which continues to function much as before.

New York has been a centre for experiment in theatre for many years but it is from its important and influential theatre scene of the 1960s that we draw some further examples. The *Zeitgeist* of the 1960s has become a subject of considerable fascination to a new generation of students. The American stage musicals *Hair* and *Godspell*, together with the British musical *Jesus Christ Superstar*, are sometimes seen as icons for the period and have been frequently revived. Significantly, none of these shows would have appeared on the London stage without the abolition of stage censorship in 1968, a moment in theatre history that led to forays into nudity, representation of the deity and obscene and profane language. The New York **Off-Off-Broadway** theatre of the 1960s tended to thrive on drug indulgence, group improvisation, racial commingling and a determination to erode the barriers between actors and their audience. This was epitomized by the Living Theatre, founded by Julian Beck and Judith Malina in a former departmental store at Fourteenth Street and Sixth Avenue, converted to seat 160 by a group of volunteers. The theatre's opening production was *The Connection* by Jack Gelber, a play that had been delivered in manuscript form by hand because the playwright could not afford the postage. Ironically, it was precisely such lack of resources that gave the work of the Living Theatre its freedom to experiment and take risks; productions were mounted at a tiny fraction of the cost of Broadway shows and, according to the actor Pierre Biner, the director insisted that the cast mingled with the audience during the interval of *The Connection* 'asking for a fix in the characteristic tone and manner of addicts' (Cohn, 1991, p. 60). The outrage expressed in some reviews merely increased the fascination of potential audiences who submitted themselves to various 'assaults' in subsequent productions.

In a 1964 production of *Mysteries and Smaller Pieces*, the Living Theatre defined its performance strategy:

> No curtain
> Performers circulate among the audience. Everyday clothes
> Performers become part of audience.

What were termed 'contacts' varied from invitations to the audience to join hands in a circle on stage for exercises in humming and meditation to surrounding the audience with moving figures shouting slogans and solicitations to join the cast for a sexual orgy. Inevitably some spectators left the performances, while others joined in, clearly liberated by these unfamiliar techniques. The experience of these years of bold experimentation led to far wider concepts of what an audience might be asked to do. By the 1970s, for example, the Cuban-born dramatist Maria Irene Fornes was dividing her audience into four groups in order to move through the living-room, study, bedroom, kitchen and onto the lawn of a New England country house, in her play *Fefu and her Friends*. In this play, the audience watch Fefu in conversation with seven different friends in the varying locations that they visit.

Robert Schuman, who founded the Bread and Puppet Theatre during the 1960s, considered that his ideal target audience was one that did not usually go to the theatre. Taking his work into the streets and **found spaces** of New York, he charged one dollar for indoor performances and nothing for outdoor work. Instead, his company distributed and shared bread with the audience. His view was that too many of his contemporaries in the experimental theatre were concentrating on shocking and insulting their audiences rather than communicating with them. He was not so much concerned with revolutionizing the theatre as with developing traditional forms for a new era. The significance of distributing bread lay in his wish to 'feed' the audience but its obvious connection to religious and sacramental acts emphasized the sense of communion. Rejecting the use of conventional theatre buildings for his plays based on both actors and huge puppets, Schuman argued that that such spaces had become 'too well known' and 'too comfortable' and that such an environment conditioned the reactions of the audience who were 'numbed by sitting in the same chairs in the same way' (Roose-Evans, 1988, p. 122).

◼ Recent concepts of the audience

We have observed a significant shift in attitudes in theatre from the centrality of the actor and the play to a new centrality of the audience. This development dates from the middle years of the twentieth century and discussion and research in this field have been influenced by the growth of **communication studies**, which see the audience as potential consumers of the products of the media, and of **critical theory** which recognizes how meanings are constructed by audiences rather than exclusively by writers and performers.

Communication studies

Students of this discipline regard the audience as a central concept in the study of mass communication and classify audiences according to such criteria as size, composition, degree of education or location. They are less likely to think in terms of ideology or beliefs and will analyse audience needs and responses with such research techniques as surveys and questionnaires. Marsen (2006, p. 117)) defines an audience as 'a group of people assembled voluntarily at a particular place and time to view and listen to a public performance of a secular nature'. The origins of such audiences as an observable and definable phenomenon lie in the world of ancient Greece and Rome where spectators gathered in large numbers to witness public theatrical and musical performances, sporting events and political gatherings. Such an audience still exists today. However, the invention first of the printed book and subsequently of newspapers, magazines, sound recording, radio, film, television, video and DVD recording, the internet and the mobile phone has created a 'mass audience' of huge proportions which has increasingly become an object of study, partly because communicators are anxious to understand and target their 'consumers'.

As we have seen, the middle years of the twentieth century were a time of great change in the theatre because of the growing influence of the mass media and consumerist philosophies. Shows such as the seminal **rock-opera** *Jesus Christ Superstar* were carefully packaged by their producers to ensure that 'hit' songs from the stage show were released as records with associated marketing strategies before the actual London production. Merchandise and logos were tightly controlled and film rights granted in such a way as to ensure that what was originally a stage show became an example of mass communication. This approach now controls much of the live theatre in such a way that stage musicals with their associated images, merchandise, recordings of all kinds and televized 'audition' shows are now seen as a global commodity designed for the new, international audience. This **mediatization** of theatre continues to present a challenge to the live interaction of performer and audience.

The sociologist Herbert Blumer (1951) offered a redefinition of the audience that took into account the changing economic and technological factors of modern society. He distinguished four types of audience composition:

The group is a collection of people known to each other and they may interact in some controlled way. Roles of the group members are clearly defined and they are bound together by common interests and ideals that enable the group to persist. **Interpersonal communication** takes place among group members.

The crowd is larger than the group but may be located in the same or similar place. It only has a temporary existence and when it disperses it is unlikely to re-form in the same way. It may have a common rhythm or mood but not in the systematic ideological fashion of the group. Its behaviour will be largely impulsive and irrational and its lack of a shared set of values will ensure that its actions are not governed by ethical standards.

The public is an audience defined by its civil practices and rights in a socio-political context. It is, accordingly, a product of the modern concept of democratic politics where open, visible discussion and debate are an agreed method of addressing issues of common concern that affect society as a whole.

The mass comprises the largest of all audiences and, like the public, exists over a large geographical area. It is anonymous and lacks group cohesion or organization. The mass audience responds to objects of interest produced in a way over which it has no control. Like the crowd, it has no structure but is different in that it has no fixed location at any one time and little or no contact with other members. The growth in the varieties of media 'texts' available enables the mass to be highly selective in what it uses and this, in turn, provokes intensive marketing strategies by producers.

Marsen (2006, p. 120) suggests that, in the process of audience analysis, (a task increasingly seen as vital for the success of a theatre company), there are three main factors to be taken into consideration:

demographics, including such objective factors as age, gender, ethnicity, education and income level;

psychographics, including subjective aspects such as values, lifestyle preferences, leisure activities and consumer tastes;

technical knowledge, an issue that becomes relevant when specialist ideas are being communicated. It refers to the level of technical terminology and understanding that an audience is assumed to have.

Demographic analysis of audiences can take many forms but one particularly interesting and relevant approach is based on the work of two American sociologists, Strauss and Howe (1991). In their book *Generations: The History of America's Future, 1584 to 2069*, they propose a cyclical model of generational change based on certain abstract principles that appeared to influence each generation. They identify four generational types to which they give the mythical names '**prophet**', '**nomad**', '**hero**', and '**artist**', suggesting that these represent certain recognizable behavioural patterns.

◆ A prophet generation is principled and righteous and approaches social issues with a sense of idealism and almost missionary zeal.

◆ A nomad generation is generally cynical and realistic, universalist and rootless, approaching social issues through cunning and strategy.

◆ A hero generation advocates social and civil rights and seeks technological change and economic prosperity and attempts to tackle social issues through rational policy-making and institution-building.

◆ An artist generation is mellow and mild-mannered and believes in fairness and equality and tends to exhibit a somewhat gullible approach to social and life issues.

Strauss and Howe suggest that the cyclic pattern they claim to have discerned can be seen in the generations now living: 1925–1942 are an artist generation; 1943–1960 are prophets; 1961–1981 are nomads; 1982–2003 are a hero generation and the cycle begins to repeat itself with the likelihood of a new artist generation, 2004–2025.

Obviously these categories take little account of individual differences or of specific contextual factors such as events that take place in particular societies. They were devised as a response to the history (in the case of the dates here, recent) of the United States but they seem to have some universal validity and are used by researchers in the media industry, of which theatre is increasingly a part, to ascribe programming to target audiences and they may be used for discussion by anyone seeking to understand generational factors involved in audiences.

The context of postmodernism

Communication studies and critical theory have often overlapped during a period when the dominant set of philosophical ideas and attitudes have been described as postmodern. This term implies that the 'modern' era with its belief in scientific rationality and the inevitable progress of humanity has been superseded by an age of far greater uncertainty. It is, however, more helpful to think of **postmodernism** as a gradual unravelling of modernism, rather than a sudden shift of emphasis and perception. Postmodernist attitudes are, inevitably, reflected in the expectations and critical responses of audiences as well as in the devising and presentation of works in the theatre and it is important at this point in our discussion to summarize some of the characteristics of postmodernism. This is admirably done by Marsen (2006, p. 30):

◆ A conception of personal identity as fragmented or dispersed, mostly owing to our participation in many, and sometimes contradictory, contexts such as career changes, relocations, the dissolution of the nuclear family or the proliferation of multiple marriages.

◆ An abandonment of the search for origins, the original, universal or transcendental cause. This includes the dissolution of the modernist-Romantic notion of genius, the inspired creator of the new. The original work is replaced by intertextuality, parody and self-parody, an acceptance of contradiction as having no resolution, and a strong sense of irony.

◆ A questioning of notions of linear reality and linear – causally based – narratives, opting for parallel universes or multiple realities. This questions modernist notions of subjectivity and stream-of-consciousness-type discourses, replacing them with a series of disconnected and/or fragmented images (collage), infinite regress-type techniques, ironic uses of sound or non-synchronized sound in multi media texts, etc.

◆ Socio-cultural developments associated with the mass media, such as internationalization and a dramatization of information that tends to blur distinctions between 'truth' and 'fiction'.

◆ Political practices based on group and cultural membership rather than on universalist and totalizing projects; for example, feminist, gay and other diversity-orientated groups form political unions that are increasingly replacing modernist ideological systems such as communism. Rather than belonging to groups identified by race or belief, people are defined by the nature of what they consume.

By now you should be entirely familiar with the concept of the *Zeitgeist* and will, no doubt, recognize many of the characteristics of our age in the list provided here. Such a list is not intended to imply that all features or trends are observable in any one situation but, if you believe with Hamlet that the 'purpose of playing (acting)' includes showing 'the very age and body of the time his form and pressure' (Act III Sc. 2), it is inevitable that the loss of confidence and meaning that seems to characterize recent times will be reflected in the plays that are written, the productions presented and the performances that you may undertake.

Critical theory

The critical theory that has emerged over the past 40 years or so in relation to theatre assigns an active rather than a passive role to the audience. This reflects the belief that, ultimately, it is the audience that constructs meanings during a theatrical performance by **decoding** the **signs** which constitute the discourse between performer and audience. Pickering and Auckland-Lewis (2004, pp. 135–6) outline the means whereby a theatrical event is given meaning by its spectators. They suggest three stages in the process:

1. *Encoding meaning*: the theatre professional takes the raw dramatic text (work) and translates it into a performance text, using performance conventions. The performance will enshrine *ideological constructions* based on the creator's concept of what theatre is and what it is for.

2. *Programme and meaningful discourse*: once constructed and in performance the text and meaning of a play are no longer tied to a single idea but are now open to re-reading during the process of the discourse, i.e., the interaction of performer and audience.

3. *Decoding*: the audience decodes the theatrical discourse or *reads* the performance. Again, **ideological** pressures come into play and the audience brings it own cultural issues that will affect the process. Spectators from broadly the same society may read the texts in any number of different ways, depending on their own ideological, cultural or political position. They may accept the **encoding** systems of the producer and decode the performance in a manner that recreates the producer's preferred meaning or totally reject that by reading the performance in an oppositional way. Most likely, the audience will enter into a **negotiated meaning**, a balance of acceptance and rejection.

The concept of ideology in the context of critical theory is important and easily misunderstood. One of the major areas of critical thinking has concerned the effect that texts can have in creating, sustaining or changing ideologies. Most people would probably define ideology as a grouping or set of beliefs but, heavily influenced by Marxist criticism, many critical thinkers now consider ideology to be a modality of power or a means by which one social group achieves and sustains dominance over another.

In employing terms like 'codes of communication' or 'sign system' we are borrowing from the school of criticism termed **Structuralism**, introduced initially into a consideration of literature in the mid-twentieth century. This method demolished the traditional assumption that the text functions like a transparent screen between writer and reader. The identity of both reader and writer and the meaning of the story had previously been (and often still is) assumed to be fixed, just *there* waiting to be discovered. The Structuralists demonstrated that the identities of both reader and writer are constructed by and through the process of communication and it is in this context that famous, and often misleading quotes from critics, such as 'the author is dead' or 'there is nothing beyond the text' have been used.

If meaning in literature is constructed rather that found then the theatre presents us with a doubly complex situation because, as we have seen, 'meaning' is constructed by both performers and spectators. The traditional view, still maintained by many actors, is that the text alone can be reliably preserved. But this has been called into question and it has been asserted that the reading of a dramatic text is no more reliable than the process of reading a performance.

◆ It was the French critic, Roland Barthes (1915–80), who initially addressed the analysis of a text as a system of **signs**. His work reminds us that we are constantly reading messages in the objects around us but that these are not in words. Applied to theatre, an audience will read and construct meaning from objects, costume, décor, physical movement, sound effects, music and the quality of light. Such signs systems may enable the construction of meanings that **denote** that is, state explicitly, or **connote**, that is, suggest by means of association.

◆ When we witness a performance, the meaning presents itself as a totality and we are unlikely to analyse the various codes of signification as a conscious process: indeed, we probably think 'alongside' the performance. However, in our final chapter, we shall be considering some of the categories under which we might conduct a reflective analysis of the kind frequently demanded of Theatre Studies students. The vocabulary of **semiotics**, which is the study of the nature of signs and their importance in our making sense of the world, still has some use in the theatre although some critics are now suggesting that it is already outmoded. For instance, in a more recent philosophical stance known as **post-structuralism**, the French thinkers Lacan, Derrida and Foucault have offered a critique of the Structuralists' concept of the 'sign' arguing that there are only arbitrary and conventionalized relations between words and meanings and that it is in the process of disassembling a text that we can explore the uncertainty of truth. Meaning, they argue, is always deferred or disguised.

We can illustrate the use of critical theory, however, if we return briefly to consider the work of Artaud. His ideas centred on the creation of a new theatre language reinforced by seeing a company of Balinese dancers who visited Paris in 1931. What particularly impressed him was the supremacy of movement and sound over verbal language and he wrote of the weakness of spoken language dialogue as seeming like 'so much stammering' (1968, p. 39). The actors, he said, were like 'moving hieroglyphs', the whole appearance one of 'theatrical conventions' with profound symbolic meaning too deep for 'logical discursive language'. In his reflection on what he saw, Artaud was groping towards understanding that 'sign systems' were in operation for him to 'read' and that his stress on the potential symbolic and metaphorical value of all elements of theatre represented an early appreciation of the meanings to be constructed in the process of the theatrical discourse. He was, in fact, searching for a 'code' with which to communicate.

■ Conclusion

In this chapter, we have argued that the live audience and its possible interaction with the performers are one of the key elements of Theatre. When we have stripped away those aspects of drama that may be more efficiently catered for by film or other media, we still have the essential chemistry between audience and performers in the theatre. In order to illustrate the many changes in the perception of the role and approach of the audience which have taken place in significant periods in the history of theatre we have provided some extensive examples that repay considerable attention. These include the writings and teaching of Artaud, who had a particular determination to control and transform the audience experience.

We then applied principles from recent Communication Studies and critical theory to the study of audiences and summarized various ways in which audiences may be categorized and discussed. This led us to a consideration of the concept that audiences have to 'read' performances and we examined this process in the light of recent ideas. We have tried to encourage you to consider the audience as one of the major determining factors in the planning of new performances, pointing out that an understanding of the originally envisaged relationship with an audience is a key to appreciating the text of a play from the past or the challenges of creating a new text.

Topics for discussion and reflection

◆ Do you support David Hare's attack on Marxist playwrights?

◆ A famous soccer team was once forced to play an important match in an empty stadium as a punishment for rule-breaking. How do you imagine this affected the players and the match?

◆ Comment on Brecht's and Hare's concepts of what transpires between actors and audience.

◆ Shakespeare and his contemporaries, Restoration dramatists, Strindberg and Chekhov appear from the evidence available to have sensed that to some extent they were 'in the audience's hands'. At what point in our discussion do you detect a shift to a point where the playwright/director aims to control the audience?

◆ Consider the practicality of Artaud's ideas if you try making works for the theatre; how do you respond to his suggestions?

◆ The ideas of having printed 'programmes' complete with notes or 'pre-show' or after-show discussions/talks are all relatively recent. What do they achieve for audiences and what were conditions like before their introduction?

◆ In Shakespeare's time there was usually only one full copy of the script and the cast only had their parts with marked cues. The audience were unable to obtain a published edition of the play. What effect on actors and audience did these facts have and how has that changed?

■ Further reading

Abercrombie, N. and Longhurst, B. (1998) *Audiences*, London: Sage. A very helpful consideration of the whole concept of audience.

Fairclough, N. (2003) *Analysing Discourse*, London: Routledge. A practical and clear guide to this important topic.

Marsen, S. (2006) *Communication Studies*, Basingstoke: Palgrave Macmillan. Provides essential insights into the issues common to Theatre and Communication.

McGrath, J. (1996) *A Good Night Out*, 2nd edn, London: Nick Hern. A perceptive and stimulating reflection on performance in various contexts.

McQuail, D. (1997) *Audience Analysis*, London: Sage. Provides a clear methodology for the task.

Pickering, K. and Auckland-Lewis, G., (2004) *Thinking about Plays*, London: Dramatic Lines. Offers an accessible introduction to the use of critical theory.

■ Website

For a discussion of audiences in relation to prologues and epilogues, see our website: www.palgrave.com/foundations/pickering

The Study of Theatre

Reflection and Analysis

From the outset, we have made it clear that this book targets the active and enquiring student and the 'reflective practitioner' who wishes to study Theatre. The single most important characteristic of a student of Theatre Studies is the ability to analyse aspects of Theatre and to both reflect upon and evaluate their own work in that field of study. Such critical thinking will draw upon all the insights and knowledge gained during a course of study supported by the kind of reading represented by this book. We shall, therefore, be drawing upon and bring together the many strands of this book as we propose forms of analysis and reflection. These may well be employed in the writing of a review, in an analytical essay or in a piece of private reflection.

Learning outcomes

By the conclusion of this chapter, you should be able to:

▶ understand what is involved in the analysis of performance;

▶ use critical skills to evaluate your own practice;

▶ write a theatre review with efficiency and clarity;

▶ appreciate the differences between analysis and evaluation;

▶ devise and use categories for analysis;

▶ adopt a holistic and integrated approach to the study of Theatre;

▶ reflect on current and possible future developments in Theatre.

Evaluation and analysis

As a student, it is inevitable that your own work with be constantly subjected to external evaluation. When this is linked to published criteria, it will be regarded as **assessment** or **adjudication**. In the case of Theatre Studies, this presents the, sometimes difficult, process of assessing both practical work, such as acting, directing or some form of performance together with academic work, which may take the form of written assignments, presentations or discussions. However, none of these activities takes place in a vacuum; for example, it is highly likely that you have supported your acting work by maintaining a journal and it is almost certainly the case that any written work undertaken will relate to the live, practical process of performance. Thus, any assessment of your work will invariably take account of more than one aspect of the 'subject' and any one area of study may consist of several elements.

As a student, it is important not to rely solely on external assessment but to develop the habit of personal evaluation and the critical skills for evaluating what you see and hear. Evaluation concentrates on the level of success achieved by a work of performance, whether it is an entire play or a solo speech delivered in a studio and, to some extent, the judgement will be subjective. It is rare for any two audiences or individuals to agree precisely on the nature or 'reading' of a performance, but, with the use of agreed objective criteria, it is usually possible to reach a consensus on the level of skill represented.

Such agreement is reached by identifying the component elements of theatre skills and involves asking particular kinds of question which we must investigate shortly.

Analysis is *not* an evaluation. The task of analysis is to establish how meaningful discourse is created. When applied to performance, it involves an understanding of all the elements of theatre and how they interact and yet it must ultimately concern itself with the entirety. In order to appreciate and analyse the *mise-en-scène*, we must break it down initially into its components for investigation prior to achieving a sense of synthesis. We suggest that the topics covered in the chapters of this book provide a useful and practical framework for analysis of performance.

Asking the right questions

Any form of critical thinking involves the constant asking of questions. For example, many students embark on preparing a performance without an appreciation of the questions that are necessary before key decisions can be made. A simple, but frequently overlooked instance is the choice of performance space. There are probably hundreds of questions that could be asked before a particular space is selected and yet this process is often overlooked in a desperate attempt to select a play. Once a play is selected, there are an equal number of questions to be considered before rehearsals can begin, and so on.

Evaluation usually depends on the judicious use of the questions 'did?' or 'was?' Did the actors inhabit their characters? Did the cast respond to each other? Did the company utilize the space imaginatively? Did the lighting enhance the mood or convey the required information about time of day? Was the actor audible? Was the attention of the audience gained and maintained? Was the material provocative or baffling? Was the quality of physical movement such that it drew attention to itself rather than to what it may have been attempting to communicate? Was meaningful discourse created?

Analysis, on the other hand, is more likely to use the questions 'how'? or 'what?' How did the production employ signs to communicate? How were the intentions of the performers encoded? How did the production seek to evoke the slums of New York? How did the company exploit the actor–audience relationship? How did the actor playing Macbeth react to the news of the death of Lady Macbeth? What codes of communication were employed? What did the actor playing Lady Macbeth do in the 'sleepwalking

UNIVERSITY OF WINCHESTER
LIBRARY

scene' and how did she do it? How did Helene Weigel speak her lines in Brecht's play *The Mother*? And to this we must add: how did these small aspects of a performance combine to allow a total production concept to achieve its **realization**?

■ The review

Just as your work in Theatre Studies must involve reflection and critical thinking in relation to your own practice, so, also, you will need to cultivate critical skills in evaluating the work of others. Visiting, and thinking about, theatre performances of all kinds are an essential part of your study and the reading of texts must also involve you in considering the performance issues raised by those texts.

Traditionally, the most common form which is a synthesis of performance evaluation and analysis is the Theatre Review, which may appear in a journal or newspaper but might also form the basis of your own reflective writing in a log book or essay. It is important to acquire the habit of regularly reading reviews in newspapers and journals so that you prepare for writing your own review of a performance you have seen. A review will normally contain: (1) information about the work, the performers, and the performance, including details of the time and place; (2) comments on the work and its realization in performance; (3) an evaluation of the performance using the same broad categories that we shall be proposing for analysis; (4) discussion of the themes and meanings that the reviewer discerned in the performance; (5) recommendations for improvement; and (6) advice for potential audiences.

A good, responsible and stimulating review will do the following:

◇ provide information about a work for those who are unfamiliar with it;

◇ offer critical evaluation of the performance;

◇ highlight any particularly notable features of the production;

◇ convey the sense of being present to those who were not;

◇ encourage audiences to attend;

◇ explore how the text was realized in performance.

The review as a record of performance

Although there are now many technical means of preserving performances for posterity, these all have their limitations because we were not actually present at the original event. One traditional, and still very effective, means of encapsulating something of the power of a live performance is the writing of a review. As examples of this process we reproduce below three varying accounts of the work of the eighteenth-/nineteenth-century actress, Sarah Siddons, generally regarded as the greatest English tragic actress of all time. Invariably known as Mrs Siddons, she dominated the English stage for a substantial period. Here she is in the role of Lady Macbeth:

> It seemed almost as if a being of superior order had dropped from a higher sphere to awe the world with the majesty of her appearance. Power was seated on her brow, passion emanated from her breast as from a shrine; she was tragedy personified. In coming on in the sleepwalking

scene, her eyes were open, but their sense was shut. She was like a person bewildered, and unconscious of what she did. Her lips moved involuntarily – all her gestures were involuntary and mechanical. She glided on and off the stage like an apparition. To have seen her in that character was an event in everyone's life, not to be forgotten.

(Hazlitt)

Now we might compare this account of her performance with her own notes for the role of Lady Macbeth in the famous 'sleepwalking scene' described by Hazlitt:

Behold her now with a wasted form, with wan and haggard countenance, her starry eyes glazed with the ever-burning fever of remorse ... whether walking or asleep the smell of the innocent blood incessantly haunts her imagination. 'Here's the smell of the blood still: all the perfumes of Arabia will not sweeten this little hand.'

(Sarah Siddons's notes on the character of Lady Macbeth)

Mrs Siddons was clearly able to transmit her ideas into practice as we read of: 'a convulsive shudder – very horrible. A tone of imbecility audible in the sigh' (a spectator describing Mrs Siddons in the same scene in 1784).

As a potential reviewer, building on your work in Theatre Studies, you might usefully ask the following questions:

◆ How do Mrs Siddons's notes appear to have been translated into live performance?

◆ Do you consider the first extract to be an evaluation, an analysis, or both?

◆ What questions have been answered by the two impressions of her performance?

◆ How is your perception of Mrs Siddons affected by our having suggested that she was 'the greatest English tragic actress'?

◆ Do the passages provide a vivid and detailed account of her performance and if so, how is that achieved?

◆ Do you need to be familiar with the play to fully appreciate the points being made?

◆ How does Sarah Siddons's preparation and execution of a role compare with your approach to acting?

Now consider the following passage in which there is a description of the performance by the popular actor Kemble in a production of *Macbeth* in 1817. The description is written by another famous actor, Macready:

In the fifth act when the news was brought, 'The Queen, my lord, is dead.' he seemed struck to the heart. Gradually collecting himself he sighed out 'She should have died hereafter!' then, as if with the inspiration of despair, he hurried out, distinctly and pathetically, the lines '... Tomorrow and tomorrow and tomorrow ...' rising to a climax of desperation that brought the enthusiastic cheers of the close-packed theatre. All at once he seemed carried away by the genius of the scene. At the tidings of the wood of Birnam moving, he staggered, as if the shock had struck at the very seat of life, and in the bewilderment of fear and rage he could just ejaculate the words 'Liar and slave,' then lashing himself into a state of frantic rage ended the scene in perfect triumph.

As you think critically about this passage, you may need to familiarize yourself with the scene from the play being described. You will notice that the performance event contains at least one substantial difference from a present-day performance, but the writer provides the necessary information to enable his reader to imagine the situation. Although this account is written in what may seem an outmoded fashion, you should note the following qualities that should be present in your own writing:

◆ careful attention to detail;

◆ an ability to recall and describe key moments of performance;

◆ an awareness of the original text and of the performance text;

◆ aural awareness of the details of performance;

◆ a blend of narrative, analysis and evaluation in evoking the performance;

◆ a clear evocation of the event.

▰ Towards analysis

There is, of course, a great deal more to the writing of a review than a desire to preserve great performances for the interest of posterity. We have seen that a review may contain descriptive, evaluative and analytical material. However, the study and appreciation of Theatre may sometimes demand a more exclusively analytical approach. If we consider two passages dealing with Helene Weigel, the actress wife of the playwright Brecht, you will see how you may draw upon your knowledge of Brecht and his attitude to acting in order to appreciate his detailed analysis and that of a leading theatre critic of the day.

> Helene Weigel spoke the sentences as if they were in the third person, and so she not only refrained from pretending in act to be or claim to be Vlassova, and in fact to be speaking those sentences, but actually prevented the spectator from transferring himself to a particular room, as habit and indifference might demand, and imagining himself to be the invisible eye-witness and eavesdropper of a unique, intimate conversation.
>
> (Brecht discussing his wife's performance in notes on *The Mother*, 1933)

> In the central part (Mother Courage) Helene Weigel is never allowed to become a bawdy and flamboyant old darling: her performance is casual and ascetic; we are to observe, but not to embrace, her. Twice, and agonisingly, she moves us: once by the soundless cry which doubles her up when she hears her son being executed; and again when, to avoid incriminating herself, she must pretend not to recognise his body. She walks towards it, wearing a feigned, frozen smile that does not budge from her lips until she has stared at the body, shaken her head and returned to her seat. Then her head slumps and we see, collapsed and petrified, the sad stone face of grief. Elsewhere, even in Paul Dessau's magnificent songs, we must never sympathise with Mother Courage; she has battened on the Thirty Years War, and must suffer for her complicity by losing her daughter and both her sons.
>
> (Kenneth Tynan, on the Berliner Ensemble's production of *Mother Courage* in London, 1956)

These two reflections on the performance methods of Helene Weigel make an interesting contrast with those on Sarah Siddons, although, considering the many years that separate them, the similarities are even more fascinating. They both constitute a form of analysis of Weigel at work: particularly of the signs with which she communicated and, inevitably, there is an appreciation and awareness of the skills being employed. Note also how the influential critic, Kenneth Tynan, draws on his understanding of the moral issues of the play in order to expand upon the meanings that Weigel has enabled her audience to create. Your own understanding of the techniques encouraged by Brecht would give you a considerable advantage over many readers of these passages and you can see how the review by Tynan adds colour and a sense of total performance when compared to the purely analytical passage on Weigel's technique in *The Mother*. It is important that you develop the ability to write both forms of response.

The process of analysing a theatrical performance is highly complex: in order to analyse a performance it is necessary to draw upon a wide range of insights and areas of understanding. By far the most important work in this aspect of Theatre Studies in recent years has been carried out by Professor Patrice Pavis and we strongly advise you to consult his book *Analyzing Performance* (2003). The approach taken by Pavis has formed the basis of several 'checklists' of features to observe in order to make a final synthesis of the disparate aspects of performance visible and audible at any one time. As a means of identifying these essential elements for analysis we propose that you take the topics on which we have focused in successive chapters as the basis for your work. To facilitate this, you should read again the opening chapter and then, as we take the various other issues into account, refer to the appropriate subsequent chapter.

▉ The event

Any piece of theatrical performance is framed by the event of which it is a part. We take the term **frame** and **frame analysis** from the social psychologist Erwin Goffman who argued that it is by perceiving the frame in which something takes place that we ultimately make sense of it. Consider, for example, this scenario.

> An Arts Festival was recently held in Brighton, a city with a reputation for artistic activity and a lively arts community. Performances, exhibitions and events of many kinds took place over a short period and one of these was a performance of plays by Shakespeare using three actors in a Pizza Restaurant. The actors presented their plays in various parts of the restaurant among the people eating and drinking at their tables.
>
> The presentation described took place during one evening and the event was reported and shown on local television.

From the news item and from various reports, it is obvious that the performances were greatly enjoyed by the audiences. The small cast showed great ingenuity in casting and in the use of various objects concerned with cooking as improvised props.

Now imagine that you had attended this performance. It is likely that you would have seen it advertised and decided it would be a rewarding experience: you might have needed to book a table and you could be pretty sure that the audience would have been sympathetic to the idea of this somewhat unusual mode of production. In other words, the performance of the actors was framed by the fact that they were part of an Arts Festival and their work would derive meaning from that fact.

Imagine, however, that you had decided to go with a friend for a pizza meal in the same restaurant and that what you really wanted was to enjoy the food and drink and to engage in an exchange of news and conversation. Suddenly, your planned evening is interrupted by the arrival of three actors who insist on acting Shakespeare just near your table. Initially you might think that this was merely a high-spirited group who had had too much to drink or that the spontaneous performance was not given with the permission of the management. Whatever your reactions, they would largely depend on the fact that your frame for the performance was entirely different from that of the audience which had anticipated seeing a play and that, for you, the nature of the event derived its features from its unexpected and unprepared aspects. Above all, the socio-political or cultural make-up of the audience may well have been significantly different from the audience which attended during the Arts Festival. That, of course, may well have been the whole purpose of the second imaginary version of events because many practitioners in theatre have a determination to reach audiences that would never willingly attend a performance. The poet and dramatist T.S. Eliot once famously remarked that he had found himself writing plays in verse for 'audiences at Arts Festivals who come prepared to be bored by poetry'.

Therefore, any analysis of performance must begin with an analysis of the event and the following are some of the aspects that should concern you:

- how the event was organized;

- how the event was publicized;

- the context in which it took place: e.g. an arts festival, part of a 'season' of plays or performances at a theatre, a 'one-off' performance by a new group, a short 'run' by an amateur company, a school production, etc.;

- where it took place;

- the social and/or generational groups evident in the audience;

- how they found out about it and why they were there for example, were they regular supporters of a particular group or theatre or were they there because a family member was involved?;

- how the event was funded;

- how many performances of the same piece took place;

- the probable 'target' audience;

- the overall scale of the production and the potential size of the audience;

- the title and familiarity of the piece performed;

- the genre of the piece and the likely expectations of the audience. for instance,was it a well-known musical attended by a large tourist audience or a new play presented to a small audience in a pub?;

- the conventions being used/flouted;

- the 'use' of the audience as participants in the event;

- the provision for comfort, refreshment and hospitality;

- any formal (e.g. pre-advertised post-show discussion session) or informal (e.g. actors in bar after show) interaction with the performers;

- the general spirit of the event: celebratory, reflective, shocking, escapist?;

- its relation to your perception of the *Zeitgeist*.

The work

The relationship between an original stage work and its realization in performance is a constant source of debate in Theatre Studies and is likely to be a recurring theme in any analysis. As part of the complete event that will frame the performance questions may revolve around:

   any information concerning the work made available through publicity or programme notes;

   the availability of a published text;

   the likely familiarity of the work: classical text; popular musical; 'set work'; new writing or devised piece; revival of well-known play, etc.;

   knowledge concerning the writer(s);

   any reputation of the director or company of actors in relation to the work;

   any stated directoral approach such as striving for **authenticity** or a contemporary interpretation of an old text;

   significant casting of well-known performers in key roles.

The space

Performances take place in a bewildering number of different spaces, to such an extent that it has led some to predict the death of the permanent theatre building. There is almost certainly no evidence that audiences have lost their appetites for the facilities and ambiance that a purpose-built theatre can provide. However, as we have seen, theatre architecture now reflects a much more flexible approach to the use of space and lately this has, to some extent, been prompted by the success of productions in **found spaces**. These may appear to offer many more options to directors and audiences.

In an analysis of performance an insight into the function and utilization of space is essential and, as a minimum requirement, you should observe and record the following factors:

◆ the precise size of the acting area and auditorium if they are separate;

   the shape of the spaces concerned;

   facilities for audience seating/standing. circles, stalls, galleries, 'gods', stools, benches, boxes, etc.;

   the form of staging used, e.g. proscenium, in-the-round, promenade;

   the design of the building, e.g. studio theatre, opera house, warehouse, church, small provincial theatre;

   the actor/audience relationship made possible by the space;

   the use of curtains or any demarcations of the acting space;

   the building's acoustics and sight-lines;

   entrances and exits to the stage and to the auditorium, how they were used;

in general terms, how the space was lit;

provision for intervals, late-comers, box-office;

general level of comfort and the optimum period of time that could be spent there;

disability access or other provision for those with special needs;

how the space is managed.

Once these factors have been taken into consideration, it becomes possible to enter into a more detailed analysis of the performance elements achieved by the various practitioners. In relation to the space it is now essential to think critically about:

the way in which the performance space is shaped, using constructions and objects;

any art installations present;

the use of scenery and décor: does this involve, for example, the construction of flats, interior settings, three-dimensional pieces, ropes, levels, steps, ramps?;

the conventions used in relation to space, e.g. the concept of a '**fourth wall**' or the use of multi-focus settings;

how the boundaries of the 'stage' are defined;

how the staging reflects the playwright's suggestions/requirements set out in the text;

any attempt to reproduce the performance conditions that existed when the play was written.

■ Signs and codes

The discussions we developed in our chapter on audiences can solidify into some observable features when you are considering the visual and aural aspects of performance. These will include:

how the setting conveys, or negates, a sense of 'reality';

the information that the setting/scenic constructions convey;

the mood that is established through the use of music and/or lighting;

how the staging suggests locations, historical periods or times of day;

the economic or social conditions suggested by the setting;

how a bare stage or empty space is transformed in the imagination;

what the costuming of the actors conveys;

how the design qualities achieve a consistent code of communication;

how lighting is used to communicate meanings;

the images created and their potential meanings;

how music/song/dance are used;

the audience reactions to the environment created.

■ Physical and vocal performance

You will recall how our two chapters dealing with performance skills initially outlined some general aspects of physical performance and then examined a number of systems of acting. The impression received from live performance will not distinguish between the various elements we have isolated for study purposes, so initially you are more likely to gain a general impression of 'good' or 'bad' or 'effective' performance rather than accurately identifying the precise reasons for these judgements. However, analysis involves critical thinking beyond the shallow and immediate reaction of 'good' or 'bad' and we would recommend that you analyse the use of vocal and physical resources as a basis for first reflections and then move on to more complex issues of character and representation.

Therefore, your initial observations of a performance will include:

the use of non-verbal communication;

the movement or dance skills employed and their purpose;

the range of gestural language and facial expression employed;

the use of stillness and focus;

specialized physical skills such as combat or aerial techniques;

the use of slapstick and other physical, comic devices;

the employment of a particular style of movement to convey period or genre;

the ability of the actors' bodies to respond to the demands of the performance text;

the audibility and clarity of the voice;

the use of accent, tone, pitch, rhythm, articulation and the establishment of aspects of characterization through the use of the voice;

vocalization in all its forms;

the employment of such devices and conventions as the '**aside**' or 'stage whisper'.

how all the above contributed to the total production: the response generated; the sense of confidence projected; the security of the performances both vocally and physically;

the elements of physical theatre demonstrated or the extent to which this constituted the main genre employed;

the handling of dialogue, verse or soliloquy by the actor(s).

Further analysis of a performance requires an understanding of acting in relation to style, specific techniques for character-creation and of stage-craft in general. A moment in a play, for example, may hinge upon the nature of the entrance or exit made by an actor. If a 'critic' or analyst is not aware of such issues, their observations will remain vague and imprecise. Analysis of acting also requires an understanding of the **conventions** and **governing idea** being used in a production; so, for instance, if a play involves the convention that several rooms are visible at once (as in some plays by Tennessee Williams or Alan Ayckbourn), the employment and utilization of that convention will explain much of the actor's performance. Recall the detail of Brecht's analysis of Weigel's technique before you embark on the analysis of a performance you have observed.

Observations will focus on some of the following:

◇ the chosen style of performance and the consistency with which it is used;

◇ the qualities of imagination evident in the acting;

◇ relationships with the audience and how they are handled/exploited;

◇ the presence in the cast of any actor who brings a level of expectation, e.g. a well-known comic playing a role;

◇ how physical and vocal skills combine to create a character or allegorical figure;

◆ how ideas and emotions are communicated;

◇ the nature and levels of interaction between the actors;

◇ performance in relation to the genre or nature of the work;

◇ the effective use of 'timing' and other technical aspects of acting;

◇ any evidence of acting theory being used to underpin performances;

◇ the sense of 'truth' achieved;

◇ evidence of listening and focus in the performance;

◇ the acting in the context of the setting and environment;

◇ the ability to inhabit a role and a costume;

◇ the clarity with which the protagonists' dilemmas are conveyed;

◇ how objects are used;

◇ memorable moments and images created by the acting;

◇ techniques used to engage and sustain the interest of the audience;

◇ any apparently indefinable 'star' qualities that require more reflection and analysis.

■ Further considerations of the work

We use the term 'work' to discriminate from the term 'text', employed by some scholars to describe what is evolved in performance. The modern theatre scene embraces a substantial range of styles of work ranging from classical plays to newly devised pieces and there is no shortage of critics predicting the death of conventional plays, narrative and, indeed, the theatre itself. However, this negative view probably tells us more about the critics than it does about Theatre and most certainly does not account for the fact that Theatre Studies is one of the fastest-growing areas of academic investigation. The structures of theatre organization may well be changing rapidly but there continues to be a stream of productions in a multiplicity of settings and situations all emanating from stage works of ancient or recent origin and, in the theatre of the West, these have increasingly embraced works from diverse cultures. Furthermore, the boundaries of performance between such areas as dance, circus, theatre sports, improvisation, opera, aerial work, classical plays, stand-up comedy and ritual have become blurred in the constant quest for new and distinctive forms of theatre and this has greatly influenced the way in which works are interpreted and devised.

Any analysis of a performance *must* include a simple, clear statement of what the work is and of how the performance relates to that work. Such statements may highlight:

- the author and date of writing of the work;
- its stage history;
- its form and genre;
- its basic requirements in terms of casting and setting;
- its setting in terms of time and location and any variations on these determined by the director;
- any distinctive qualities of the writing/devising;
- specific aspects of the written/spoken text;
- world events which might have been relevant at the time of the work's origins;
- social, moral and philosophical attitudes evident in the work;
- any evidence of the use of improvisation/workshopping/devising in creating the work;
- any performance traditions relating to the work;
- evidence that the work might have been conceived as piece of 'total theatre';
- evidence that a work emanated from particular theories or styles of performance or as a reaction to these.

■ The total performance

The process whereby the work is staged within a particular production concept, a process we prefer to call the *mise-en-scène*, only becomes apparent through an understanding of the different elements involved. When these have been identified and examined, it is possible to reflect on the work as a whole. As we have seen in our chapter on varieties of performance, the possibilities are considerable and will operate within the frame of the particular event. The event itself may reveal attitudes adopted by the production team and audience, for example, the presentation of a play by Shakespeare to a group of students studying the play for an examination may not be the most appropriate time to make substantial changes to the spoken text and transfer the setting to outer space! Again, any analysis should begin with a simple, clear statement of the general nature of the *mise-en-scène*. This will include such aspects as the choice of venue, the governing idea of the presentation, (e.g. in the style of a Japanese Nō play or an entertainment staged in a café), and the situation of the audience. More detailed observation and reflection will then need to focus on:

- where the physical action takes place;
- the involvement of the audience;
- the dominant style of performance and the images employed;
- the choices made in relation to the work;
- the use of moving images, puppets, projections, multi-media, animals or vehicles;

◇ the number and gender of performers;

◇ any ideology seeming to drive the production;

◇ the integration of modes of performance;

◇ the relationship between staging and characters;

◇ stage entrances and exits as an integral part of the total concept;

◇ the concept of 'off stage' or any liminal spaces employed;

◇ the performance as **commodity** as part of a global phenomenon, e.g. its similarity to a DVD version, the use of the same images or costumes;

◇ its quality as a stage piece in relation to a possible origin in another form, e.g. novel, film, TV programme, children's literature.

■ Meanings

Critical thinkers were asking what a play or a performance 'meant' long before the Structuralists suggested that meanings were constructed by de-coding the signs of performance. It is a perfectly reasonable question to ask, given that a meaningful discourse involves the exchange of ideas in spoken and visual language and that impressions gained attending a performance can be both stimulating and baffling. Any analysis of a performance will need to focus initially on *how* meanings are encoded or presented and ultimately on the personal meanings constructed and deduced by the critical thinker. In considering these issues, the following factors will be taken into account:

◇ any **thesis** or set of ideas that appear to underpin the action;

◇ the use of **archetypes** and metaphors;

◇ the obvious direct or indirect influence of a practitioner or theorist;

◇ influences from other cultures;

◇ ritual qualities of action;

◇ the use of parable or fable;

◇ realistic detail;

◇ references to the subconscious, dreams or visions;

◇ political systems or situations;

◇ symbolic action;

◇ themes and issued explored in action and dialogue;

◇ moral dilemmas and personal journeys.

Suggested activity

Write an analysis of a performance you have recently attended under the following headings: The Event; The Work; The Space; Signs and Codes; Physical and Vocal Performance; The *Mise-en-scène*; Meanings.

◼ Conclusion

This book has aimed to enable you to accumulate a critical vocabulary to draw upon. We have stressed the necessity of reflecting upon your own practice and that of others. The skills of observation and analysis and the ability to learn from every experience of Theatre, however apparently inadequate, should now be firmly established in your mind as part of the discipline of Theatre Studies. The range of skills a student of Theatre Studies is asked to develop can seem daunting but no one aspect can be seen in isolation. Rather, the entire process of Theatre can be seen as relating to both art and to life in such a way as to ensure that it provides a constant source of interest, challenge and enlightenment and a way of making sense of the business of being human in today's world.

Topics for discussion and reflection

◆ Do reviewers have too much power in the contemporary theatre?

◆ Who is currently writing the most informative and helpful reviews in your national or local press?

◆ Does an attempt to record your impressions of a production improve or spoil your experience of the event?

◆ How has analysis of your own practice helped to develop your competence?

◆ Who are the 'greatest' living actors in your opinion and why are they 'great'?

◼ Further reading

Auslander, P. (1997) *From Acting to Performance: Essays in Modernism and Postmodernism*, London: Routledge. A very useful collection reflecting aspects of recent thinking.

Billington, M. (2008) *One Night Stands: A Critic's View of Modern British Theatre*, London: Nick Hern. Stimulating material from one of the finest critics of the modern theatre.

Counsell, C. and Wolf, L. (2001) *Performance Analysis: An Introductory Course Book*, London: Routledge. A carefully contructed approach to the task of analysis.

Leach, R. (2008) *Theatre Studies: The Basics*, London: Routledge. A lucid and compact volume, ideal for gaining an overview of the subjects introduced in this book.

Pavis, P. (2003)*Analyzing Performance Theater, Dance and Film*, Ann Arbor, MI: University of Michigan Press. An advanced but very rewarding text which explores the theoretical basis of analysis in the theatre.

Pickering, K. (2007) *From Page to Performance*, London: Trinity College. A practical guide to performances derived from various kinds of text.

Glossary

'A' effect	Brecht's idea of alienation or distancing in acting technique.
Action	The broad sweep of what happens in a play.
Activities	The detailed things that characters in plays do, such as sitting, smoking or walking across the room.
Adaptation	The process of transforming a work for one medium into a work for another medium.
Adjudication	The evaluation of a performance by a visiting expert, frequently in the context of a competitive festival or event.
Aerial	A performance on high wires, ropes and trapezes. Sometimes requiring the use of harnesses and involving 'flying' high above the stage. Skills are derived from circus.
Affective memory	Both Stanislavsky and Meisner used this term to indicate the personal memories stored in the subconscious mind of the actor.
Afterlife	The idea, taken from Jonathan Miller, that a play must be recreated in production for new times and situations.
Analysis	The breaking down of a work into its component parts for the purpose of study.
Apron	Normally an extension to the front of a proscenium stage allowing action to be brought out from behind the proscenium arch and nearer to the audience. Sometimes used to describe the front of any stage that projects into the auditorium.
Archetypes	Characters who represent particularly distinctive and typical forms of behaviour (e.g. an archetypal bully).
Arena	A central acting area surrounded by the auditorium.
Art installation	Now used to describe a three-dimensional art object placed in almost any situation other than a conventional art gallery.
Artefacts	Objects such as Theatre programmes or playbills which have survived from an event being researched.
Articulation	The shaping of sounds into words by the actions of the tongue, teeth, lips and palate.
Artist	The first of four cyclic generations defined by Strauss and Howe.
Aside	A device in a play whereby an actor steps briefly out of the action to address the audience confidentially.
Assessment	The evaluation of work using agreed and published criteria.
Authenticity	Acting that is totally truthful.
Backcloth	A large canvas, painted cloth hung at the rear of a proscenium stage, usually showing a landscape. Backcloths may be changed by a system of rollers and pulleys. The rear wall of the stage is termed the 'cyclorama'.

Beats	The individual small transactions that add up to make a scene.
Booth	A small enclosed stage, usually created with curtains and mounted on a wooden, elevated base. Used for travelling theatre, fairground shows and puppets from antiquity to the present day.
Box set	A solid-looking room constructed on a proscenium stage by joining together canvas flats and inserting doors and windows.
Cabaret	A performance for guests at a restaurant or café.
Capta	Data for research, such as overheard conversation, which can be obtained by observation and listening.
Carnivals	Public celebrations involving colourful processions with elaborate costumes and frequently including exhibits and music groups mounted on vehicles. For the discussion of carnival by Boal and Bahktin, see Chapter 5.
Centring	Focus and gathering of energy in the physical centre of the body.
Ceremony	An event that has deep symbolic meaning for participants and spectators.
Chamber play	A small-scale play intended for intimate performance.
Chorus	A group of performers or an individual performer who address the audience directly, commenting on the action.
Circle of attention	Stanislavsky's term for the intense concentration needed by the actor.
Closed question	A question for which the answer is a simple 'yes', 'no' or some similar response.
Cobbling	Piecing together parts of a play or plays to make a new version.
Commedia dell' Arte	An art form originating in Renaissance Italy in which troupes of performers took on 'stock' roles and presented improvised plays based on outline plots. The origin of such figures as Harlequin and Columbine.
Commodity	A term used to imply that a work of art can be marketed like any other product.
Communication Studies	A subject area that has grown in university education since the middle years of the twentieth century. It is concerned with the entire range of situations in which forms of communication take place and has drawn heavily on social psychology, research and textual analysis.
Community theatre	A term with various meanings. In the USA, it is usually taken to mean 'non-professional theatre' whereas in the UK it implies theatrical activity facilitated by professionals but that springs from, and involves, a local community.
Compilation	A programme created from different elements such as songs, speeches or poems.

Connote/connotation	Roland Barthes' second order of signification in the transmission of a message. For example, the word 'green' can connote either the countryside or the permission to 'go ahead' (i.e. a 'green light').
Construct	A thing constructed in the mind, an image of thought.
Context	The entire set of circumstances surrounding either the creation of a work or an incident within that work. These circumstances may include the personal, historical, social or philosophical. Contextual Studies explores these features of various Theatre works.
Convention	A framework in which performers and audience have tacit agreements. For example, that the edge of the stage is the wall of a room.
Courtesan actor	Grotowski's term to indicate an actor who remains merely a craftsperson who sells his or her trade.
Critical response	A carefully considered verbal or written reaction to a performance or text using clearly recognized criteria for evaluation. This may involve the creation or use of an already existing framework for analysis.
Critical Theory	A fairly recent area of investigation which has expanded from both literary theory and communication and media studies to influence critical approaches to the way in which theatre communicates.
CRQ	Term used in research to mean Central Research Question. To be kept in mind in the design of interviews and questionnaires.
Cultural spaces	Purpose-built areas dedicated to the Arts.
Cycles	Sequences of short plays written in medieval Britain and Europe to tell the Biblical story of humankind's creation, redemption and judgement. Often comprising over 30 plays, the performances of these cycles were a feature of cathedral cities in Britain until the Reformation and have been widely revived in more recent years.
Cyclorama	The plain wall at the rear of a stage. This may be used for projection, silhouettes and other effects.
Decode	In the theatre, this is the process whereby the audience creates meanings from the performed text.
Deductive technique	Grotowski's term for the actor who merely relies on an accumulation of skills.
Demographics	The study of statistics, such as age, gender or sexual orientation, to reveal the condition of a particular society.
Denote/denotation	Barthes' first order of signification in the transmission of a message. In this case it is simply a case of identification; for example, the word 'green' represents a colour (cf connotation).
Desk-based research	Research conducted through the use of books, journals and the internet.

Devised	A work for the theatre created through workshops, improvisation or rehearsal using various documentary and imaginative sources. The end product will probably be an agreed text.
Devising	A way of creating a play that does not begin with a set script.
Dialogue	Conversation between characters in a play.
Discourse	A term now used to describe any use of words in relation to a particular topic.
Discourse analysis	Method of analysing the language used in relation to a topic as a means of research.
Documentary	A play in which facts and real events are presented by various means. Often based on documentary sources, including film.
Dramatic concept	The all-embracing idea of a play in the mind of the playwright.
Dramatic theatre	Brecht's term to describe the kind of theatre event that follows the traditions of Aristotle and which demands the emotional involvement of the audience.
Dramaturg	Usually used in the European Theatre for a person who helps in the development of the script. This may include research into other productions and advice to the director.
Dramaturgy of the actor	The creation of text and drama by actors rather than by playwrights or directors.
Dumb-show	In the Elizabethan/Jacobean theatre, a short mimed presentation, often foreshadowing the following spoken scene, e.g. in *Hamlet* and *A Midsummer Night's Dream*.
Durational	A theatre performance that has no distinct moment of beginning and ending. The audience may arrive at any time and remain for as long as they wish.
Emblem	A picture, object or person representing something other than itself.
Emotional memory	The store of personal experience from which an actor draws.
Encode	A Structuralist term used in theatre to describe the process whereby actors and directors select ways of conveying their intended meaning.
Environmental Theatre	A term used by Richard Schechner to describe what has come to be known a 'site specific' theatre.
Epic theatre	Brecht's form of theatre event: episodic, narrative and demanding a political and considered response from the audience.
Episodic	A play that advances in episodes or short, self-contained scenes that do not always progress sequentially.
Evaluation	An aspect of criticism in which a performance is judged according to agreed values.

Event	The word now most commonly used to describe a performance in order to convey the idea that every aspect of it, from the gradual arrival of the audience to the communal participation in what happens, is part of a totality.
Exhalation	Breathing out
Experiential research	Research in which the researcher is actively involved in 'doing'. In Theatre Studies, this might mean participating in acting workshops or productions.
Expressionism/Expressionistic	An artistic movement concerned with creating images of the inner self, very often of a dream-like quality.
Farce	A play with high entertainment value that relies on fast-moving physical action and uncomfortable situations for the characters. Particularly popular in France where farces are invariably acted with wit and style.
Field-based research	Research which involves going out to obtain data. This may include experiential activity, such as visiting theatre sites.
Flying	The process whereby scenery or characters are lowered to the stage or raised out of sight using wires, ropes, pulleys and counterbalances. These were originally operated by hand but now operate mechanically. The process is only possible if there is a Fly Tower above the stage.
Form	When applied to Theatre, this usually describes the basic shape and lay-out of the building and its associated use. (e.g. 'thrust stage').
Forum theatre	A technique employed by the director Augusto Boal whereby a community is empowered by proposing alternative strategies as a result of watching a devised play.
Found objects (*Objets trouvés*)	Any random object that is utilized in the course of a performance: such objects may include things discovered lying round in a 'found space'. They are entirely distinct from manufactured 'props'.
Found space	A space that is considered suitable for a particular performance and which will profoundly influence the nature of that performance. It is invariably not a purpose-built theatre and may never be used more than once.
Fourth wall	A term usually associated with the nineteenth-century French director, Antoine, who asked his actors to rehearse on a proscenium stage with the proscenium opening blocked by canvas 'flats' to

create the fourth wall of the imaginary room in which the action took place. This structure was removed for the performance. The term is now used to imply the imaginary wall of a room that exists in the proscenium opening. Ask yourself where the 'wall' is from the perspective of (1) the audience and (2) an actor working in a 'box' set 'room'.

Framed/Frame analysis	A concept developed by the social psychologist Goffman to explain the way in which we make sense of events by seeing them in a particular setting.
Fringe	Theatre activity taking place outside the mainstream commercial and subsidized theatre.
Functional traits	A term taken from Aristotle to describe a character's modes of behaviour.
Fusion	The bringing together of two or more art forms or cultures to create a new type of work.
Generata	Data for research obtained through the careful design of interviews or other formal methods.
Genre	The kind or style of a work of art.
Gesamtkunstwerk	Literally a 'whole art work', an expression used by Wagner to describe a new Theatre form that would represent an integration of drama, music, design and movement.
Gestus	Brecht's term to describe an action or episode that conveys the 'gist' of the scene.
Gist	The basic idea of something.
Governing idea	The underlying idea developed by a director of a play, which shapes the nature of the performance.
Groundlings	The standing audience that gathered near to the stage in an Elizabethan theatre. They were probably noisy and certainly occupied the cheapest part of the playhouse. Direct eye contact and repartee with the groundlings were aspects of the performance of Elizabethan actors.
Hero	The fourth of Strauss and Howe's cyclic generations.
Holy actor	Grotowski's term for an actor who sacrifices his or her whole being to the acting process.
Ideology	Used in critical theory to describe beliefs and attitudes that enable one section of society to dominate another.
Image	A visual representation of an idea or mood.
In the moment	Meisner's term for an actor's total sensitivity and response to each event in a play, however small.
Inductive technique	Grotowski's recommended approach to acting.
Inhalation	The current technical term for breathing in.
Inspiration	An ancient term for breathing in.
Intention	One of the major determinants for a character's behaviour that must be understood by an actor.
Inter-culturalism	Creating performances that draw upon a number of cultural traditions.

Intercultural Theatre	The use and blending of material from different cultural traditions in an attempt to understand other ways of living and doing. In theatre work, this has usually involved the exploration of performance styles and practices and the use of texts from a wide variety of cultures and ethnic groups.
Interpersonal communication	The communication, both verbal and non-verbal, which takes place between individuals or small groups. Now an important part of Communication Studies.
IQ	Used in research design to mean 'Interview Question'.
Lehrstück	A teaching or learning play.
Liminal/Liminality	A state of being neither 'here nor there' an 'in-between existence'.
Linear	A play where the action progresses in sequence.
Literature review	The survey of current literature relevant to a chosen topic at the beginning of a research project.
Magic 'if'	The fundamental premise of all acting, according to Stanislavsky: the idea that the fiction is true.
Mansions	Small individual stages used in medieval Mystery Plays to represent different locations. When the Mysteries were presented in revival in Canterbury Cathedral during the late twentieth century, the mansions proved invaluable for assisting with the sight lines and acoustics.
Masques	Elaborate court entertainments involving acting, dancing and singing together with ingenious scenic devices. These were a feature of the Italian Renaissance and became an essential part of the life of Queen Elizabeth I and of her successors. Themes were usually classical and attracted the leading architects, poets and musicians of the day.
Mediatization	A recently invented term to describe the process whereby aspects of the 'live' theatre are affected by the developing media.
Melodrama	Originally defined as 'music drama' but now more generally used to describe the nineteenth-century plays which showed idealized heroines, evil characters and noble male characters in desperate situations. Acted with what would now seem to be an exaggerated and overtly emotional style of performance.
Meta-narrative	A grand idea that explains existence or gives it a purpose.
Method, The	A system of actor-training devised by followers of Stanislavsky, especially Lee Strasberg, in New York. The intense identification of actors with their characters can be seen in many American films.

Mise-en-scène	Every aspect of staging a play.
Monodrama	A play for a single character.
Monologue	An uninterrupted speech for a single character. This might constitute an entire play.
Motivation	Factors determining and explaining a character's action.
Multi-focus staging	Forms of staging that enable the audience to see a large number of varying locations simultaneously.
Music hall	A form of entertainment, or place of entertainment, particularly popular with the urban working classes towards the end of the nineteenth and beginning of the twentieth centuries in Britain. Consisting of 'acts' such as singing, comic turns and circus skills, this form of entertainment provoked the building of hundreds of proscenium theatres, many of which are now defunct.
Mystery play	A play written in medieval times telling a Bible story. The term 'Mystery' comes from an old French word meaning 'the know-how' because these plays were originally staged by the Trades Guilds. However, the term tends to refer to 'holy mysteries' in its more recent usage.
Narrative	The vital, story-telling element of Theatre.
Naturalism/Naturalistic	A movement in the late nineteenth century that focused on showing more realism in literature, drama and the visual arts. It aimed to provide an accurate or lifelike representation of the real world through a careful observation of nature.
Negotiated meaning	Used in Critical Theory to describe the way in which an audience both accepts and rejects aspects of the creators' intended meanings of a piece.
Neo-classical	In any art work, a rediscovery and re-introduction of techniques and approaches from the classical past. Literally, 'new-classical'.
Nomad	The third of the generations identified and described by Strauss and Howe.
Off-(off)-Broadway	The American equivalent of the experimental 'fringe'.
Open question	A question to which the answer may contain complexly structured expressions of opinion.
Open stage	A stage with no proscenium or wings and with no 'flats' to conceal entrances and exits.
Pageants	In medieval times, these were carts on which performances took place, enabling plays to move from one location to another. Term has more recently been used to describe a form of entertainment involving processions or sequences of historical events or characters. The emphasis in this latter meaning is on spectacle and colour.
Palate	The roof of the mouth.

Pantomime	In its British usage, this describes a form of entertainment, which is a blend of storytelling, acting, singing, dancing, stand-up and slapstick comedy. It is usually based on a romantic fairy tale and presented around Christmas time. For many theatres it is the single most lucrative event of the year and, for a substantial percentage of the population, their only visit to live theatre. In the USA, pantomime means acting without the use of words (described as 'mime' in the UK).
Paradox of acting	The fact, identified by Diderot, that, in order to move an audience, an actor must remain unmoved
Performance indicator	A feature (such as punctuation) within a text that gives an indication as to how it might be performed
Performative	A term originating in Communication Studies and having a rather slippery definition. It is used widely now to imply almost anything that has a 'performance-like' quality but derives from the idea that some words and language initiate action and change: those employed in the theatre have the potential power to do this in contrast to the language used in everyday conversation.
Performative text	A text that has particular qualities suggesting action
Piece	A section of a play for the close study of the actor as part of preparation.
Platea	A central acting area surrounded by an audience used in ancient theatre forms.
Play-within-a-play	A play that is presented as part of the action of another play, the 'audience' being the on-stage cast.
Playwright as performer	The situation in which playwrights, such as David Hare or Usha Ganguli, elect to perform their own plays rather than entrust them to another actor. This raises issues as to whether or not this situation produces 'definitive' performances.
Plot	The story line of a play.
Political Theatre	Very often from a Socialist or 'left-wing' perspective, this term covers plays that tackle issues of social, gender, national or international concern. Such plays seek to pose questions and, sometimes, provide solutions by challenging the attitudes and/consciences of audiences. There was a considerable explosion of political theatre in Britain in the 1960s and 1970s, many of the playwrights and theatre companies involved deriving their inspiration from the work of Bertolt Brecht.
Popular theatre	Theatre that draws on the traditions of popular entertainment such as Music Hall or Cabaret.
Postmodernism	A set of ideas, usually associated with the French philosophers Derrida, Foucault, Lyotard and Baudrillard that

came into prominence in the 1980s. 'Modernism' is usually thought to have been initiated by the Renaissance and brought to its summit in the eighteenth-century Enlightenment. In place of the rationality and certainties of modernism, postmodernism is characterized by a deep suspicion of language, a loss of meaning and a belief that there is nothing outside of human life to provide a set of values.

Post-structuralism	A philosophical movement that has superseded structuralism through a critique of the Structuralists' use of the concept of the 'sign'.
Practice as research	The acknowledgement that engagement in theatrical activity, such as improvisation, vocal or physical work constitutes a valid form of research.
Predictable theatre	Theatre productions that conform to the expectations of an audience.
Primary source	An object, document or other artefact dating from the precise time of an original event or work being studied.
Promenade	A performance in which the audience shares the space with the actors and moves to various locations throughout. Permanent seating is not provided and the audience invariably 'gathers round' the performers, creating a special kind of directness and intimacy.
Prophet	The second of the generations defined by Strauss and Howe.
Protest theatre	Plays designed to shock and stir the conscience of audiences with a sense of injustice.
Protocol	Term used in social science to imply 'the proper way of conducting this'.
Psychographics	Used as a research tool in audience analysis to collect subjective data to include attitudes, lifestyles, etc.
Psycho-technique	Stanislavsky's system that depended on an understanding of such issues as motivation and the subconscious.
Public solitude	The fundamental experience of the actor on stage.
Purpose-driven behaviour	Behaviour that results from a deep seated wish, ambition or objective.
Qualitative research	Research concerned with ideas and attitudes which cannot be measured objectively.
Quantitative research	Research which deals with issues that can be accurately and objectively measured.
Realization	A term used to describe the process whereby a dramatic text is transformed into a live performance.
Recitation	An occasion or process involving a public presentation of texts by a speaker. Such events might now be described as 'platform performances'. In the nineteenth century actors would hire a hall for this purpose and many famous actors published books of their favourite 'recitation pieces'.

Resonance	The amplification of sound originating in the vocal folds (cords).
Restoration	Used to describe plays and theatre that came into being at, and just after, the time of the restoration of the monarchy in England in 1660. King Charles II came from exile at the French court and, following a period of closure of the theatres during the Commonwealth, introduced the idea of actresses and a more controlled form of Theatre for a society elite.
Review	A descriptive evaluation of a play or other theatre piece in performance published in a newspaper or journal or broadcast. The writing of a review demands critical thinking and a knowledge and understanding of Theatre.
Ritual	Repeated physical and/or speech acts with profound, spiritual significance for the participants.
Rock opera	A stage musical usually 'sung through' (or with limited dialogue) exclusively using rock music.
Role-play	Actors playing various characters in given situations and then, possibly, changing to play another character.
RSVP Cycles	A term developed by Anna and Lawrence Halpin in the late 1960s and later used by Lepage. It means Resource, Score, Valuation and Performance and the word Cycle implies that the process continues.
Ruling idea	The idea that has dominated a playwright's creation.
Secondary source	A form of information about a topic created by a source other than the object of study.
Semiotics	In relation to theatre, this is used to describe the analysis of signs both aural and visual.
Sign	Any element of a performance that communicates messages which may be 'read' by an audience.
Site-specific/ site-sensitive theatre	Performances devised to exploit the particular qualities and associations of a specific, invariably non-theatrical, place.
Situation comedy	A play in which the humour derives from ludicrous situations.
Sprechgesang	A form of half-spoken, half-sung stage language.
Stage directions	The instructions left by a playwright in a play text concerning the settings and the movements, expressions or vocal delivery of characters. Often placed at the beginnings of scenes but also interspersed in the text.
Stock characters	The character-types of the Commedia or British Pantomime: predictable and with recognizable characteristics.
Street theatre	Performances, usually by small groups, of politically or 'issue' motivated theatre groups designed to attract passers-by in any public place.
Structuralism	A movement initiated by the Swiss linguistics scholar, Ferdinand de Saussure, and later diversified by Roland Barthes and Claude Lévi-Strauss, to embrace the study of sign systems. It has placed an unprecedented emphasis on the role of the reader/audience.

Studio	A theatre space where works are devised, developed, rehearsed and presented. The productions are usually small scale and may be known as Chamber Theatre.
Sub-text	The real meaning that lies beneath the words spoken by a character in a play.
Super-objective	The dominant aim of a character in a scene or entire play.
Symbol	An object or act representing an unconscious idea or repressed conflict.
Tableaux	The process whereby actors make a picture of an event or situation and remain static.
Technical knowledge	This refers to the level of technical terminology and understanding that an audience is assumed to have.
Text	In Theatre Studies this is usually taken to mean the words designed to be spoken by actors and the stage-directions printed with them: hence 'textual analysis' will involve a detailed consideration of the language and actions indicated in the published script. In Communication Studies, 'text' is taken to mean almost anything that communicates meaning and some Theatre scholars like to think of aspects of created performance, such as lighting and sound, as elements of the text.
Theatre Anthropology	The study of the universal phenomenon of Theatre and Performance usually involving a consideration of rituals, traditions and performance styles unique to certain regions and an exploration of cultural diversity. Theatre practitioners such as Eugenio Barba and Peter Brook have sought to promote international understanding and to rediscover the essence of Theatre through celebrating ethnic and performance variety.
Theatre for resistance	Theatre devised in communities as an expression of their resistance to oppression in any form.
Theatre-in-the round	This term is usually hyphenated. It describes a form of theatre in which the audience surrounds the actors but within a carefully delineated space. The actual acting area may be square, rectangular or circular but the performance techniques must be adapted to embrace the entire audience.
Theatre of Cruelty	A term introduced by Artaud to describe a form of theatre in which the audience participates in the actors' suffering and experience.
Theatre of testimony	Theatre that bears witness to truth and to events.
Theatre of the Absurd	A term first used by the critic Martin Esslin to describe plays that seem to make no logical sense. The collective title is now frequently used to label many of the plays of Beckett, Ionesco, Adamov, Pinter, Albee and Campton.
Thesis	Used to describe a belief or conviction lying beneath the surface of a play and expounded in the action and dialogue.

Through-line	The sequence of a character's objectives that run through a play rather like a spine of connected vertebrae.
Thrust stage	Any stage that extends substantially into the auditorium.
Tone	The particular quality of the voice resulting from resonance and vowel sounds.
Total theatre	Another term from Artaud but also used by Walter Gropius of the Bauhaus to describe an art form that completely engulfs the spectator and uses multiple genres and forms.
TQ	Theory Question.
Traits	Noticeable aspects of character.
Transformation	Meisner's term for the process whereby an actor adopts a character.
Transitional space	Spaces which are full of possibilities and new ideas (a term taken from child psychotherapy).
Transverse stage	A stage designed to be viewed from two sides in the form of a central passage or 'catwalk'.
Tribute show	Usually a 'musical' or concert devoted to celebrating the work of a famous performer or group but not performed by the original performer or group.
Units	A section of action in a play that appears to have some unity and which might make a convenient section for close study and rehearsal
Upstage	As a verb used to describe the process whereby one actor makes performance difficult for another by occupying a position nearer to the rear of the proscenium stage. With 'raked' stages, this area was traditionally higher than the front part of the stage and considered to be a dominant position. Acting with other actors 'upstage' of you may mean that you have to turn away from the audience in order to address them and this can constitute a weak position for performance.
Variety theatre	Any form of entertainment that includes a series of 'acts' on stage. The likely content is stand-up comedy, singing, dancing, conjuring or circus skills using both solo and chorus.
Vaudeville	A word of French origin describing plays of a light or satiric nature interspersed by songs and dance routines. Used in the USA as synonymous with British Music Hall.
Verbatim theatre	A play text that uses the actual original words of an event, usually preserved in the media or documents.
Weekly rep.	In the UK, stood for 'weekly repertory'. This system in which a new play was presented each week by the same company in the same theatre, was once the base from which actors and other theatre professionals launched their careers although some stayed in it for ever.
Wings	The areas at both sides of a proscenium stage where actors can wait to make entrances. The wings may be formed by curtains (drapes) or flats and may be able to swivel to produce various perspectives and angles of entry.

Work	The term used by postmodernists to differentiate between the original piece written down (the work) and the text, that might evolve in performance and include no verbal elements.
Workshop	This term was made famous by the director Joan Littlewood and her 'Theatre Workshop' based at Stratford, East London during the 1950s and 1960s. It is now used as both a noun, describing an experimental theatre organisation or space, or a verb, describing the process whereby drama is developed through experiment.
Zeitgeist	A concept taken from the German philosopher Hegel meaning the 'spirit of the age' or 'spirit of the times'.

Bibliography

▪ Plays

The details supplied here, including dates of publication, are for recommended editions and/or translations. You should not hesitate to use alternative versions if these are more easily available.

Ackland, R. (1990) *Absolute Hell*, London: Oberon.

Anon. (1975) *The Second Shepherds' Play*, ed. Happe, in *English Mystery Plays*, Harmondsworth: Penguin.

Beckett, S. (1986) *Waiting for Godot*, in *The Complete Dramatic Works*, London: Faber and Faber.

Bennett, A. (1991)*Forty Years On*, in *Alan Bennett: Plays*, London and Boston: Faber and Faber.

Boucicault, D. (1987) *London Assurance*, in *Selected Plays*, Gerrards Cross: Colin Smythe.

Brecht, B. (1987a) *Mother Courage and her Children; The Good Person of Szechwan*, in *Plays: Two*, London: Methuen.

Brecht, B. (1987b) *The Life of Galileo*, in *Plays: Three*, London: Methuen.

Breur, L. (2005) *Red Horse Animation*, in *Theatre of Images*, New York: PAJ Publications.

Cabal, F. (2003) *Tejas Verdes*, trans. Robert Shaw, London: Oberon.

Carriere, J-C. (1985) *The Mahabharata*, trans. P. Brook, London: Methuen.

Chekhov, A. (1980) *The Evils of Tobacco; The Seagull*, in *Collected Plays*, Oxford: Oxford University Press.

Chilton, C. and Littlewood, J. (1963) *Oh, What a Lovely War!*, London: Methuen.

Congreve, W. (2006) *The Way of the World*, London: Nick Hern.

Coward, N. (1939) *Fallen Angels*, in *Collected Plays of Noel Coward: Play Parade*, Vol. II, London: Heinemann.

Coward, N. (1960) *Peace in Our Time*, in *Collected Plays of Noel Coward: Play Parade*, Vol. V, London: Heinemann.

Coward, N. (1979) *Post Mortem*, in *Plays Two*, London: Methuen.

Etherege, G. (2007) *The Man of Mode*, London: Nick Hern.

Farquar, G. (2008) *The Beaux Stratagem*, London: Nick Hern.

Fo, D. (1992) *Accidental Death of an Anarchist*, in *Plays 1*, London: Methuen.

Fornes, I.M. (1977) *Fefu and Her Friends*, in *Wordplays 1*, New York: PAJ Publications.

Ganguli, U. (2005) *Staging Resistance: Plays by Women in Translation*, ed. T. Mukherjee, New Delhi: Oxford University Press.

Genet, J. (1960) *The Blacks*, London: Faber and Faber.

Guare, J. (1977) *Rich and Famous*, New York: Dramatists Play Service.

Hall, W. (1961) *The Long and the Short and the Tall*, in *New English Dramatists 3*, Harmondsworth: Penguin.

Hare, D. (1997) *Via Dolorosa*, London: Faber and Faber.

Harnetiaux, B. (2005) *York*, unpublished play. See www.BryanHarnetiauxPlays.com

Herzog, M. and Pickering, K. (2000) *Sir Gawain and the Green Knight*, Colwall: J. Garnet-Miller.

Howard, Sir R. and the Duke of Buckingham (1976) *The Country Gentleman*, London: J.M. Dent.

Ibsen, H. (1980) *A Doll's House* and *Hedda Gabler*, in *Ibsen Plays: Two*, trans. M. Meyer, London: Eyre Methuen.

Ionesco, E. (1962) *The Bald Prima Donna*, Harmondsworth: Penguin.

Leigh, M. (1977) *Abigail's Party*, Harmondsworth: Penguin.

Lowe, S. (2006) *Touched*, London: Nick Hern.

Luckham, C. (1964) *The Choice*, in *Plays by Women: 10*, London: Methuen.

Mamet. D. (1978) *A Life in the Theatre*, New York: Grove Press.

Marlowe, C. (1969) *Dr. Faustus* and *The Massacre at Paris*, in *Complete Plays*, Harmondsworth: Penguin.

Maugham, S. (1931) *For Services Rendered*, in *The Collected Plays*, Vol. III and *The Breadwinner*, in *The Collected Plays*, Vol. II, London: Heinemann.

McGrath, T. (2005) *Laurel and Hardy*, Edinburgh: Capercaillie Books.

Nelson, R. (1989) *Some Americans Abroad*, New York: Faber.

Nichols, P. (1987) *Privates on Parade*, in *Plays 1*, London: Methuen.

Osborne, J. (1993) *The Entertainer*, in *Plays 1*, London and Boston: Faber and Faber.

Pinero, Sir A.W. (1995) *The Second Mrs. Tanqueray*, in *Trelawny of the 'Wells' and Other Plays*, Oxford: Oxford University Press.

Rattigan, T. (1981) *Flare Path*, in *Plays 1*, London: Methuen.

Rattigan, T. (2006) *Separate Tables*, London: Nick Hern.

Robertson, T. (1972) *Caste*, in G. Rowell (ed.) *Nineteenth-Century Plays*, Oxford: Oxford University Press.

Ruhl, S. (2006) *Clean House*, in *Clean House and Other Plays*, London: Nick Hern.

Schiller, F. von (1829) *William Tell*, Oxford: Bibliobytes. An adaptation was also made by Stephen Lowe for performance at the Crucible Theatre, Sheffield.

Shakespeare, W.(2008) *A Midsummer Night's Dream; As You Like It; Hamlet; Henry V.; Julius Caesar; Macbeth; The Tempest*, individual plays in *The RSC Shakespeare*, London: Palgrave Macmillan.

Shaw, G.B. (1965) *Arms and the Man; Candida; Major Barbara*, in *The Complete Plays*, London: Paul Hamlyn.

Sheridan, R.B. (2006)*The Rivals*, London: Nick Hern.

Simon, B. ed. Ndlovu (1986) *Woza Albert?*, in *Woza Afrika*, New York: Braziller.

Strindberg, A. (1976a) *A Dream Play*, in *Plays Two*, London: Eyre Methuen.

Strindberg, A. (1976b) *Miss Julie; The Father*, in *Plays One*, London: Eyre Methuen.

Taylor, C.P. (1984) *Good: A Nightingale Sang*, London: Methuen.

Taylor, T. (1972) *Ticket of Leave Man*, in G. Rowell (ed.) *Nineteenth-Century Plays*, Oxford: Oxford University Press.

Udwan, M. (1995) *That's Life*, in S.K. Jayyusi, and R. Allen (eds) *Modern Arabic Drama: An Anthology*, Bloomington, IN: Indiana University Press.

Vanbrugh, Sir J. (1988) *The Provoked Wife*, in M. Cordner (ed.) *Four Comedies*, Harmondsworth: Penguin.

Wedekind, F. (1993) *Spring Awakening*, in *Plays 1*, London: Methuen.

Weiss, P. (1965) *The Marat/Sade*, London and New York: Marion Boyars.

Whelan, P. (2003) *The Accrington Pals*, in *Plays*, London: Methuen.

Wilmer, S. (1980) *Baby Killer*, unpublished and first performed at the Croydon Warehouse.

■ Other works

Abercrombie, N. and Longhurst, B. (1998) *Audiences*, London: Sage.

Adams. Y. (2008), 'Elizabethan Theatre in Cambridge', *Newsletter*, London: The Marlowe Society.

Alfreds, M. (2008) *Different Every Night: Freeing the Actor*, London: Nick Hern.

Allain, P. (2003) *The Art of Stillness: The Theatre Practice of Tadashi Suzuki*, New York: Palgrave Macmillan.

Allain, P. and Harvie, J. (2006) *The Routledge Companion to Theatre and Performance*, London: Routledge.

Ang, I. (1991) *Desperately Seeking the Audience*, London: Routledge.

Artaud, A. (1968) *Collected Works*, 2 vols, trans. V. Corti, London: Calder and Boyas.

Artaud, A. (1970) *The Theatre and Its Double*, trans. V. Corti, London: Calder and Boyars.

Auslander, P. (1997) *From Acting to Performance: Essays in Modernism and Postmodernism*, London: Routledge.

Ayckbourn, A. (2002) *The Crafty Art of Playmaking*, London: Faber and Faber.

Bakhtin, M. (1984) *Rabelais and His World*, trans. H. Iswolsky, Bloomington, IN: Indiana University Press.

Barba, E. (1994) *The Paper Canoe: A Guide to Theatre Anthropology*, trans. R. Fowler, London: Routledge.

Barker, C. (1977) *Theatre Games*, London: Methuen.

Barkworth, P. (1991) *About Acting*, London: Methuen.

Bartow, A. (ed.) (2008) *Handbook of Acting Techniques*, London: Nick Hern.

Baugh, C. (2005) *Theatre Performance and Technology*, Basingstoke: Palgrave Macmillan.

Bell, J. (1999) *Doing Your Research Project*, Milton Keynes: Open University Press.

Benedetti, J. (2005) *The Art of the Actor*, London: Methuen.

Benedetti, R. (1994) *The Actor at Work*, New Jersey: Prentice Hall.

Berghaus, G. (2005)*Avant-garde Performance*, Basingstoke: Palgrave Macmillan.

Billington, M. (2008) *One Night Stands: A Critic's View of Modern British Theatre*, London: Nick Hern.

Blumer, H. (1951) 'Collective Behaviour', in A.M. Lee (ed.) *New Outline of the Principles of Sociology*, New York: Barnes and Noble.

Boal, A. (1979) *Theatre of the Oppressed*, trans. C. Leal and M. McBride, London: Pluto Press.

Brecht, B. ([1965] 1974) *The Messingkauf Dialogues*, trans. J. Willet, London: Methuen.

Brockett, O. (1994) *The Theatre: An Introduction*, 4th edn, New York: Holt, Rinehart and Winston.

Brockett, O. (1995) *History of the Theatre*, Boston and London: Allyn and Bacon.

Brook, P. (1988) *The Shifting Point: Forty Years of Theatrical Exploration*, London: Methuen.

Brown, L. and Gawthorpe, A. (2007) *Teach Yourself: Writing a Play*, London: Hodder Education.

Bruder, M., Cohn, L., Olaek, M., Pollack, N., Previto R., and Zigler, S. (1986) *A Practical Handbook for the Actor*, New York: Vintage.

Bryman, A. (2004) *Social Research Methods*, Oxford: Oxford University Press.

Bryman, A. and Burgess, R.G. (eds) (1994) *Analysing Qualitative Data*, London: Routledge.

Carey, D. and Clark Carey, R. (2008) *Vocal Arts Workbook and DVD*, London: Methuen.

Cassady, M. (1988) *Playwriting Step by Step*, Studio City: Players Press.

Cohn, R. (1991) *New American Dramatists*, Basingstoke: Macmillan.

Cole, T. (ed.) (1961) *Playwrights on Playwriting*: New York: Hill and Wang.

Counsell, C. (1996) *Signs of Performance*, London: Routledge.

Counsell, C. and Wolf, L. (2001) *Performance Analysis: An Introductory Course Book*, London: Routledge.

Courtney, R. (1987) *The Quest*, Lanham, MD: University Press of America.

Darwin, C. (1962) *Origin of Species*, new edn, London: Macmillan.

Diderot, D. (1957) 'The Paradox of Acting', in L. Strasberg (ed.) *The Paradox of Acting and Masks and Face*, New York: Hill and Wang.

Dostoyevsky, F. ([1866] 1951) *Crime and Punishment*, trans. D. Magarshak, Harmondsworth: Penguin.

Emmet, A. (1975) 'The Actor's Dilemma', *Theatre Quarterly*, vol. V, no. 18, p. 21.

Emmet Long, R. (ed.) (2008) *Writing: Working in the Theatre*, New York: Continuum.

Esslin, M. (1976) *Artaud*, London: Fontana.

Eyre, R. (2000) *Changing Stages*, London: Bloomsbury.

Fairclough, N. (2003) *Analysing Discourse*, London: Routledge.

Fountain, T. (2008) *So You Want to be a Playwright*, London: Nick Hern.

Frome, S. (1990) *Playwriting: A Complete Guide to Creating Theatre*, North Carolina: McFarland.

Gilbert, N. (2001) *Researching Social Life*, London: Sage.

Greig, N. (2005) *Playwriting: A Practical Guide*, London: Routledge.

Grotowski, J. (1968) *Towards a Poor Theatre*, London: Methuen.

Hare, D. (1999) *Acting Up*, London: Faber and Faber.

Hare, D. (2005a) *Obedience, Struggle and Revolt*, London: Faber and Faber.

Hare, D. (2005b) 'The Second Intifada', in *Obedience, Struggle and Revolt*, London: Faber and Faber.

Harris, R.A. (2005) *Using Sources Effectively: Strengthening Your Writing and Avoiding Plagiarism*, New York: Pryczak Publishing.

Hill, L. and Paris, H. (eds) (2005) *Place and Placelessness in Performance*, Basingstoke: Palgrave Macmillan.

Hodgson, A. (ed.) (2000) *Twentieth Century Actor Training*, London: Routledge.

Hoggart, R. (1996) *The Uses of Literacy*, London: Beacon Press.

Hoggart, R. (2000) *First and Last Things*, London: Aurum Press.

Holland, P. (1977) *The Ornament of Action: Text and Performance in Restoration Comedy*, Cambridge: Cambridge University Press.

Holland, P. and Orgel, S. (eds) (2004) *From Script to Stage in Early Modern England*, Basingstoke: Palgrave Macmillan.

Holland, P. and Orgel, S. (eds) (2005) *Performance to Print in Shakespeare's England*, Basingstoke: Palgrave Macmillan.

Houseman, B. (2008) *Tackling Text and Subtext*, London: Nick Hern.

Kachur, B.A. (2004) *Etherege and Wycherly*, Basingtoke: Palgrave Macmillan.

Kermode, L. and Scott-Warren, J. (eds) (2005)*Tudor Drama Before Shakespeare, 1485–1590*, Basingstoke: Palgrave Macmillan.

Korty, C. (2006) *Writing Your Own Play*, Studio City: Players Press.

Kruger, L. (1999) *The Drama of South Africa*, London: Routledge.

Laban, R. von (1960) *A Life for Dance*, New York: Theatre Arts Books.

Landes, W. (2008) *How to Get Your Play Published*, Studio City: Players Press.

Lanyado, M. (2004) *The Presence of the Therapist: Treating Childhood Trauma*, London and New York: Routledge.

Leach, R. (2008) *Theatre Studies: The Basics*, London: Routledge.

Lennard, J. and Luckhurst, M. (2002) *The Drama Handbook: A Guide to Reading Plays*, Oxford: Oxford University Press.

Linklater, K. (1988) *Freeing the Natural Voice*, New York: Quite Specific Media Group.

Luckhurst, M. and Moody, J. (eds) (2005) *Theatre and Celebrity in Britain, 1660–2000*, Basingstoke: Palgrave Macmillan.

Magarshak, D. (1950) *Stanislavsky, A Life*, London: Macgibbon and Key.

Mamet, D. (1997) *True and False: Heresy and Common Sense for the Actor*, New York: Vintage.

Marranca, B. (ed.) ([1977] 1996) *The Theatre of Images*, Baltimore, MD: Johns Hopkins University Press.

Marsen, S. (2006) *Communication Studies*, Basingstoke: Palgrave Macmillan.

May, T. (2001) *Social Research: Issues, Methods and Process*, 3rd edn, Buckingham: Open University Press.

McAuley, G. (2000) *Space in Performance: Making Meaning in the Theatre*, Ann Arbor, MI: University of Michigan Press.

McCarthy, G. (2005) *Representation and the Actor*, Basingstoke: Palgrave Macmillan.

McGrath, J. (1996) *A Good Night Out*, 2nd edn, London: Nick Hern.

McQuail, D. (1997) *Audience Analysis*, London: Sage.

Meisner, S. and Longwell, D. (1987) *Sanford Meisner on Acting*, New York: Vintage.

Miller, J. (1986) *Subsequent Performances*, London: Faber and Faber.

Mudford, P. (2000) *Making Theatre: From Text to Performance*, London: The Athlone Press.

Neuman, W. (2006) *Social Research Methods*, Boston: Pearson International.

Nothedge, A. (1990) *The Good Study Guide*, Milton Keynes: Open University Press.

Oxenford, L. (1974) *Playing Period Plays*, Colwall and Chicago: J. Garnet Miller.

Palmer, R. (1992) *Write in Style: A Guide to Good English*, London: Spon.

Parker, D. (1994) *Tackling Coursework: Assignments, Projects, Reports and Presentations*, London: DP Publications.

Pavis, P. (ed.) (1996) *The Intercultural Performance Reader*, London: Routledge.

Pavis, P. (1998) *Dictionary of the Theatre: Terms, Concepts and Analysis*, Toronto: University of Toronto Press.

Pavis, P. (2003)*Analyzing Performance Theater, Dance and Film*, Ann Arbor, MI: University of Michigan Press.

Perret, G. (2007) *Comedy Writing Workbook*, Studio City: Players Press.

Pickering, K. (1997) *Drama Improvised*, Colwall: J. Garnet-Miller.

Pickering, K. (2005) *Key Concepts in Drama and Performance*, Basingstoke: Palgrave Macmillan.

Pickering, K. (2007) *From Page to Performance*, London: Trinity College.

Pickering, K. (ed.) (2008) *The Performer's Anthology*, London: Janus Publications.

Pickering, K. and Auckland-Lewis, G. (2004) *Thinking about Plays*, London: Dramatic Lines.

Reinhaz, S. (1992) *Feminist Methods in Social Research*, London: Oxford University Press.

Roose-Evans, J. (1988) *Experimental Theatre from Stanislavsky to Brook*, London: Routledge.

Schechner, R. (1994) *Environmental Theatre*, New York: Applause Books.

Schlemmer, T. (ed.) (1972) *The Letters and Diaries of Oskar Schlemmer*, Connecticut: Weslyan University Press.

Seale, C., Gobo, G., Gubrium, I. and Silverman, D. (2004) *Qualitative Research Practice*, London: Sage.

Shapiro, J. (2005) *1599: A Year in the Life of William Shakespeare*, London: Faber and Faber.

Spickard, J. (2006) *How to Construct an Interview Protocol*, London: University of East London.

Spickard, J. (2007) *Module Study Guide for Research Methods*, London: University of East London.

Stanislavsky, K. ([1950] 1967) *On the Art of the Stage*, trans. D. Magarshak, London: Faber and Faber.

Stanislavsky, K. (1968) *Stanislavsky's Legacy*, trans. E. Hapgood, London: Eyre Methuen.

Stanislavsky, K. (2008a) *An Actor Prepares*, in *An Actor's Work*, trans. J. Benedetti London: Routledge.

Stanislavsky, K. (2008b) *My Life in Art*, trans. J. Bendetti, London: Routledge.

Stanislavsky, K. (2008c) *Building a Character and Creating a Role*, in *An Actor's Work*, trans. J. Benedetti, London: Routledge.

Strauss, N. and Howe, W. (1991) *Generations: The History of America's Future, 1584 to 2069*, New York: William Morrow and Co.

Striff, E. (ed.) (2003) *Performance Studies*, Basingstoke: Palgrave Macmillan.

Taylor, G. (1989) *The Students' Writing Guide for the Arts and Social Sciences*, Cambridge: Cambridge University Press.

Tynan, K. (ed.) (2008a) *Kenneth Tynan: Profile*, London: Nick Hern.

Tynan, K. (2008b) *Theatre Writings*, London: Nick Hern.

Wengraf, T. (2001) *Qualitative Research Interviewing: Biographic Narrative and Semi-structured Method*, London: Sage Publications.

Willet, J. (1964) *Brecht on Theatre*, London: Methuen.

Wilson, M. (2005) *Storytelling and Theatre*, Basingstoke: Palgrave Macmillan.

Wolf, W. (1973) 'A Designer Works with Brecht', *Theatre Quarterly*, vol. II, no. 6, p. 15.

Worthen, W.B. and Holland, P. (eds) (2003) *Theorizing Practice: Redefining Theatre History*, Basingstoke: Palgrave Macmillan.

Index

Note: Pages listed in **bold** indicate a Glossary definition of the term listed.

UNIVERSITY OF WINCHESTER
LIBRARY